SPACIOUS MINDS

SPACIOUS MINDS

Trauma and Resilience in Tibetan Buddhism

SARA E. LEWIS

CORNELL UNIVERSITY PRESS
ITHACA AND LONDON

First published 2019 by Cornell University Press

Library of Congress Cataloging-in-Publication Data

Names: Lewis, Sara E., 1981– author.
Title: Spacious minds : trauma and resilience in Tibetan Buddhism / Sara E. Lewis.
Description: Ithaca : Cornell University Press, 2019. | Includes bibliographical references and index.
Identifiers: LCCN 2019015733 (print) | LCCN 2019016998 (ebook) | ISBN 9781501709562 (pdf) | ISBN 9781501712203 (epub/mobi) | ISBN 9781501715341 (cloth) | ISBN 9781501715358 (pbk.)

Subjects: LCSH: Tibetans—India—Dharmsala—Religion. | Tibetans—Mental health—India—Dharmsala. | Buddhism—India—Dharmsala. | Suffering—Religious aspects—Buddhism. | Psychic trauma—India—Dharmsala. | Resilience (Personality trait)—India—Dharmsala. | Cultural psychiatry—India—Dharmsala. | Tibetan diaspora.
Classification: LCC BQ7594.D53 (ebook) | LCC BQ7594.D53 L49 2019 (print) | DDC 294.3/923—dc23
LC record available at https://lccn.loc.gov/2019015733

This book is dedicated to the memory
of Dr. Ali Pomponio (1953–2012)

Contents

ACKNOWLEDGMENTS

It is impossible to convey my gratitude for all who have helped make this book a reality. Kim Hopper believed in my work and gave careful guidance from the earliest days of this project's conception. I am deeply influenced by his quest to understand the mind and humbled by his authentic and profound respect for human beings. To Lesley Sharp: it must have been my good karma to find myself in your writing group. There is an idea in Buddhist culture that the right teacher always appears at the right time; I am exceedingly grateful for her ongoing mentorship. I wish to offer deep thanks to Vincanne Adams, who graciously took me on as a student from afar and has continued to offer invaluable mentorship in the early stages of my career. I also wish to thank Jack Saul and Ana Abraido-Lanza, as well as Jennifer Hirsch for her fierce encouragement, mentorship, and friendship. An intensive workshop with Kim Hopper, Lesley Sharp, and Jennifer Hirsch supported by Wellesley College was instrumental in reworking the manuscript; I am so grateful for this ongoing support.

The person to whom this book is dedicated, Alice Pomponio ("Dr. P," as we called her), was my mentor at St. Lawrence University and the person with whom I discovered the field of anthropology. I will never forget her. Thank you also to a lifelong friend and teacher, Cathy Shrady. My appreciation goes to Emily Mendenhall for reading early chapter drafts, as well as the members of my beloved writing group at Columbia University: Nancy Worthington, Chris Alley, Kirk Fiereck, and Jen Van Tiem. Thank you to my academic big sister, Neely Myers.

This research would not have been possible without generous support from the Lemelson Society for Psychological Anthropology Fund, Foreign Language Acquisition Scholarship (FLAS), Fulbright IIE, Weatherhead East Asian Institute, Sasakawa Young Leaders Fellowship Fund (SYLFF), and the Mellon Foundation. Thank you as well to Ted Lowe, editor of *Ethos* and the Condon Prize committee for helpful suggestions in the early development of the project. Portions of this study's data have been previously published in "Trauma and the Making of Flexible Minds in the Tibetan Exile Community," *Ethos* 41, no. 3 (2013): 313–36 and "Resilience, Agency, and Everyday *Lojong* in the Tibetan Diaspora," *Contemporary Buddhism* 19, no. 2 (2018): 342–61.

Thank you to the Department of Anthropology at the University of Oregon for time and support for writing, and especially to Daphne Gallagher, Angela Montague, Carol Silverman, and Diane Baxter for their friendship. I am grateful for the support I have received at Wellesley College in the Department of Religion, thanks to generous support from the Luce Moore Foundation. In particular, I wish to thank my supportive friends and colleagues, with special appreciation for Ed Silver and Susan Ellison. A year's fellowship at the Wellesley College Newhouse Center provided an invaluable opportunity to workshop portions of the book and work alongside more senior colleagues who offered friendship and advice. A Wellesley College faculty research award allowed me to hire an undergraduate research assistant, Eva Duckler, to work on editorial tasks. A fiercely creative, rare, old soul— she is someone who will go on to do something beautiful in this world. To all my students and the women of Wellesley College, your refusal to take knowledge at face value before deeply, and sometimes ruthlessly, interrogating it, gives me hope that a lineage of thinkers and seers will not be lost.

I also wish to acknowledge and thank my colleagues at Naropa University in the Contemplative Psychotherapy and Buddhist Psychology Program:

Janneli Chapin, Karen Kissel Wegela, MacAndrew Jack, Ugur Kocataskin, Caroline Leach, and Lauren Casalino. You appeared at just the right moment and I am grateful and humbled to join this compassionate and spirited community I now call home.

My deepest thank you to my friends and neighbors in Dharamsala. Thank you, especially, to all the Tibetan grannies for your endless scoldings on proper Tibetan grammar and the dangers of cold drinks. Thank you for finally nodding with approval when I wore no less than four sweaters and a large piece of sheep's wool tied around my waist (to protect my organs from getting cold). And thank you to my young Tibetan friends for falling down with laughter at the sight of my granny apparel. I have immense gratitude for my research assistant, Abo Gakyi, who worked tirelessly in assisting me with recruiting interview participants, translation, and Tibetan language transcription. Additional translation assistance (and lovely homemade butter lamps) came from Aksel Lyderson. Kesang Chhoden Lama assisted with Tibetan spell-checking and transliteration. Thank you to Gen Dekyi and my dearest friends, Josh and Nicolette, and to Ruth Sonam and the late Geshe Sonam Rinchen. I have immense gratitude for Sakyong Mipham Rinpoche, Sakyong Wangmo, Dzongsar Khyentse Rinpoche, Dilgo Khyentse Rinpoche, and Chögyam Trungpa Rinpoche.

From the moment we began corresponding I felt a special connection to my editor at Cornell University Press, Jim Lance. A critical thinker and deeply kind soul, Jim has encouraged and guided me in seeing this book come to fruition. I am so very grateful for his support. I also wish to thank the scholars who reviewed the manuscript, providing critically important feedback. In particular, I appreciate them pushing me to think more deeply about resilience and the moral good in anthropology. I am deeply humbled and appreciative for their close reading of this work.

Writing a book has also provided a unique opportunity to count the blessings in my life. Thank you to Ericka Phillips, Whitney Joiner, Sarah Kimball, Ashley Dinges, Martina Bouey, Shelly Webb, Ella Reznikova, Sarah Lipton, Alison Pepper, Ian Bascetta, Dan Glenn, Kelly Lehmann, Alexis Shotwell, Mitchell Levy, Andrew Sacamano, Toby Sifton, Anna Weinstein, Jesse Grimes, and the entire Trident Core Group. My deepest appreciation for the Shambhala Interim Board who will long remain in my heart. Thank you to David Desmond, Ashley Hodson, Jade Kranz, Ian McLaughlin, Jessyca Goldstein, Megan Mack, Jess Wimett, Anita Shepherd, Brendan

xii   *Acknowledgments*

Shea, Mark Winterer, Anne Montgomery, Brendan Hart, Brooke West, Noga Zerubavel, Hillary Schiff, Erick Howard, Chris Hiebert, and many other friends and colleagues. With all my heart, I thank Brett Knowles for coming into my life.

Finally, thank you to my parents, Tom and Sandy, and my sister, Emily, whose unwavering support sustains me through it all.

Abbreviations

FRO	Foreign Registration Office
HSCL	Hopkins Symptom Checklist-25
HTQ	Harvard Trauma Questionnaire
IRB	Institutional Review Board
NGO	Nongovernmental organization
NKD	New Kadampa Movement
PRC	The People's Republic of China
PTSD	post-traumatic stress disorder
RCs	residential certificates
SSRI	selective serotonin reuptake inhibitor
SYLFF	Sasakawa Young Leaders Fellowship Fund
TAR	Tibetan Autonomous Region
TCHRD	Tibetan Center for Human Rights and Democracy
TCV	Tibetan Children Village
TPO	Transcultural Psychosocial Organization

TTS   Tibetan Transit School
TTSP   Tibetan Torture Survivors Program
UNHCR   United Nations High Commissioner for Refugees
VCD   video compact discs

Note on Transliteration

Many Tibetan scholars use a method of transliteration called the Wylie system, which corresponds to the spelling rather than pronunciation of Tibetan words. For example, the word "Kagyu" (a school of Tibetan Buddhism) using the Wylie transliteration is: bka' brgyud. Wylie is a standardized and convenient method for those who know the language, but for non-Tibetan speakers it is largely unintelligible. Therefore, in this book I use a mixture of Wylie (bka' brgyud) and transliteration based on pronunciation (*kagyu*), preferring the pronunciation style when citing or describing actual conversations. I will use Wylie when describing concepts or terms that may hold particular significance to Tibetan scholars.

Central Characters

Sonam Tashi[1]: A fifty-five-year-old monk and ex-political prisoner who has lived in exile for nearly twenty years.

Tashi Lhamo: A twenty-two-year-old Tibetan woman who spent nine months in a Tibetan prison and has lived in Dharamsala for three years as a maid at an Indian-run hotel.

Dolma: An eighty-year-old Tibetan woman who came with the first wave of Tibetans who followed the Dalai Lama into exile in the early 1960s.

Palden: A twenty-four-year-old man who disrobed as a monk when he came to India four years ago. He works at a coffee shop in Dharamsala and lives with an American girlfriend.

Yangzom: A thirty-five-year-old mother of two, raised in the Tibetan Children's Village (TCV) boarding school.

---

1. A pseudonym, as with all names herein. Study participants' ages at the time of fieldwork between 2011 and 2012 in Dharamsala, India.

Ani Dawa: A seventy-one-year-old nun who lives outside a traditional nunnery and is known around town as mentally ill.

Dekyi: A sixty-year-old mother of a *tulku* (reincarnate lama) who just arrived at the refugee reception center.

SPACIOUS MINDS

INTRODUCTION

Sipping chai at a tea stall, Sonam Tashi, a fifty-five-year-old monk, re-counts his experience in a Chinese prison after being arrested for posting photographs of the Dalai Lama around his monastery in Tibet. Knowing him as a staunch political activist and survivor of torture, I expect the inter-view to center around human rights. But he tells a more complex tale. "I had to stay as a prisoner," he explains. "But I just thought of it as a retreat house. I was given food, and other than that, all I had to do was practice. Some said: 'If we have to stay our whole lives here and die in prison, then it is not really prison if we use this experience to develop compassion.'" The monk does not deny pain and hardship. Yet seemingly with ease he changes the way he re-lates to the situation, using his time in prison to engage in Buddhist prac-tice. How could an ordinary Buddhist monk reimagine a prison as a retreat house, I wondered. And was this resilience real, or performed?

I was not the first researcher to whom Sonam Tashi has told his tale. In fact, we were introduced by an American friend who invites the monk every semester to guest lecture to his students studying abroad in Dharamsala,

India. Sonam Tashi speaks excellent English and is often found meeting with foreign travelers, disclosing gruesome details of torture he experienced while inside a Chinese prison. He has written two memoirs inspired by Palden Gyatso's autobiography (1998), *Fire under the Snow: True Story of a Tibetan Monk*, where Gyatso famously declares that his biggest fear during thirty-three years in captivity was that he would lose compassion for his torturers. Remarkably, these accounts of imprisonment center around humility, human connectedness, and nonviolent resistance, creating a heroic image. And yet I hoped that over the course of my fieldwork within the Tibetan exile community, I would come to discover the more ordinary experiences of Tibetans living in Dharamsala. Over time, I thought, I would learn the ways everyday people suffered and recovered as they rebuilt their lives in exile.

I surmised that Tibetans were compelled to perform this heroic resilience and the kind of Buddhist serenity Westerners hope to encounter (Lopez 1998). I suspected that once I was better acquainted with ordinary Tibetans who do not meet routinely with journalists and students, those who do not speak English or have much to gain from interacting with an anthropologist, more stories of trauma and hardship would emerge. I came to Dharamsala wanting to understand local processes of resilience and recovery, with particular interest in how Buddhist practices might shape responses to traumatic events. As a researcher interested in learning about resilience, it seemed logical to prod my Tibetan interlocutors to speak about their trauma symptoms. But as I became acquainted with Tibetan friends and neighbors more intimately, I realized that no one much liked to talk about distress, often insisting that others were much worse off. In fact, it was the norm for people to downplay personal suffering and explain that distress needed to be refashioned and reframed through Buddhist ideals such as compassion. Here, the trauma narrative is not a culturally sanctioned form of expression. What at first glance might be read as repression, I came to read as a form of refusal,[1] a conviction that viewing oneself as a trauma survivor with chronic and intractable suffering will thwart recovery. And yet, simultaneously, the Tibetan exile community is embroiled in a human rights campaign, which they have come to learn is predicated on crafting and circulating trauma narratives.

In this book, I investigate this apparent paradox. How and why does this community create narratives of suffering with the intention to circulate them publicly when these same individuals, on the personal level, tend to downplay and even deny their own trauma? To answer this puzzle, I set out to understand Tibetan approaches to resilience and found that local notions of stress and trauma (a construct that needs to be fully contextualized in place and time) are wholly different from assumptions embedded within biomedicine. Namely, for Tibetans, suffering is the rule and not the exception. The First Noble Truth, the truth of suffering, is taken for granted and the entire Buddhist path is, in some sense, dedicated to instructing practitioners on what to do in the face of this unavoidable reality. And as I will argue in this book, accepting the universal truth of suffering is key to building resilience in Dharamsala.

Getting Out of Tibet

Tibetans began migrating to Dharamsala, a town located in the foothills of the Himalayas in the northern Indian state of Himachal Pradesh, ten years after the Chinese first invaded Tibet in 1949. When the Dalai Lama fled to India, around 85,000 Tibetans followed (Ketzer and Crescenzi 2002). Temples, monasteries, and Buddhist artifacts were destroyed and many forms of Tibetan culture (particularly religious ones) remain restricted or banned today. When the Dalai Lama settled in Dharamsala in the early 1960s, he established the Tibetan government-in-exile along with the Central Tibetan Administration, a central body composed of specialized departments, including the Department of Security, Department of Education, and Department of Health. Today, more than 150,000 Tibetans live in exile—in India, Nepal, Europe, North America, and beyond. Dharamsala is home to approximately 11,000 Tibetans, most of whom live in McLeod Ganj, an enclave perched on a steep hill above a busy Indian town.

Life in Tibet today is strained and difficult for many, and those who leave do so for a variety of reasons. Some hope to find better work opportunities in exile, including the chance to come to North America or Europe. Parents make difficult decisions to send their children into exile, often with monks or nuns from their county who are planning the arduous journey by foot over the Himalayas. Many Tibetan schools have been systematically converted to Chinese-speaking ones and China has created economic incentives to recruit more Han Chinese to move into the area, making everyday cultural life more

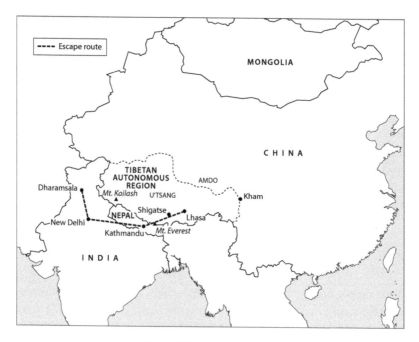

Figure 1. Map of escape route.

and more Chinese. Thus, Tibetans must learn to speak Chinese for survival and many do their best to secure work despite discrimination and hostility within their homeland. Many of the major monasteries and nunneries have reestablished themselves in India and Nepal because of restrictions within Tibet, and some monks and nuns leave Tibet seeking religious, linguistic, and cultural freedom.

The legality around leaving Tibet is murky, but in general Tibetans cannot obtain the funds, permission, or social capital to emigrate legally to other countries. In the 1980s, an informal agreement was struck with Nepal and the United Nations High Commissioner for Refugees (UNHCR) that allowed Tibetans to temporarily travel through Kathmandu en route to India. The Tibetan government-in-exile established refugee camps along several borders, and buses carry those who are able to cross the border into Nepal over land to India. This informal agreement grows increasingly strained as China continues to threaten both Nepal and India with economic sanctions for helping Tibetan "political dissidents." Most Tibetans who flee leave in small groups, traveling at night across the Himalayan Mountains. Some save money for bribing border police and manage to find rides hiding in Jeeps. Others walk the entire distance.

Life in Dharamsala

Although not all who come to Dharamsala are necessarily political refugees, the plight of this highly marginalized ethnic group is, in some sense, always political. Those found carrying photographs of the Dalai Lama may be convicted as political "separatists," even if their intent is merely devotional. As Carole McGranahan argues, "Tibetans are not refugees on individual terms but as part of a nation-state community or, more accurately, a nation-state in exile" (2010a, 13). Meeting "His Holiness" the Dalai Lama, the spiritual leader of Tibet, is often cited as a primary reason for leaving. Indeed, all Tibetans who come to Dharamsala are granted an audience with him, usually at his private residence, upon their arrival. This experience is treasured. Devotion to the Dalai Lama also orients and affirms new arrivals as "really Tibetan": a status that is ambiguous and contested back home in Tibet.

Despite the propensity to characterize Dharamsala and its Tibetan inhabitants as uniform, they are not a homogeneous group and are highly diverse in terms of language, socioeconomic status, culture, and education. Many coming from the eastern Tibetan regions of Amdo and Kham speak dialects that are not easily understood by those speaking so-called standard Tibetan in U-Tsang, colloquially called, *Lhasa-ke* or *Ü-ke*. Some scholars argue that there is good reason to consider what is spoken in Ü-Tsang, Amdo, and Kham (the three major regions of Tibet) as distinct languages rather than dialects (Roche and Suzuki 2018; Tournadre 2014). In addition to rivalry and mistrust among those who hail from different regions of Tibet, there is significant derision among old-timers and new arrivals, both questioning the authenticity of the others' "Tibetanness"—those living in India have mixed with foreigners, whereas Tibetan new arrivals have inevitably been influenced by the Chinese. As in Tibet, women remain in marginalized positions in Dharamsala, although their status in society is far more equal to men than is generally the case in India. Youth who grow up within the Tibetan Children Village (TCV) boarding schools—currently 16,726 children aged five to eighteen years old are schooled and housed in branches across North and South India (TCV 2017)—come to speak a hybridized form of Tibetan infused with Hindi and English words.

But it is not merely foreign researchers who mistakenly conceive of Tibetan exiles as a homogenous group. There are bitter divisions within the diaspora and yet Tibetans are highly motivated to present themselves as a cohesive community; in fact, it may be economically and politically dangerous to acknowledge diverse voices and perspectives that could threaten resistance discourse and the campaign for political sovereignty (Brox 2016; Yeh 2013). Political posters of events back in Tibet, many with graphic photographs of self-immolation and bloodied victims of police brutality, span sides of buildings and community bulletin boards in Dharamsala. Sometimes there are hunger strikes in town where people sit in public view while their compatriots give speeches about human rights abuses using a bullhorn. Popular Tibetan films and pop music feature lyrics calling for the Dalai Lama's return to Tibet and lament the oppression of Tibetan language and culture in what has become China's Tibet (Diehl 2002). This iconic discourse is rendered by pastoral landscapes of humble yak herders who have come to represent a fetishized nostalgic past of "real" Tibet (Gayley 2013; Upton 1996). Much of exile culture in Dharamsala centers around performing a Tibet imagined not merely for foreigners, but to confirm and reestablish a culture Tibetans fear losing.

The town of Dharamsala—a cool, misty mountain refuge from chaotic Indian streets—has seen a number of shifts over the past hundred years. It is the indigenous home of the Gaddhi villagers who lost much of their land in the early 1860s when the British established a military cantonment. In 1959, Prime Minister Nehru gave the land to the Dalai Lama and the Tibetan people who followed him into exile. Today, Dharamsala has become an intriguing hodgepodge of monasteries, nunneries, boarding schools, government-in-exile offices, and home to lay Tibetans. Makeshift and poorly constructed concrete houses dot the sides of winding streets that flood (sometimes with sewage) during the monsoon summer months. For both locals and visitors, everyday life centers around the Dalai Lama's temple. Despite the arduous twelve-hour bus ride from New Delhi, the town of Dharamsala has become a popular destination for backpackers, Western Buddhism students, study abroad programs, and activists. As I describe in more detail in

Figure 2. Dharamsala. Photo by Megan Joan Mack Photography.

the next chapter, engagement with the West has also shaped how Tibetan activists engage human rights discourse by circulating trauma narratives, a new genre of discourse, refashioned and repurposed for global consumption.

Everyday Suffering

Living in India is not easy and there were many occasions when I relied on Tibetan friends and neighbors for support. As many ethnographers will attest, most of what I learned came not from formal interviews, which can produce formulaic responses, but through everyday social engagement. When I had problems of my own (mostly mundane annoyances like ongoing battles with Indian visa officials who periodically tried to deny my research visa), my Tibetan interlocutors gave me advice on how to cope. Complaining about my difficulties to Dolma, my elderly neighbor, she used the Tibetan political situation to explain why I needed to toughen up. "Whether someone is happy or not depends on how spacious their mind is—not what is happening externally," she explains.

> It depends on their way of thinking. Whether or not they have a wide and spacious mind and are able to think very broadly—not only about oneself, but about others and the country and whole planet. Not narrow thinking. Inside Tibet, there is no freedom. People are tortured very brutally by the Chinese police, but they try to deal with these problems and get on with life. They don't give up, but they try to persevere.

So why, then, I asked, shouldn't I try to persevere? In this particular instance, I was certain my ill treatment at the visa office was due to sexist attitudes about a female researcher. But Dolma was hearing none of it. "You lose in the end, with anger. It only hurts *you*," she emphasized. "The perseverance is within your own *sems* [heart-mind]. Your own refusal to give up *btang snyom* [equanimity]."

Admittedly, at the outset I looked at the Buddhist concept of equanimity with some skepticism and long wondered if this were not some kind of internalized oppression. But Dolma's usage of equanimity did not sound at all like floating on a tranquil lake or a denial of emotion. This kind of *btang snyom* was more engaged, active, and intentional. It was a way of refusing to be dragged down—an unwillingness to pick up that ball of negative emotions.

Dolma continues: "no matter the problem—small annoyances like Indian visa offices or large ones like torture and imprisonment—you should apply the same method. The method of seeing that problems come from our own minds, and not from the outside." There are formal Buddhist practices known as *lojong* (mind training) that coach practitioners in how to train the mind, but Dolma speaks of this cultural wisdom in wholly ordinary ways. She says, "You create space in the mind, you make the mind more vast by thinking about others, and by thinking that it is only natural to have problems in life." Talking about mental distress only solidifies it, she argues. "And it can make you sick." What Dolma and many others implored me to understand is what is known as *sems pa chen po* (vast or spacious mind)—what I argue in this book is the hallmark of resilience among Tibetans in exile.

Spacious Mind: A North Star Principle

Like many of the 150,000 Tibetan citizens currently living in exile, Sonam Tashi and Dolma are reticent to frame personal experiences in terms of trauma. Instead, they deploy shared cultural understandings, often infused with Buddhist doctrine, to reframe the mental distress associated with loss, violence, and displacement. These cultural practices encourage letting go of distress rather than holding on to or solidifying it. The process of letting go is both a pathway to and evidence of *sems pa chen po*. My argument is that *sems pa chen po* acts as a kind of north star principle guiding the way, even among those who are struggling. A spacious mind is not merely an outcome but a pathway, a method, a view, and a horizon, orienting those who are suffering toward recovery.

But whereas biomedical notions of trauma are tightly woven with the practices of testimony, narrative, and a therapeutic imperative to debrief, many Tibetans insist that talking too much about problems will only make things worse. As it is understood today, trauma does not necessarily refer to difficult events themselves—witnessing violence, surviving an earthquake, exposure to war—but the enduring and relentless suffering in the aftermath. Indeed, the chronicity of trauma is seen as inevitable: devastation endures. But is this perspective universal? Although medical professionals view trauma as a taken-for-granted category of human existence (Desjarlais 1995; Felman and Laub 1992), myriad societies across the globe do not recognize trauma disorders as a psychiatric category. Many Tibetans who come to India seeking a better life have faced severe oppression and discrimination; some are survivors of torture. But members of this community are reticent to share their personal accounts as ones of chronic suffering. Instead, those living in Dharamsala argue it is best to move on rather than depict details of past horror through debriefing.

We might ask, then, is it the case that Tibetans experience trauma but do not talk about it? Or is their experience altogether different? And if resilience in the face of political violence and resettlement is not sufficiently defined by the absence of psychological symptoms, what might it be like? What defines resilience for Tibetans? Furthermore, this book investigates what there is to learn about resilience from a culture that thinks about stress as something that is inherently workable, and in fact, can be a great teacher. How does this frame what scholars call the moral good and why might an anthropology of ethics and moral experience more aptly explain what Tibetans do in the face of adversity than the dichotomy of trauma/resilience?

Resilience and the Problem of Trauma

Spacious Minds argues that resilience is not a mere absence of suffering—in fact, my work with Tibetan exiles suggests that those who cope most gracefully may indeed experience deep pain and loss. But whereas anthropologists have demonstrated how social structures produce subjectivities marked by suffering, there are few studies that investigate the potential for zones of recovery and sociocultural practices that bolster communities under duress. Although the term "resilience" has become a buzz word in public health, education, and global humanitarianism, this book challenges perspectives that liken resilience to the hardiness of physical materials, suggesting people should "bounce back" from adversity. Such metaphors do not work because they are static and ahistorical (Allen et al. 2013; Kirmayer et al. 2009); they also fail to account for ways that vulnerability may actually promote recovery—which is different from neoliberal notions of resilience that implore individual grittiness in the face of inequity. More broadly, *Spacious Minds* reveals how one community attempts to mitigate structural problems of forced migration, calling into question the tendency to use trauma as an organizing principle for all studies of conflict where suffering is an individual problem rooted in psychiatric illness.

Many important thinkers within the humanities and social sciences have contributed to a growing literature on the historical and social construction of trauma. Anthropologists in particular have critiqued the universalizing of post-traumatic stress disorder (PTSD), showing how while trauma is taken to be a natural human experience, it is a relatively new concept brought into existence at a particular moment in history (Fassin 2009; Hacking 1998; Young 1995). But beyond merely articulating the ways that Tibetan categories of distress are different from biomedical ones, I seek to push back against theoretical boundaries by showing how alternative systems of appraisal contribute new possibilities for understanding resilience. Whereas the experience of trauma among Americans is articulated and reinforced by biomedicine, the social world of Tibetans encourages those exposed to violence to see past events as impermanent and illusory. In Dharamsala, debriefing, working through, or processing past events is not considered to be a particularly efficacious way to manage distress and people believe it might even cause illness.

Within biomedicine, PTSD is understood as a specific set of reactions to a stressful event that lead to prolonged debilitation and impairment. There are specific criteria that must be met. First, the person must have been exposed to actual or threatened serious injury, violence, or death. Next, the traumatic event must be reexperienced as intrusive thoughts, nightmares, flashbacks, or physical reactivity. Avoidance of trauma-related stimuli and "negative thoughts or feelings," such as isolation and negative thoughts about oneself and the world, are also required for one to be diagnosed with PTSD (American Psychiatric Association 2013). Finally, to be diagnosed with PTSD, the person must also demonstrate increased arousal and reactivity, such as engaging in risky or destructive behavior, a heightened startle reaction, and difficulty concentrating.

But within the Tibetan psychiatric nosology, there is no particular gloss for such a disorder.[2] This is not to say that Tibetans never experience prolonged and intractable mental distress with some of these features, but the notion of "trauma"—understood as psychic or somatic harm that lingers from past injury—is not a specified mental illness. Trauma as disorder is not reinforced by social institutions such as insurance companies, clinics, and psychiatric experts, as in Euro-American contexts (Fassin 2009; Foucault 1965; Young 1995). And yet researchers from the Global North continue to investigate rates of post-traumatic stress disorder among Tibetans with perhaps unsurprisingly mixed results.

The purported prevalence of PTSD and other psychiatric disorders varies widely across studies of mental illness among Tibetans in exile, ranging from 25 to 70 percent for anxiety and 14 to 57 percent for depression (Crescenzi et al. 2002; Holtz 1998; Keller et al. 1997; Sachs et al. 2008). Assessing PTSD, a specific category of anxiety disorder, proved difficult for researchers, raising questions about its cultural utility. As Sachs et al. (2008) point out, many studies deliberately oversample torture survivors, so while these studies find that 20 percent of refugees meet criteria for PTSD (Crescenzi et al. 2002; Keller et al. 1997), this reveals little about the general population. Using the same instruments, when Lhewa and colleagues (2007) conducted a similar study with a comparable sample of Tibetan refugees they found that only 5.3 percent met criteria for PTSD.

Many of these studies used the Harvard Trauma Questionnaire (HTQ) to measure PTSD, and the Hopkins Symptom Checklist-25 (HSCL) for anxiety and depressive symptoms. Researchers at the Bellevue/NYU Program for Torture Survivors sought to translate and validate these instruments for use in a Tibetan refugee population. They found that while the sensitivity and specificity of the HSCL were high, the HTQ generated low sensitivity, which they hypothesize is due to low rates of PTSD (Lhewa et al. 2007). Many of these studies note that Tibetan clinicians themselves challenge the cultural utility of PTSD, further troubling the validity of these studies. There are many prescribed ways of understanding and coping with distress in Dharamsala. They are not easily "back-translated" into psychiatric categories, however. Nor do Tibetan medical categories correlate and align with biomedicine, particularly within the realm of mental illness (this is discussed further in chapter 2). While some biomedically oriented researchers wonder if a type 2 error (a false negative) is at play due to cultural factors, others surmise that Tibetans may indeed have lower rates of psychiatric illness than would be expected.

But this supposition leads to somewhat dangerous territory. To complicate matters, scholars must always fight against the long-standing romanticizing of Tibetans as inherently peaceful, serene, and altogether spiritual (Lopez 1998; Said 1978). And thus, a study on resilience among this cultural group may be easily misconstrued as Orientalist or naïve in its conception. What is interesting about the Tibetan case is not that Tibetans are more remarkable than other groups, but that they understand human resilience as rather basic and ordinary—not at all remarkable, in their view. By basic I do not mean simple, but rather they understand the human capacity to mitigate stress through mind training as something that anyone can learn and be trained in. In her studies of war and atrocity, Carolyn Nordstrom (1997) urges readers to pay attention to ordinary processes of resilience—not because they negate suffering, but because they offer a realistic picture of the creative solutions average people find to thrive.

After more than fifty years in existence, Dharamsala has become home to multiple generations of Tibetan migrants. Tibetans fleeing their homeland arrive to a relatively thriving and stable community where they are free to educate their children in the Tibetan language, practice their religion, seek education, and establish informal businesses. But whereas it is important to note that not all Tibetans are resilient on the individual level (and that there may be marked differences across gender, generation, time since migration, and birthplace), at the cultural or population level, there seems to be remarkable geographies of resilience.

I borrow this idea of a "geography" or "landscape" from Angela Garcia (2010), who frames her study of drug addicts in the American Southwest in these terms. Rather than looking to individual psychology, she considers how a geography of despair and hopelessness has been built, and how it molds a lived world where extraordinary numbers of people succumb to drug addiction. João Biehl (2005) articulates a different kind of geography in his ethnography of zones of abandonment in Brazil. Such landscapes (in these cases, demoralizing ones) shape the lived experiences of those unfortunate enough to be born there, cutting sharply across lines of inequity. Here I ask: Might the inverse be true? Are there ways that cultures can produce resilience just as they produce moral injury? And if so, might it be the case that suffering and resilience can be evoked simultaneously—such that resilience is not necessarily the inverse of suffering? The Tibetan case is instructive in this regard because it demonstrates how communities can train in resilience not in spite of suffering, but because of it, and through it. Indeed, in this book I go so far as to ask: can a person be resiliently traumatized? Such a question will no doubt elicit critique.

Social scientists—perhaps anthropologists in particular—are wary of studies on resilience, or what might be called "the anthropology of the good" (Desjarlias and Throop 2011; Mattingly 2014; Mattingly and Garro 2000; Robbins 2013; Throop 2010). To this end, Joel Robbins argues that anthropology in the twenty-first century has been defined largely by its fascination with "the suffering subject," using trauma "as a bridge between cultures" (2013, 453). Political theorists argue that the ubiquity of *resilience* as the concept du jour only further entrenches the neoliberal subject in a "responsibility of vulnerability" endemic to the Anthropocene (Evans and Reid 2014). Social critics reject the notion that individuals should "bounce back from the experience of catastrophe unscathed" (Evans and Reid 2014, 6), which implicitly implicates the subject in his or her own oppression and failure to withstand the blows of injustice. In other words, if a person cannot bounce back from a devastating natural disaster, unemployment, or serious illness, then it is thought to be because of their own moral failing (see Adams 2013 and Myers 2015 for ethnographic studies that illustrate this problem).

Armed by critical studies of race, gender, and sexuality, anthropology as a discipline values investigation that reveals injustice and structural inequities. And yet it is important to avoid writing about people as if they are *only* vulnerable victims of structural violence. At times, the entire Global South is framed in this way. Robbins implores his anthropological colleagues not to abandon social suffering, but to use it as a launching point to go onward, asking how people in different societies strive to create good in their lives. But somehow, studies of hope, forgiveness, humor, recovery, happiness, and love are precarious in anthropology; scholars fear they may disavow injustice (or worse, that people seek a false "Pollyannaish" capital *G* "good" [Robbins 2013, 457]), wishfully touted as something universal.

That the Euro-American style of practicing anthropology is comfortable with writing on suffering and ambivalent to venture into exploring the moral good reveals more about us as scholars than about our interlocutors. Why are medicine, politics, and suffering foundational concepts worthy of rigorous investigation but compassion is not? As Jason Throop argues, "What becomes recognized as 'cultural' in the concrete practice of ethnographic encounters is precisely that which destabilizes our otherwise unnoticed assumptions, that which unsettles our usual modes of typification" (2010, 224). Readers, in this regard, may vacillate in their understanding of Tibetan Buddhist forms of resilience, which appear in stark contrast to Euro-American tendencies to emphasize, reinforce, diagnose, and testify suffering, enhancing its veracity. Feelings of disbelief, admiration, skepticism, and wonderment may arise in readers who struggle to see how trauma and what one ought to do about it could look different from afar. For many anthropologists, what is most at stake in their ethnographies is suffering, and to that end, Don Kulick has urged us to think about exactly why there is a "long-standing anthropological interest in powerless or disenfranchised people" (2006, 933). Those working within the anthropology of moral experience urge researchers to see their own reflexive commitments as deeply moral (Mattingly 2014; Taylor 1989) insofar as what we see as significant in "the other" may indeed reveal our own phenomenological and epistemological anxieties.

Although a vigilant focus on inequity may momentarily safeguard against naïve (and sometimes racist) formulations of how oppressed people can withstand pain, it ultimately backs our interlocutors into a narrow corner of marginalization if we disavow resilience. This is a great danger for scholars of forced migration. As anthropologist Michael Jackson warns: "If we are to avoid the trap of becoming infatuated with our own intellectual-cum-magical capacity to render the world intelligible, then the vocabulary 'we' all too glibly project onto 'them' must be tested continually against the various and changing experiences of actual lives. Otherwise we risk becoming complicit in the social violence that reduces the other to a mere object—a drudge, a victim, a number, assimilated to a category, a class, or a global phenomenon" (2013, 4–5). What Jackson advocates is for scholars to resist defining our interlocutors by their struggles. This relates not only to how we write, but how we conceive of research questions and study design in the first place.

For as Nancy Scheper-Hughes asserts, "While anthropological references to vengeance, blood feuds, counter-sorcery, and witch hunts are many, descriptions of individual or collective rituals of remorse and reparation are few indeed" (1998, 114). In this light, the major contribution I wish to make with this ethnography is to demonstrate how suffering and resilience fit together and to show what we can learn from looking at the specificity of how cultures both imagine and practice resilience. In this book, I do not deny the existence of suffering within Dharamsala, but rather I start from that place and ask: what happens next?

The Anthropology of Ethics and Moral Experience

I situate this book within the anthropology of ethics and moral experience, an approach that commits to understanding "the good" on its own terms. What this ethnography contributes is a case study in how suffering itself may be a launching point for the good. Whereas it may feel intuitive that suffering, illness, and pain should be eradicated as quickly as possible, Tibetan Buddhists argue that a willingness to sit with suffering opens a special kind of door; it is a threshold. As cancer survivors, survivors of war, and the bereaved attest, there is something about deep loss that yields transformation and a connection to what Michael Jackson (2009) calls "the real," that deep truth that came before and that endures. This notion of "the real" is instructive in that moral good is much more expansive than quotidian understandings of goodness, which are framed only by positive traits. The moral good, or "the real," includes pain and human suffering. In fact, they are intricately linked.

Cheryl Mattingly (2010, 2014) serves as an intellectual beacon for understanding the good within suffering—or perhaps, the goodness *of* suffering.

Her work reveals how people take extraordinary events (murder, incarceration, disability, assault, displacement) and fold it into everyday experience. Through ordinary engagement, Mattingly argues that it is important to learn how suffering "demand[s] a transformative effort to reimagine not only what will happen, but also what ought to happen, or how one ought to respond not only to difficulties and suffering but also to unexpected possibilities" (2014, 5). Whereas concepts such as "trauma" and "resilience" are evaluative terms coming from the outside, anthropologists engaged with phenomenological understandings of pain ask us to drop this language of assessment and instead walk directly up to first-person experience. Whereas those from the outside slide the experience of Tibetans in exile into familiar registers such as "trauma" and "resilience," it is critical to underscore the ways such concepts do little to illuminate what pain is like and how it may serve to open transformative doors.

Research Study Design

Through an ethnographic study of Tibetans living in Dharamsala, India, *Spacious Minds* investigates how community members cope with adversity, asking first what counts as resilience, and second, how in practice Tibetans in Dharamsala thrive in exile. My work as an anthropologist is also shaped by my training in clinical social work. Having worked as a psychotherapist in psychiatric hospitals and in community mental health settings, my understanding of trauma is shaped not just by reading studies, but through intensive clinical engagement. My clinical training, not typical for an anthropologist, has sensitized me to notice nonverbal cues and other subtle signs of distress among my interlocutors on which I might not otherwise pick up. My training, for example, in how to conduct a mental status exam, as well as a learned sensitivity in asking about traumatic events, influences my approach and interpretive frame. It is not uncommon for researchers working on torture and violence to experience what is known as vicarious trauma, where they become emotionally distressed by exposure to horrific and upsetting narratives. As a social worker, I had received specialized training in how to manage such reactions, which I found useful in conducting this long-term ethnographic research project. My clinical experience with Americans diagnosed with PTSD and other anxiety disorders also served as stark backdrop of difference to how Tibetans coped with atrocity and hardship.

The results of this study are based on extended ethnographic fieldwork I conducted since 2007, with a continuous fourteen-month period from 2011 to 2012. During that time, I lived in the Tibetan area of McLeod Ganj, or "upper Dharamsala," in the state of Himachal Pradesh. I mixed into the fold of everyday life in Dharamsala, drinking tea and cooking meals with neighbors, joining in daily *khora* (circumambulating around the Dalai Lama's temples and spinning prayer wheels), and participating in political marches and candlelight vigils for Tibet. I spent time with older Tibetan men and women as I helped them round the *khora* or drag heavy wooden prostration boards into the *tsuklakhang* (temple). The Tibetan new arrivals reception center clinic encouraged those recovering from their arduous journey from Tibet or Nepal to talk with me. I also interviewed several dozen monks and nuns, inside their monastic compounds and around town. In addition, many students at the Tibetan transit school and within the TCV high school shared their stories over biscuits and chai. Although there were common themes related to resilience that emerged across disparate groups, I did not seek to find consensus across my sample. Instead, I allow the Tibetan exile community, which is highly diverse, and even disjointed across its mobile population, to stand unresolved on issues where there is divergence. Although my analysis focuses on the vast majority of Tibetans in Dharamsala who are Buddhist, there are those who are atheist, Christian, or Muslim. As well, many concepts and practices I describe in the book are applicable to a much broader population of Tibetan Buddhist practitioners who may be Mongolian, Nepali, Chinese, or Bhutanese.

In addition to extended participant observation, I also conducted eighty semistructured interviews with a range of different kinds of people living in Dharamsala. This research did not rely on well-being scales or other clinical instruments to measure resilience. Rather, my aim was to investigate how Tibetans living in Dharamsala identify and understand resilience from their own view. During this first phase of interviews, I conducted what is known as a "cultural domain analysis," which asked interview participants to respond to the following question: "How would you know that even in the face of difficulty, someone is doing okay?" Using a free-listing methodology, participants were asked to list as many items as they could think of that would provide evidence that a person was doing okay (and what they think "doing okay" looks like) despite difficulty. I analyzed responses according to both frequency and salience across the sample. This is where I first encountered the notion of *sems pa chen po* (vast and spacious mind), which seemed to define what it meant to be resilient in this context. Within this same group ($N = 40$), I also asked each person to make a list of three or four difficult situations in their lives. Then, we discussed how they coped with each problem listed. Taking seriously Cheryl Mattingly's imperative that to understand the moral framings of suffering a researcher must look "upon events, some large and dramatic, others small and almost invisible" (2014, 8), this ethnography grapples with distress ranging from the everyday to the life changing.

In phase 2 of interviews, I used the data I already collected to develop a semistructured guide to interview another set of Tibetan participants ($N = 40$). The aim of these interviews was to explore in greater depth the practices and processes of resilience in Dharamsala. As with every other aspect of my fieldwork, these interviews were conducted in the Tibetan language. A local research assistant helped to transcribe interviews, and we jointly translated interview transcripts into English to ensure my translation captured the nuance of subtle concepts. This research was approved by the Columbia University IRB (Institutional Review Board) as well as local Indian authorities, and was funded by a Fulbright award, a Lemelson Society for Psychological Anthropology award, the Sasakawa Young Leaders Fellowship Fund (SYLFF) in conjunction with the Columbia University Weatherhead East Asian Institute, and the Mellon Foundation.

Organization of the Book

Beginning with chapter 1, "Life in Exile," I introduce the setting of the study and context of the research problem. I also describe Tibetan political history from the early 1900s until the present day, with particular emphasis on political activism and migration out of Tibet. This chapter describes the journeys Tibetans undertake to get to Dharamsala, India, and how this small hill station has changed over the last fifty years. The identity and meaning of being a refugee living in exile varies across this community, which some researchers have mistakenly characterized as static and uniform. I explore here some important differences with regard to gender, age, and time since migration.

Chapter 2, "Mind Training," argues that the Tibetan notion of resilience is characterized by spaciousness, a willingness to let go, and a sense of flexibility. Rather than debriefing or processing details of past events, the support that Tibetan refugees give to one another often follows the sensibility of a Buddhist approach known as *lojong*, or "mind training," which emphasizes changing the way you think rather than changing the external environment. Here, resilience is an approach for meeting life's inevitable problems with openness and the conviction that everything in life is workable. As my neighbor Tashi Lhamo teased good-heartedly: "Foreigners are such big complainers! They always want to talk about problems. Instead, we should try to have *sems pa chen po* (big or vast mind) and not focus on ourselves." This chapter shows how alternative ways of appraising trauma contribute new possibilities for understanding resilience. In this context, compassion is not just a moral value but a practice or technology of the self, particularly in times of crisis. For Tibetans in exile, pain and misfortune, while difficult, can also be an opportunity for transformation.

In chapter 3, "Resisting Chronicity," I argue that distinctive cultural concepts of time frame Tibetan understandings of traumatic memory and the sense of what one ought to do in the face of difficulty. In North America, the therapeutics of trauma work often involves a retrospective stance—a past revisited in the name of recovery. Whereas Euro-Americans expect trauma to be chronic and debilitating, Tibetans exposed to violence understand their distress as impermanent and fleeting, which changes the impact and durable effects of the ordeal. The notion of "going back" and debriefing, working through, or processing past events is not seen as a useful way to manage distress. The imperative is instead to "hold lightly" and look flexibly at emotions—to see them as impermanent. The north star ideal of *sems pa chen po* lights the path ahead when people (inevitably) struggle to leave a harmful past behind. The way people recover—reinforced through Buddhist practice more than clinical treatment—is to drop one's attachment to the ways one was wronged altogether. Unlike public truth commissions or psychotherapy, which are technologies to work with narrative, mind-training principles woven into Tibetan cultural understandings of what to do in the face of suffering actually implore one to deconstruct both the legitimacy and the utility of holding tightly to "my story." To solidify one's experience is to be narrowly trapped by it.

Chapter 4, "The Paradox of Testimony," articulates an intriguing paradox that emerges as a result of the Tibetan political resistance campaign. Scholars detail the ways that the "Americanization of Mental Illness" (Watters 2010) has spread across the globe, usually usurping local practices. And yet in this community, something unusual has transpired. Rather than becoming postcolonial victims of Western trauma concepts, Tibetan political activists have appropriated foreign ideas and fashioned them not for psychological healing—indeed, they largely reject foreign mental health services—but as a political device to fuel their human rights campaign. With a keen awareness of how testimony and narrative give legitimacy to their political aim, Tibetan activists have revamped local sensibilities of "telling trauma" by encouraging their countrymates to disseminate their stories of violence to the world. While on the personal level Tibetans do not see much therapeutic utility in recounting details of torture and imprisonment, they readily distribute bloodied photographs and trauma narratives to journalists and foreign researchers with hopes of garnering international support. This is a flexibility of another kind: in experimenting with globally circulating media on YouTube, Twitter, and human rights platforms, Tibetan activists use foreign psychiatric concepts to enhance political visibility.

In chapter 5, "Open Sky of Mind," I chronicle how the Tibetan practice of creating a spacious and flexible mind promotes agency. As such, I move beyond the social suffering paradigm to open new possibilities for studies on collective and social resilience. In North America, there is a sense of entitlement to constant health, happiness, and well-being. Becoming sick, feeling unhappy, or losing a loved one feels not just painful, but somehow wrong. "Why do bad things happen to good people?" some ask. Taking seriously the notion that suffering is intimately shaped by culture, *Spacious Minds* grapples with a collective view that insists that difficulty and disruption are just part of life. Far from implying that anyone who is imprisoned or violated somehow deserves it, the Buddhist system of karma reminds this community that in the endless sea of past lifetimes, we have all been oppressors at one time. Accepting suffering as a natural part of life (and thus, not particularly remarkable when we, in fact, encounter adversity) does not lead to victim mentalities or internalized oppression in the Tibetan exile community. In fact, I argue the opposite—that such perspectives actually promote agency in the face of structural violence. This perspective pushes critical medical anthropology to dialogue with an anthropology of the good. If suffering, oppression, and inequity are the starting place, what happens next? How do communities thrive and how, as scholars, can we understand resilience in a way that does not silence suffering?

This inquiry concludes with a discussion on how resilience in Dharamsala arises through a purposeful practice of viewing stress as inherently workable. Resilience is considered rather ordinary in Dharamsala, prompting people to *expect recovery* rather than expecting chronic distress and disability. While specific Buddhist practices may not be transferrable to other populations, I argue that this culture's propensity to view stress as inherently workable may, indeed, be a useful takeaway for outsiders. The community members who generously shared their time and personal stories with me were motivated by the idea that Tibetans could help other refugee groups. My interlocutors were especially interested in learning about the Holocaust and the plight of Syrian refugees, as well as others across the globe embroiled in political turmoil. In particular, they saw their Buddhist approach to mitigating problems as potentially helpful for outsiders (often pointing out how inept Westerners seem at coping with problems).

The medical anthropologist Arthur Kleinman asks: "What are the limits of trauma as an organizing idea, especially as it is employed to make sense of mass violence? And what are the leading alternative candidates for this role?" (2015, xv). The story of resilience in *Spacious Minds* responds to this query, presenting a new way of understanding suffering that can offer lessons for combatting the effects of violence and loss around the world. Based on Buddhist sensibilities, this community sees loss, disruption, and even violence as a taken-for-granted aspect of human existence. And when it inevitably happens, it is not an anomaly or an affront to the sanctity of life. That is, people expect hardship in samsara. But rather than hardening and stoically withstanding the blow as "grit," Tibetans contend that life's atrocities can be a training ground for compassion.

Chapter 1

LIFE IN EXILE

In premodern Tibet, there was a largely semibureaucratic governance marked by regional and religious alliances (Samuel 1993). Tibet's exact geographic boundaries are contested and varied across historical maps, but most regional provinces fell under the rule of the Dalai Lama's administration in Lhasa, beginning with the fifth and extending to the present—the fourteenth Dalai Lama, Tenzin Gyatso. Of the four schools of Tibetan Buddhism (Gelug, Kagyu, Nyingma, and Sakya), the lineage of the Dalai Lamas is associated with the Gelugpa tradition, which rose to power above other schools. Throughout Tibet's history, the rise and fall of these various Buddhist schools was synonymous with political rule. Systems of governance were not uniform in Tibet; some regions were governed as kingdoms, others as chiefdoms, and some were ruled by religious leaders (McGranahan 2010a; Tuttle 2005).

By the time Chairman Mao Zedong came into power in 1949, he announced his intention to "liberate" Tibet. Despite an appeal by the Tibetan government to both the United States and Great Britain to support its application for membership in the United Nations, little was done to stop the People's Republic of China, which was rapidly becoming a world power. The United States, focused on the Korean War, did not speak out against the invasion. As McGranahan (2010a) details, however, the United States has a long history of working quietly behind the scenes for the Tibetan political cause, including covert CIA training of Tibetan civilian militia. In 1950, forty thousand Chinese troops moved into the capital city of Lhasa, prompting the state oracle[1] to determine that because of the mounting political crisis the sixteen-year-old Dalai Lama should assume power immediately rather than waiting until the customary age of eighteen. Despite a number of appeals to the United Nations, the international community did not intervene and over the next decade Tibet was systematically taken over by China.

In 1959, the Dalai Lama, in a disguise, fled to India. The journey took three weeks by horseback, traversing the Himalayas. Over the next several years, eighty thousand Tibetans followed the Dalai Lama, the political and spiritual leader of Tibet, into exile. The Dalai Lama was invited to India by Prime Minister Nehru, who provided the Tibetan leader and his people a safe haven in Dharamsala. This remote hill station in Himachal Pradesh was abandoned by the British, who had formerly established a military cantonment in the region. Although it was treated as a remote no man's land, the local Gaddhi people were displaced when the British colonized India, and still today are marginalized in their native land. Upper Dharamsala, known as "McLeod Ganj," is almost entirely a Tibetan enclave and remains the seat of the Tibetan government-in-exile.

Central Tibet today spans an area of China known as the TAR—Tibetan Autonomous Region; much of eastern Tibet, Amdo and Kham, has been incorporated into the Gansu, Yunnan, Sichuan, and Qinghai provinces. The official statement from the Chinese government is that Tibet has always been a part of China, thus justifying the invasion and subsequent rule over it. While today's political disputes focus on human rights, in the early days of conflict, Tibetans resisted the characterization of the struggle as a violation of individual or human rights, instead insisting that the focal problem was to regain the sovereignty of the Tibetan state (McGranahan 2010a). But as described later in chapter 4 of this book, a new and intentional focus on human rights has become more prominent today as activists seek to join global narratives of resistance. And whereas there are discernable disagreements among Tibetans, most take the Dalai Lama's lead and have given up hope of independence and instead seek cultural, linguistic, social, and religious freedom and autonomy.

The Tibetan government-in-exile, housed in Dharamsala, is composed of the *kashag* (executive cabinet) and a forty-four-member Parliament. By his own hand, the Dalai Lama relinquished his title as political leader of Tibet and pushed government leaders to develop a more secular and democratic political system. In 2011, the *sikyong* (political leader), Lobsang Sangye, a Harvard-educated lawyer, was elected to the newly formed cabinet of the government-in-exile as the prime minister and new political leader of the Tibetan people. The Dalai Lama remains a spiritual leader of Tibet, although there are many other lesser-known lamas, such as the seventeenth Karmapa, head of the Kagyu school, who are also deeply influential in social and cultural life.

Beginning in the late 1970s and early 1980s, the government-in-exile, led by the Dalai Lama, attempted to engage China in a series of peaceful negotiations. Despite being termed the "Tibetan Autonomous Region," Tibetans claim they continue to face religious, cultural, and ethnic persecution. The Dalai Lama hoped that through compromise and peaceful dialogue, an agreement could be reached. Along with the *kashag*, he developed what is known as the "Middle Way Policy," which does not ask for independence, but rather "meaningful autonomy." The policy evokes the following:

> The central government of the People's Republic of China has the responsibility for the political aspects of Tibet's international relations and defense, whereas the Tibetan people should manage all other affairs pertaining to Tibet, such as religion and culture, education, economy, health, ecological, and environmental protection; the Chinese government should stop its policy of human rights violations in Tibet and the transfer of Chinese population into Tibetan areas; to resolve the issue of Tibet, His Holiness the Dalai Lama shall take the main responsibility of sincerely pursuing negotiations and reconciliation with the Chinese government. (Dalai Lama 2019)

The People's Republic of China (PRC) does not acknowledge Tibetan sovereignty and has refused dialogue with the Tibetan government-in-exile, maintaining that the Dalai Lama is a terrorist who encourages separatism among Tibetans (who should pledge allegiance to the Chinese government).

Despite wide admiration for the Dalai Lama across the globe, there are no countries that recognize the Tibetan government-in-exile as a legitimate government. Even the government of India, despite its own ambivalent tolerance of Tibetan settlements inside its country, does not formally recognize Tibet as a sovereign nation. When countries like Germany or the United States host the Dalai Lama, even in his role as religious figurehead, the People's Republic of China blasts them for doing so, sometimes threatening economic sanctions. This tension also plays out in more subtle instances, such as when a Tibetan undergraduate student at the University of Massachusetts Amherst was barred from carrying a Tibetan flag at her graduation ceremony in 2017 because, she was told, "Tibet is a part of China" (*Boston Globe* 2017). There are few countries that publicly acknowledge the Tibetan situation as a crisis and none are willing to risk upsetting the PRC to offer much to help.

The flow of migrants out of the Tibetan plateau has fluctuated over the last several decades, but it is estimated that nearly 150,000 are living in India, Nepal, Bhutan, and elsewhere across the world. Although it is difficult to document current trends in the diaspora, it is estimated that approximately 2,500 to 3,500 Tibetans leave the country each year (International Campaign for Tibet 2019). Some leave legally on temporary visas and do not return. For example, 300,000 people came to Bodhgaya, India, in January 2012 when the Dalai Lama led the Kalachakra Empowerment;[2] many were Tibetans on a three-month religious pilgrimage visa. I attended the initiation where I observed many older people who arrived covered in dirt and torn clothing, having traversed the Himalayas and undertaken arduous journeys to attend the teachings, underscoring what people are willing to sacrifice for a chance to connect with their spiritual leader. Many Tibetans with whom I spoke told me they saw this as their last opportunity to see the Dalai Lama and to receive the special Kalachakra empowerment. Some had only loose plans of where they would go next and many had only enough money for a few weeks. The Tibetan settlement communities throughout India support new arrivals with funds that comes, in part, from foreign aid. Indeed, the new arrivals did not seem to worry much about how they would get by.

Exile communities in India are relatively thriving; however, Tibetans living in India are not granted citizenship or political asylum. Tibetans can obtain residential certificates (known as RCs), which must be renewed every year, but Indian officials may deny them arbitrarily without recourse. Some Tibetans who are born in India are able to procure Indian passports, yet this is highly variable and depends on the mood of Indian government officials;

giving *baksheesh* (bribes) to secure one's paperwork is sometimes effective. My neighbor, a retired government official said: "Now thousands of Tibetan refugees don't have an RC. Therefore, they have many problems in their daily life, such as finding jobs. Without an RC, you can't buy cooking gas or rent rooms from Indians. But if they have money, it will be easier for them to solve these kinds of problems." It is known around Dharamsala that monasteries and nunneries are filled with Tibetans whose RCs are lapsed, having been denied renewal. There is no governing body to which they may appeal, so people simply stay in a quasi-legal situation in India unable to travel. There are rumors that one day the Foreign Registration Office (FRO) connected to the local police department will canvass the monasteries demanding registration cards. Although these ambiguities are unsettling, most Tibetans in Dharamsala feel they are under less scrutiny than they were in Tibet.

At the same time, Carole McGranahan (2016b) makes the case that citizenship refusal among Tibetans in India is a complex dance for those who insist their loyalty remains in Tibet—a homeland to which they vow to return. "Tibetans refused citizenship, but were they ever offered it?" (McGranahan 2016b, 336). For members of the Tibetan diaspora, although living in India affords a degree of pragmatic freedom, the refusal to pledge their citizenship (first to China, and now to India or Nepal) is a power move to stake their own claim to future citizenship in a free Tibet. Renouncing their citizenship, even if it would make daily life easier in India, sits closely alongside the experiences of their countrymates in Chinese prisons and detention centers. The director of a social service agency in Dharamsala explained to me:

> When I was in my county in Kham, no one could say anything about the history of Tibet. My parents can't explain the history or say very much about Tibet being an independent country. If they tell us about history, then children might not be able to keep the secret and they might get in trouble with authorities. My uncle is in a Chinese prison right now. He was sentenced to fifteen years. He was supposed to be released in 2011, but during his time in prison he never gave up his love for Tibet. He was asked to renounce his love for Tibetan culture and religious practice, but he wouldn't comply. So he was given three years extra. The reason that Tibetans have so much hope is because the Chinese always discriminate against Tibetans for jobs and education. They are very strict in their policy. This caused Tibetans to unite, giving us strength to resist the Chinese.

And thus, there is great ambivalence in the meaning of acquiring, renewing, and being denied an RC in Dharamsala. It is at once a tedious hassle and an index of their precarious ties (or lack thereof) to citizenship.

One might ask why China cares so much about Tibet. Some of these reasons are described below, but there has also been ongoing controversy over Taiwan and many lesser-known territories throughout Mongolia, Russia, and the South China Sea have been embroiled in land disputes over the last sixty years; Tibet is not unique in this respect. And yet because of the fascination with Tibetan Buddhism and admiration of the Dalai Lama, the occupation of Tibet has garnered international interest. Today, Tibet is valuable because of its untapped territory for Han Chinese settlers; during the 1970s, Tibet's vast, open space was used for different purposes: the storage of nuclear weapons. There is also an abundance of natural resources in Tibet, such as lithium, copper, and rare minerals. As well, it houses a great mass of underground water that is increasingly controversial in its usage and conservation. Over the last decade, the People's Republic of China has built a series of hydroelectric dams on rivers in Tibet to export electricity back to Chinese cities. Many Tibetan activists today have become increasingly concerned with the environmental destruction of the land; for instance, many protest the development of a hydroelectric construction project on Yamdrok Tso, a sacred lake between Lhasa and Shikatse (International Campaign for Tibet 2014).

A new arrival I interviewed at the Tibetan reception center explained: "Me and my husband had to leave Tibet because my husband took photos of the Chinese taking aluminum out of the ground near Nari. Many trucks took the metals out of the ground to take back to China. Also in my county, many places were destroyed by this digging. And the rivers were destroyed by harmful chemicals. Many animals and even people died because of the chemicals. My husband tried to protest against this. Later we found out that the Chinese were planning to arrest us for exposing them." Similarly, another new arrival explained:

> The Chinese are destroying the environment. Many areas are destroyed. Mandrojama, the birthplace of Songtsen Gampo [king of Tibet who was instrumental in bringing Buddhism to the land], held many resources. The Chinese dug out many precious metals and gems, completely destroying the land. From Mandro to Drikung Monastery, there is one mountain, which the Chinese tuned into a giant hole, removing all the treasures. During the digging,

Tibetans were not allowed to come near the site. Also, there is one small electricity base built by the Chinese. This is how they found the precious stones and metals. The Chinese government also built a huge dam in one river. Everyone says if the dam is destroyed, many Tibetan villages will be wiped out by a flood. Near the Drikung Monastery, each day the Chinese took out thirty truckloads of natural resources. I got a small piece of the treasure from another person. The rock is multicolored and very beautiful. This stone is precious, so I put it in my offering bowls [small bowls kept on one's religious shrine].

As of June 2017, over forty Tibetans in Qinghai Province had been arrested for protesting water rights when Chinese officials announced their plans to divert a river from a Tibetan settlement (Phayul 2017). China dismisses these protests, arguing it owns the right to these resources.

The PRC state government is also concerned with Tibet for cultural reasons. The Tibetan people are counted as one of fifty-five ethnic minority groups within the Han-dominated PRC. Besides these issues of ethnicity that are shared among other territories that have been subsumed into the PRC, Tibet has long been a source of particular tension because of the pervasiveness of religion. Not all Tibetans are religious; however, Buddhist holidays, rituals, and institutions, such as monasteries, are central forces in everyday sociocultural life. Local monasteries and nunneries hold a great deal of responsibility within communities, such as conducting daily rituals to appease local deities and managing funeral rites and care of the dead. Lay Tibetans make offerings to monasteries to perform purification practices on their behalf in times of sickness, financial hardship, or suspicion of spirit harm. Unlike in other religious traditions where monasticism is dying out, the tradition in Tibet remains strong.

Many families continue to send at least one child to a monastery or nunnery, at least for a period of time where they receive religious training and learn to read and write. Tibetan Buddhism is considered an "unregistered religion" that is not sanctioned by the PRC, and thus it is easy for government officials to deny routinized registration to monasteries and *shedras* (monastic colleges), citing their technically illegal activities. While many unregistered religious groups are active across China—notably a massive upswing of Pentecostal and Evangelical Christian groups—Tibetan Buddhists continue to face systematic discrimination, as the Chinese government deems them a dangerous "splittist" group (Cabezón 2008) under the guidance of the so-called Dalai Clique (a pejorative term for the Dalai Lama and his supporters). At the same time, the Chinese government has issued statements that it intends to take control of the Tibetan Buddhist religious institutions, such as those that name the reincarnation of the Dalai Lama and other leaders.

It is estimated that thousands of monasteries, nunneries, and religious monuments have been destroyed across the Tibetan Plateau. This was done in the name of modernizing Tibet, and particularly during the Cultural Revolution, to liberate its people from the "opiate of religion," because Tibetans' worldview "presumes the existence of deities and other planes of existence, the efficacy of magic, the existence of past and future lives, and the possibility of human perfection" (Cabezón 2008, 266). Initiatives to modernize and develop Tibet continue today. With a railroad now joining Beijing to Lhasa (a forty-eight-hour journey), Han Chinese are rapidly moving in to the region as they enjoy economic incentives to work and settle in the TAR. Tibetans heavily opposed the railroad construction because it destroyed large areas of wilderness, including sacred lakes, rivers, and mountains, and provided easy access for young Chinese developers to flood into Tibetan areas. Many who left Tibet describe how difficult it was to get work without good Chinese-language skills, and those who did find work made significantly lower wages than their Han Chinese peers.

Across the Tibetan plateau, the PRC continues to threaten religious and cultural freedom. The degree of persecution is variable, however, and some Tibetans live good, self-determined lives without discrimination. But still, in many regions of the TAR and within the eastern provinces, there are restrictions on Tibetan cultural practices (particularly those that are religious in nature), prompting many Tibetans and Tibet supporters to characterize China's political activities within Tibet as a cultural genocide. For example, many Tibetan schools have been converted to Mandarin-speaking schools, and in some areas it is impossible to educate one's children in one's native language. It is dangerous for Tibetans to publicly display photos of the Dalai Lama in their places of business, for example, which might be interpreted as political activism against the state. It is immediately noticeable in Dharamsala how prominently shopkeepers display photos of the Dalai Lama in every restaurant, shop, and tea stall—an act of defiance, allegiance, and devotion.

Nearly all the major Tibetan monasteries have reestablished themselves in India or Nepal. Local monasteries across Tibet still function, but many have restrictions on how many monks can be there at a time. Monks in Kham and Amdo—now part of Sichuan, Yunnan, Qinghai, and Gansu Provinces—are restricted in freely traveling to larger *shedras* (monastic colleges) in Lhasa for higher studies, something that was common before the Cultural Revolution (Cabezón 2008). There are also reports of reeducation campaigns using schools, radio, television, and the restructuring of monasteries to quell "backward" ways of life (Laird 2006). Many people I interviewed shared stories from childhood recounting how they were forced to leave Tibetan schools and travel great distances to attend Chinese government–sanctioned schools where Buddhist ideology was referred to as "separatist political propaganda."

At any given time, there is friction between monastics and Chinese authorities somewhere within Tibet. In December 2013, for example, protests erupted in Driru County after Drongna Monastery was closed following the arrest of Kalsang Dhondrup, the monastery's debate master. It is unknown what the precise charges are against him (Phayul 2013), but some reports indicate that the monasteries and local villagers refused to fly the government flags that were issued to them. After a number of monks failed interviews to assess their political allegiance, two more monasteries in the Nagchu region, Tarmoe and Rabten, were shut down (Tibetan Review 2014). Laypeople have also been targeted, including a number of Tibetan pop musicians, such as Lolo and Gongpo Tsezin, who were arrested and imprisoned for singing about self-immolation protests (Free Tibet 2017).

Since the early 1950s, it is estimated that hundreds of thousands Tibetans have been imprisoned for engaging in political activities, such as distributing proindependence literature, displaying the Tibetan flag and images of the Dalai Lama, and more recently, involvement in a self-immolation. Not all who are imprisoned by the Chinese government are tortured. However, the UNHCHR found torture, particularly among monks and nuns, to be widespread (United Nations 2013). Torture activities include beatings, exposure to severe cold, being forced to stare at the sun for extended periods, starvation, suspension in the air, attacks by dogs, solitary confinement, and sexual assault (Hooberman et al. 2007); some report being forced to watch others being tortured, such as watching others receive electric shocks as a warning (Benedict, Mancini, and Grodin 2009). Many describe being forced to denounce the Dalai Lama, even to stomp on his photograph, which they found particularly devastating.

A Buddhist Way of Life

Numerous ethnographic works detail the ways that Buddhist beliefs are internalized in the lifeworlds of everyday people throughout Asia (Cassaniti 2015, 2018; Dreyfus 2003; Makley 2007). The differences across regions in South Asia, Southeast Asia, Japan, China, and Mongolia also reflect the diversity of Buddhist traditions. Buddhism is generally divided into three major schools, or *yanas* (Sanskrit: path, or vehicle): the Hinayana, Mahayana, and Vajrayana. The Theraveda traditions of Sri Lanka, Thailand, Laos, Burma, and Cambodia, which are part of a Hinayana school of thought, emphasize personal liberation and practice focused on renunciation. Within these traditions, it is argued that when a person becomes an *arhat* (a Buddha), his or her karma is extinguished, leading to a state of nirvana, where the endless cycle of rebirth finally comes to an end. The Mahayana[3] traditions of China, Korea, and Japan (including Zen and Pure Land), emphasize that Buddhist practitioners should work for the benefit of all sentient beings. Mahayana Buddhists take bodhisattva vows, the vow to remain in samsara (endless cycle of rebirth) until every living being has attained enlightenment. Between the sixth and eighth centuries in northern India, the Mahayana teachings coalesced to form the basis of what are known as the Vajrayana (diamond vehicle), based on tantra teachings. Today in Tibet, Mongolia, and Bhutan, Vajrayana traditions are practiced that use deity practices to achieve enlightenment quickly with the aim of helping other beings. Known as the "resultant path," Vajrayana practitioners start from a place of visualizing themselves as enlightened deities as a way of training the mind to see through the seductive illusion of samsara.

The Mahayana and related Vajrayana paths rely on a concept known as *bodhichitta* (Sanskrit: *Bodhi*, meaning "awake," and *Chitta*, meaning "heart-mind"), the awakening of enlightened mind. Bodhichitta merges expansive compassion with a direct realization of emptiness. Tibetan Buddhists make aspirations through prayer to awaken *bodhichitta* in their hearts, and this concept remains a touchstone in moments of difficulty. Elsewhere, Julia Cassaniti (2015) argues that ordinary Buddhist practitioners (in the case of her research, Thai laypeople) do not necessarily know the philosophical workings of concepts such as *anicca* (impermanence), and yet this concept fundamentally shapes how people think about life events. I found something similar in Dharamsala, where the notion of *bodhichitta* seems to frame the lives of ordinary Tibetans even when they cannot explain the high philosophical concept of emptiness. In the next chapter, I give more detail about how this mind of enlightenment orients Tibetan community members toward recovery in times of difficulty.

The Dalai Lama

The importance of the Dalai Lama to the Tibetan people cannot be overstated. In interviews, the Dalai Lama—known as Gyalwa Rinpoche—tirelessly reminds his audience that he is a "simple Buddhist monk." While arguably one of the most widely recognized world leaders alive today, he is a man who was born to a humble nomad family living in a yak-skin tent in eastern Tibet. As a Nobel Prize laureate and admired world figure, his central message to his audience is the interconnectedness of all sentient beings. Despite his fame, he still lives within the walls of Namgyal Monastery and wakes each day at 3:30 a.m. to engage in several hours of meditation practice. But while the Dalai Lama emphasizes that he is no different from other simple Buddhist monks at heart, he is keen to interact with a remarkable array of people—from meetings at the White House, to audiences with poor Indian families who travel days by bus to seek his council. Politicians, religious leaders, and scientists across the globe have developed collaborative partnerships with the Dalai Lama. For instance, he has teamed with Emory University to create the Science for Monks Program, which brings scientists to monasteries and nunneries in India to introduce biology, chemistry, mathematics, and physics into monastic education. In addition, a partnership with scientific researchers through The Mind and Life Institute supports new developments in contemplative science, and scientific research on meditation and mindfulness.

During my time in the field, I had the opportunity to briefly visit the Dalai Lama's private residence. He held my hand (as he often does with visitors) and said in English: "You are a researcher. This is good. Very good!" He then explained how the Buddha was a scientist. "Buddhism," he said, "it is better to think of it as a science—not a religion. You have to closely investigate and ask questions. The Buddha said not to accept anything on blind faith. We have to check and investigate for ourselves. All scientists and researchers are doing the same. You foreigners are very good, very intelligent, about investigating outer reality. And we Tibetans have excelled in studying inner reality—the mind."

When asked by journalists about the situation involving "the Chinese," the Dalai Lama is quick to point out the distinction between the Chinese people and government policies, noting that Chinese people are reasonable and kindhearted. He cautions against equating government policies with individual people. His messages often challenge false dichotomies, encouraging his audience to relate to others first and foremost as decent people. In a televised interview,[4] Piers Morgan asked the Dalai Lama to describe a person who has most impressed him over the years. His response, which shocked an incredulous Morgan, is emblematic of his style of teaching:

DALAI LAMA: I think . . . Nelson Mandela; he is quite impressive. And then, then of course as an individual person, I love President Bush.

MORGAN: Which one?

DALAI LAMA: The younger one.

MORGAN: *Really?*

DALAI LAMA: Yes!

MORGAN: *Really? Really?*

DALAI LAMA: Yes. Not as president of America, but as a human being. Sometimes his policies may not be very successful. But as a person, as a human being, very nice person. I love him.

MORGAN: But how did you feel when Bush went to war so much, and was responsible for so many deaths if you are a man of peace?

DALAI LAMA: Oh, after he started the Iraq crisis, in my meeting with him, I expressed to him, I love you. But where your policies are concerned, I have some reservations, I told him.

In this way, the Dalai Lama challenges a simplistic reading of what is true. This style of seeing that there is no true story has also informed the kinds of political policy he has attempted to perpetuate, and as will be explained later, is an essential aspect of Tibetan forms of resilience.

In advising the Tibetan people, he has consistently stressed for over fifty years the importance of nonviolence and peaceful negotiation. And yet, increasingly there is a growing multiplicity of perspectives among Tibetans regarding their political situation; some are unfaltering in their commitment to nonviolence, whereas others increasingly advocate for stronger forms of political action. But Tibetans as a whole seem to have a common goal: to see the Dalai Lama one day return to his homeland in Tibet.

I do not think I conducted any interviews at all without the Dalai Lama being evoked as a protector, precious teacher, and guru. Just being near him was a comfort to people. A typical statement of resettlement was something like what Sonam Dawa, a middle-aged woman said:

> Since I married my husband in Lhasa, we stayed there to do business and then we came to India. So I never saw my parents again. I had great sorrow. When I was in Lhasa, I told a lie to my parents to conceal my involvement in protesting the environmental destruction. I had to lie to my parents. I felt so much regret about lying to them after they died. We don't have freedom and cannot go back to Tibet, which also makes me very sad. Sometimes when I display some small items near the street, the Indian police will come and demand bribes so we don't get shut down. But I comfort myself and try to be patient. If the Dalai Lama can go back to Tibet, then we will go, too. Otherwise, we are okay here since we are with His Holiness. Since I work very hard to make money for my family, I won't starve.

The phrase "otherwise we are okay since we are with His Holiness" is often evoked as if it were self-evident why just being in his proximity brings comfort. It affirms their cultural identity as Tibetan, but more than this, it brings a sense of home, refuge, and safety.

Life in Dharamsala

There are thirteen Tibetan settlements in the northern Indian state of Himachal Pradesh, which are home to 20,000 Tibetans (Bhatia, Dranyi, and Rowley 2002; Proust 2008); around 9,500 of this total live in Dharamsala. Many Tibetans living in India earn their living making handicrafts and selling sweaters, wool shawls, and Tibetan jewelry. Others work in the service industry in hotels, restaurants, and tourist venues. Whereas some Tibetans in Dharamsala are able to start their own businesses, nearly all of these ventures have an Indian partner behind the scenes. Indian policy is ambiguous on whether Tibetans can legally own property and businesses there.

State-level ambivalence about Tibetans living in India is mirrored in everyday life in Dharamsala, where conflict between Tibetans and their Indian hosts is commonplace. There is resentment among Indians in the region that so much international aid goes to Tibetans, while their Indian neighbors are sometimes even worse off. Some Tibetans find foreign sponsors who send money every month. From the Tibetan point of view, they often feel cheated and discriminated against by local Indian shopkeepers, police, and government officials. I observed some poor treatment, but there is also a culture particular to India that foreigners (including Tibetans) are not always adept at managing, such as paying bribes and negotiating payment. In fact, rather than trying to adapt to local norms in India, many Tibetans resent these customs, and in some cases, believe they are morally superior to their Indian hosts who routinely bargain for services.

I experienced these tensions when for five months there was water for only one hour per day in my Tibetan-managed flat. The building was owned by a Tibetan woman who lived in Dheradhun, some ten hours away; it was managed by her brother, a Tibetan doctor. I was told that the pipes were "not good," which was why there was such a limited supply. However, a neighbor, the wife of a retired Tibetan government official, confided in me that the owner does not want to pay *baksheesh*[5] to the Indian water company. It seemed that everyone else in the neighborhood had paid, and they had water. I called my landlord to inquire further about the problem. He admitted that they refused to pay extra. Instead, they applied for a permit to build a new water tank. "We have dignity," he said, and then added, "not like the Indians. They are always cheating each other." The permit for the new tank never arrived. Sometimes I fantasized about finding the Indian water guys and paying the *baksheesh* myself. Forget dignity; I wanted water. After the five-month standoff, my landlord called and said, "Sara-la,[6] water is coming now." The water was back, and I never got a straight answer about what happened.

Little Lhasa

Otherwise another Indian town, Dharamsala is known as "Little Lhasa" for a reason. With thirteen monasteries and four nunneries in the greater Dharamsala area, there is near-constant sounding of drums, trumpets, bells, and cymbals echoing through town as part of the *pujas* (ceremonial offering to avert obstacles) and daily rituals required for Buddhist practice. Outside the monasteries, lay tantric yogis (*ngakpas*) perform exorcisms, divinations, and elaborate rituals to cure illness and bring fortune. Such a picture might conjure up what Lopez (1998) calls the "Myth of Shangri-la," the romantic idea that to be fully Tibetan is to be steeped in holy and mystical Buddhist practices. But alongside all of this, one finds endless Internet cafes, young Tibetan teens cruising around on motorcycles (often with a young Western girl on the back), monks chatting on cell phones, and rowdy arguments over the price of cooking gas.

While not particularly easy to get to (it is a twelve-hour bus ride through winding mountain passes from New Delhi), it remains a thriving tourist destination for foreign and Indian tourists alike. Offering a welcome respite from the hot, crowded stress of India, many come to Dharamsala to relax. Alongside the variety of Buddhist courses and retreat centers, Indians and Western expats have set up shop offering reiki, yoga, crystal healing, and massage. Tibetan Buddhism has long been naïvely equated with peace, serenity, and love (Khyentse 2008; Lopez 1998), prompting Western seekers to engage in what Chögyam Trungpa called "spiritual materialism" (1973). It comes as no surprise that the home of the Dalai Lama would attract such spiritual seekers. And yet alongside this hodgepodge are functioning government offices and rigorous Buddhist institutes of study, debate, and practice. Many important lamas and abbots reside in Dharamsala, making it an attractive place for young monks and nuns to complete their studies. With its mix of Tibetans, Indians, and foreign expats, this makes for an unusual community. There is indeed a certain arbitrariness here. This small Indian town became an epicenter of Tibetan culture merely by chance when Prime Minister Nehru offered the remote land to the Dalai Lama in 1959.

Some Tibetologists avoid conducting research in Dharamsala, seeing it as an "adulterated field of anthropological inquiry" (Proust 2008, 7). It is not only researchers from outside who question the authenticity of these new forms of Tibetan culture. Many "old-timers," that is, those who left Tibet decades ago—particularly those who left Lhasa with the Dalai Lama— complain about exile culture. The *shey-sa* (honorific language) style of Tibetan I learned to speak in graduate school was rarely used among young people—especially those born in exile who spoke slang Tibetan mixed with Hindi and English. Some of my most fascinating fieldwork was con-

Figure 3. Monks in Dharamsala. Photo by author.

ducted at dawn when I joined the *mo-lags* (grannies) in daily prostrations on long wooden boards positioned inside the Dalai Lama's temple. "You are a good girl! A very nice girl," two ladies said. "You speak Tibetan very politely."

"But your prostrations!" said another one, giving me a good-natured whack on the behind. "You shouldn't stay on the ground so long. You are young! Not old like me. Don't be lazy." She picked up a fleece jacket I had set down next to me, yanked me close to her and tied it tightly around my waist. "Your kidneys!" she cried. "You will get sick. It is cold." The other ladies nodded in agreement. "But good speaking. You are not rude like those exile girls." The old-timers even questioned the extent to which newcomers from Tibet were even *really* Tibetan, having grown up in China. And derision existed on the side of those born in exile as well, who saw the old-timers as backward and unsophisticated.

There has long been regional elitism inside Tibet. A language teacher from Lhasa once explained to me rather innocently, "You see, those from Amdo and Kham [regions in eastern Tibet] . . . they are a little bit rough.

They are a little like, how do you say? Like hillbillies!" Many "minority languages" (Roche and Suzuki 2018) throughout Tibet are so variable that
some Tibetans cannot communicate with one another. Many new arrivals
to Dharamsala not only want to learn English but also need to learn "standard" Tibetan to communicate with those from other regions. Young adults
often spend several months upon arrival to Dharamsala engaged in language
study at the Tibetan Transit School (TTS) before moving on to join friends
or relatives in other Tibetan settlements elsewhere in India. Although knowing English, standard Tibetan, and even some Hindi is useful, many people
tend to cluster together with people from their own regions of Tibet, holding somewhat derogative views of other regions.

A similar elitism can be found within the long and complex history of
sectarian conflict across the schools of Tibetan Buddhism. Often the heart
of these debates is at once philosophical and political. Reflecting again on Lopez's (1998) assertion that there is fascination and romanticism associated
with Tibet among Westerners, some might be surprised to learn that monasteries are not the peaceful and serene settings they imagine. Monks do not sit
quietly in meditation; rather, they are on strict schedules that dictate a rigorous
daily routine involving recitation, debate, exams, and elaborate ritual responsi-
bilities for *pujas*. Anthropologist Michael Lempert (2012), who conducted ethnographic research at Sera Mey, one of the largest and most important monastic colleges in South India, found that these settings are highly restrictive and
morally conservative. The *ge-kos* (discipline masters) routinely use public sham-
ing and reprimand to enforce order and motivate young monks by encouraging competition. In smaller monasteries, monks may need to conduct trade
outside their monastic training schedules unlike their counterparts inside
"mega monasteries" (Sullivan 2013) who are supported by patrons.

There have also been troubling and dangerous instances among monastic sects that go beyond acts of symbolic violence. Because the religious clergy
often assume political positions of power, during struggles over land, money,
and power, monks as well as their lay patrons have been known to engage in
violent warfare (Lempert 2012; Lopez 1998). A contemporary example of the
dark side of monastic institutions is the Dorje Shugden affair. Dorje Shugden is a protector deity who has been historically connected to the Gelukpa
tradition (the lineage of the Dalai Lama); however, in the 1970s the Dalai
Lama was advised by his council that the practice had dangerous implica-

tions for him (he reportedly received similar messages in dreams from the Nechung Oracle as well as his previous incarnation, the fifth Dalai Lama). Because the deity promotes extreme sectarianism, the current Dalai Lama, a notable proponent of *ri me* (a nonsectarian movement across all Tibetan schools) banished practices associated with Shugden—also making a political statement that angered conservative Gelukpa leaders who believed they should prevail over other schools. In the 1990s, the Dalai Lama made a formal statement (which I heard him repeat during teachings in Dharamsala) that Shugden practitioners cannot receive tantric empowerments from him. In 1997, the principal of the Institute of Buddhist Dialectics and two students were stabbed to death by known Shugden practitioners in front of the Dalai Lama's temple in Dharamsala.

The gravity of this situation is palpable. Tibetans avoid speaking Shugden's name; if they must, it is whispered. During religious teachings and empowerments in Dharamsala, the Dalai Lama mentions this harmful deity imploring people not to engage in the practice. The Dorje Shugden sect continues to grow as part of the New Kadampa Movement (NKD), an organization that is known for beautiful and welcoming Dharma centers in North America and Europe. They often protest outside the Dalai Lama's public talks around the world, claiming religious discrimination. Recently, it has come to light that the Chinese government gives large sums of money to NKD as part of their anti–Dalai Lama campaign.

I include descriptions of conflict to dissuade readers from romanticizing—a trap that one could easily fall prey to in a study of resilience among this cultural group. These accounts also portray the long-standing divergences across various Tibetan factions. Like any other society, Tibet has its share of violence and corruption. And yet, many community members told me that they believe they are more resilient than other cultural groups—that they can handle life's problems better than most. My research does not aim to demonstrate that this group is any more or less resilient than other communities, but I found this belief to be very prevalent among the residents of Dharamsala and an interesting data point for my study. "We have a very special way of thinking," explained one woman. "And thinking that the rest of the world could benefit from how we approach life's difficulties inspires us to continue fighting for our country and way of life. If your motivation is to help others, you will never give up."

Tibetan Resistance

For more than sixty years, there has been significant political protest both among Tibetans and foreign human rights activists aimed at gaining political autonomy for Tibet (or complete independence). March 10, 1959, marked what has since been known as "Tibetan Uprising Day"; on this day, thousands took to the streets after rumors began circulating that the Dalai Lama would be arrested or abducted by the police following a theatrical performance in Lhasa (to which he allegedly received an invitation from the Chinese government but was told he could not bring his usual entourage of security and advisers). Thousands of Tibetan protesters surrounded the Dalai Lama's palace to protect him and within a week the Tibetan militia planned and successfully orchestrated the Dalai Lama's escape out of Lhasa. As with his people who followed, the Dalai Lama traveled at night in secret over the Himalayan mountain range into Nepal and then India.

The time of the Cultural Revolution beginning in 1958 and into the 1970s was a devastating period, not only for Tibetans but for many other ethnic minorities within the region. From 1987 to 1989, members of the Tibetan Independence Movement staged large-scale protests across the TAR; this was a particularly violent period and eventually martial law was declared and foreign journalists were restricted from entering the country. To mark the thirty-year anniversary of the uprising in 1959, monks from Drepung Monastery took to the streets and thousands of laypeople followed suit. Over the next few years, aggression bubbled beneath the surface on both sides until erupting in 1995 with a historic kidnapping.

In 1995, a six-year-old boy named Gendun Chokyi Nyima disappeared from his home shortly after being recognized by the Dalai Lama as the eleventh incarnation of the Panchen Lama. The relationship between the lineages of Panchen Lamas and Dalai Lamas is important in that they have historically located and recognized one another's next incarnation. The previous Panchen Lama (the tenth) had been arrested and imprisoned for publicly supporting the Dalai Lama in the mid-1960s and died in 1989. The Dalai Lama spent six years searching for his incarnation. When the newly named six-year-old boy disappeared (the Chinese government openly admitted to detaining him for security purposes), the Tibetan people revolted, leading to more uprisings. The Chinese responded by enthroning a young boy of their own—the son of a Chinese security officer—as the Panchen

Lama, who would name the next Dalai Lama. The current Dalai Lama, Tenzin Gyatso, has openly stated that he will not take rebirth in Tibet (if he takes rebirth and continues his lineage at all), and the Panchen Lama remains a missing person. In many protests today, Tibetans call for the return of the Dalai Lama to Tibet and the release of the Panchen Lama, who, if alive at the time of this book's publication, would be in his thirties. These struggles reveal the ways that Buddhist practice is tightly woven with politics in Tibet.

Every year since 1959, Tibetan Uprising Day is observed on March 10. During the observance in 2008, there were a series of usual protests in Lhasa except this year the tension was exacerbated by the Beijing Olympics, which Tibetans found reproachable given China's history of human rights abuses. During the protests, riots erupted and six thousand Tibetans were arrested (Free Tibet 2017). Many monasteries throughout Tibet led the protests in their region and soon Tibetans across the globe joined in, hoping to draw more international support. Nearly twenty Chinese embassies across North America and Europe became sites of fervent protest, which the Chinese government claimed were orchestrated by the Dalai Lama, whom it deems a terrorist (China View 2013). Hunger strikes sprung up around the United Nations building in New York City and there was significant media coverage; yet there were no discernable advances in Tibet's political aims.

The summer following the March 2008 uprising, I arrived in Dharamsala to begin preliminary fieldwork. It was here that I first observed notable disagreement with the Dalai Lama's stance on nonviolence and the Middle Way, particularly among young people. While the official stance of the Tibetan government-in-exile backs the Dalai Lama and his insistence on peaceful negotiation, there is a significant segment of the population pushing for stronger and more active responses. At this time, the Summer Olympics had just begun in Beijing. The atmosphere in Dharamsala was one of betrayal. *How could the world give China this honor?* people wondered. Students for a Free Tibet distributed sweatshirts resembling those won by a sports team that said: "Team Tibet"; they were proudly worn in the weekly protests and candlelight vigils held for those who were recently killed or imprisoned during the uprising. It was an unusual sight to see the *mo-lags* (grannies) wearing black zip-up sweatshirts over their *chupas* (traditional Tibetan dress).

During the 2008 protests, foreigners were again shut out of Tibet. Since this time, the restriction on foreigners traveling into Tibetan regions has waxed and waned. Currently, restrictions have relaxed somewhat, but this

Figure 4. Panchen Lama billboard in Dharamsala. Photo by author.

changes frequently. While visiting the TAR, tourists are encouraged to stay with official tour guides, and during times of restrictions may be required to do so. Some Tibetans inside the TAR are reticent to associate with foreigners, which might rouse suspicion that they are engaged in political activity. Likewise, some in Dharamsala worried that their family inside Tibet might be harmed if their faces were shown on television or in photographs, insinuating political involvement. As a researcher in Dharamsala, it was palpable how concerned people were that their anonymity be protected. Association with a foreign researcher would be seen as suspect, and my Tibetan research assistant often had to vouch for my word that their identities would not be revealed in the research.

For many residents in Dharamsala, life remains unresolved in myriad ways. Their citizenship is unsubstantiated—both spatially and temporally caught in borderlands without the social capital to land anywhere permanently—a plight that defines many forced migrant experiences (El-Shaarawi 2015; Holmes and Castañeda 2016). Socially and politically, it seems unlikely that Tibet will gain the kind of autonomy it seeks despite an unrelenting political campaign for freedom. In a seeming paradox, while they fight for social justice there is a simultaneous insistence that people are ultimately responsible for their own happiness or misery. Dorjee, a young monk who was the nephew of a neighbor said:

I think people can cope with problems depending on their individual way of thinking and experiences. If someone who has never had problems before develops even small difficulties, they become very discouraged and think, "I'm going to die!" If someone grows up dealing with many different problems and difficulties in life and has experience coping with problems, then when something difficult develops, their minds are accustomed to dealing with things so their minds remain very stable. They know if they have problems, then there are ways to resolve them. The Dalai Lama said that in foreign countries even those with many resources and wealth still have depression. They do not have many physical problems, but when they cannot get what they want, they easily become frustrated and unhappy. Anyway, whatever happens, it is very important to do *lojong* (mind training) and keep one's mind very spacious. Sometimes when people lose something valuable, they become quite upset. But this is just a part of life—everything is impermanent. Recently, I had a very good mobile phone sent to me from my family in Tibet. Unfortunately, one day I knocked my elbow against a car and the mobile broke. At first, I was very disappointed, but then when I thought about it more carefully I realized there is nothing that doesn't eventually become damaged and changes. I am sure from my experience if we make great effort to cope with problems, it becomes very obvious or apparent once we have made progress.

What Dorjee references here—*lojong*, or "mind training"—is a built-in cultural way of thinking about what one ought to do when facing problems.

One part of *lojong* is reflecting on emptiness and impermanence, and remembering that everything changes. Everything is fundamentally illusory, so we should loosen our grip on things. He continues, explaining: "If people have many experiences in life and hardships in life such as poverty, then they can cope easily with problems in the future. For example, if someone lost a family member or their house burnt down, or they failed an exam, then this person can endure problems. They don't turn it into a big situation. Sometimes even if something very special happens, they do not get overly happy. Likewise, if something bad happens they also don't get too upset. They are very stable." The point is to understand that human life is in some sense defined by suffering and therefore mind training helps in developing mental and emotional agility in times of trouble.

But as I describe in more depth in the next chapter, not everyone is capable of flawless mind training. Of course it is only natural to become sad, angry, enraged, depressed, and despondent. How, then, does *lojong* work? Is this not merely an idealized practice that is unrealistic for ordinary Tibetans? What I describe next is how *lojong*-inspired thinking helps to light the way in dark times. It is more path than destination. The inspiration for what to do—however imperfectly—is what I argue drives resilience.

Chapter 2

Mind Training

Dr. Dawa, a practitioner of *sowa rigpa* (the science of healing), has lived in Dharamsala for nearly thirty years. There has been a growing interest in investigating *sowa rigpa*, or traditional Tibetan medicine, but she says, "although people want to know about the power of Tibetan medicine, foreign researchers do not understand the way the *sems* (heart-mind) works. In *phyi lugs smen* (foreign medicine, or biomedicine), they think you can just take pills, which will do all the work, paying no attention to the patient's state of mind. But medicine becomes more effective if both the patient and the physician are compassionate. The most powerful medicine human beings have at their disposal is the medicine of compassion." This notion that compassion should be regarded as medicine is a long-standing idea in Buddhist scriptures. In fact, the historical Buddha told his followers to regard him as a physician and to think of themselves as very sick people, trapped in samsara, the endless cycle of rebirth. The Buddhist teachings and practices should be applied, then, as medicine, with compassion as a potent elixir. Dr. Dawa continues:

If a person who practices *Buddhadharma* properly has some difficulties, then they will automatically think that samsara is the ocean of suffering, so of course we will face difficulties. And we understand that when we have problems in this life, it is only the result of *lé* (karmic past actions). Therefore, we cannot blame others for our problems. Like this, the advice of *Buddhadharma* is to be selfless and put others before self. This is very beneficial. For example, if we are not able to get what we want, we should think, "oh, no problem," even if others have what we want. Also, when we become unhappy or have problems with the mind, if we can think, "there is no problem," and we don't mind if others are happy. Actually, you can do a little trick in your mind and think, "oh! I willingly offer these good things to that person." The motivation in thinking in this way is very positive and it transforms the situation. In our life, the biggest problem we face is desire and attachment. If we cannot get what we want, we have many problems. If we try to be content, then we never have these problems. Others may harm us, and this disturbs the mind. Even if someone is a [Buddhist] practitioner, still, they have problems. So mainly they have to train their minds; there is no way around this.

This kind of training—to think that problems are not really so bad, to willingly offer happiness to others even when one is struggling—is a radical approach, and one that may be off-putting for people in the Global North. From an ultimate point of view, Tibetan Buddhism coaches people to see the illusory nature of samsara, and within this, that problems themselves—and even the "self" who is having the problem—is fundamentally an illusion. In this way, there is nothing from the outside that causes distress; distress can only come from inside the mind. This fact of life is something that Tibetans in Dharamsala seem to experience as empowering. "It is up to you," they say.

Using the Tibetan exile community as a case study, this chapter argues that resilience is not a mere absence of suffering. Rather, it is *the way* a person copes with adversity that is evidence of resilience. Like suffering, resilience is also culturally shaped and defined. In the United States, for example, we tend to think of resilient individuals as those who can withstand pain and injustice, emerging unscathed from adversity. But for Tibetans, those considered most resilient are often those who are deeply affected and transformed by adversity. Resilience here is not defined as the ability to "bounce back," like a physical material that can withstand brunt force. It is not grit. Instead, those who are most resilient use their vulnerability as a way to deepen compassion. In this way, compassion is both the result of resilience and a method to train in resilience. Similar to what researchers call "post-traumatic growth" (Tedeschi and Calhoun 1996), Tibetans in their practice of resilience use suffering as a transformative opportunity. Because suffering is seen as an unavoidable aspect of everyday life, this approach is not limited to remarkable individuals. Instead, the resilience practices I elucidate in this chapter are considered to be pragmatic and part of life's journey.

During my fieldwork in Dharamsala, I conducted what is known as a cultural domain analysis, a method for identifying particular cultural idioms used to describe a given concept. In this case, I wanted to learn how Tibetans in exile defined resilience. Although I could roughly translate the word "resilience" into the Tibetan language, I did not assume its cultural meaning would be the same as in English. Some translations of this concept may include, *ten-po* (resolute), *she chen-po*, or *shug chen-po* (strong). But these terms do not fully capture the essence of resilience processes among Tibetans, in their view. Indeed, the results of the cultural domain analysis revealed that the qualities associated with resilience in Dharamsala are quite different from Euro-American notions, which tend to center around productivity in the face of difficulty (e.g., being productive in work, school, running a household). For Tibetans, resilience is evident based on how a person *relates* to suffering itself; it is defined by the qualities of spaciousness, openness, a willingness to let go, and flexibility. Rather than processing details of past events, the support that Tibetan refugees give to one another often follows the kind of sensibility found in what is known as *lojong*, or "mind training," a set of Buddhist teachings that emphasize changing the way you think (rather than changing the external environment).

Dolma

Waking up every morning around dawn was choiceless for eighty-year-old Dolma, who lived in a tiny one-room shelter underneath a print shop near Kirti Monastery. The cold, cement floor and walls had no insulation, and during monsoon, a thick layer of mold covered her belongings. Wedged between Kirti Monastery and Jamyang Chöling Nunnery, the cacophony of morning *pujas* begin at dawn and the loud cymbals, drums, horns, and chanting echo the neighborhood.

"*Drig ge re* [no matter, it's okay]," says Dolma. "*Chak tsal* [prostrations] are my main duty as an old granny, and they should be done very early."

Dolma left her birthplace in eastern Tibet in the middle of the night in 1960. A wave of neighbors, friends, and a few family members had already left the previous year. It was not until a *tulku* (incarnate lama) at a nearby monastery went missing that Dolma, at the time twenty-eight years old with three children, thought to leave. She had not received any formal schooling and lived a nomadic life herding yak with a band of several families in the region. Dolma recalls how she used to climb a high mountain, and from the top, she assumed that the whole world was below her. She says, "I didn't realize that the world was much bigger than what I could see from this high mountain." When the political situation escalated, Dolma and her family were terrified but took direction from a trusted friend they saw as more worldly because he had previously traveled to Ü-Tsang, the Tibetan province where Lhasa, the capital city is located. The family friend had described the people in Ü-Tsang as "dried crops," people without good heart and decent morals. "Those from Kham, we call Kham-pa and those from Amdo, Amdo-wa," she explained. "I actually didn't know that we are all Tibetans! And I really did not know there were people elsewhere in the world with yellow hair." Even venturing into the capital of Lhasa seemed foreign and difficult, let alone fleeing into another country.

It took nearly four weeks to complete the journey by foot. By the time Dolma's family traversed the Himalayas into Kathmandu, and finally into India, one member in their party had died. Others suffered frostbite. All experienced near starvation. In many ways, Dolma was ill equipped for life in India. She could not speak English or Hindi, or earn a living. In those early days, there was no support, no services, and very little to eat in Dharamsala. But she, like her countymates, were equipped to deal with suffering. Dolma had no formal religious training, but the cultural milieu in which she was raised was steeped in the Buddhist tradition. Her parents and grandparents taught her from an early age that suffering in life is not only natural—it is to be expected. And the best thing to do when something difficult happens is to "think broadly" about others who are also suffering. "You can even think, at this very moment of all the others who are experiencing the same thing as you," explains Dolma. Feeling that you are not alone helps to generate compassion, and simultaneously shows you that your struggles are not such a big deal. This notion of "no big deal" may be off-putting, and even offensive—

particularly for Western scholars concerned with social justice. But people in Dharamsala do not see this kind of attitude as internalized oppression.

The practice of *lojong*, or "mind training," and the everyday cultural wisdom based on it, dictates two major approaches for resilience: (1) generating compassion for others (often in one's same situation), and (2) reflecting on emptiness. This way of relating to difficulty helps to create what Tibetans call *sems pa chen po* (a spacious, flexible mind), a mind-set that encapsulates their view of resilience. In this community, resilience is an active process— an approach for meeting life's inevitable problems with openness, humor, and compassion. There is a sense that if people are dependent on external circumstances for happiness, their lives will be a constant roller coaster of ups and downs. Instead, it is more effective to generate inner stability and strength that can weather life's challenges (and successes) without being swept away.

Resilience and Coping

The term "resilience" is often defined as one's ability to thrive or maintain equilibrium in the face of adversity (Walsh 2006), and thus more than the simple absence of psychopathology. In fact, psychologists such as George Bonanno (2004) and others argue that resilient individuals may experience transient periods of intense suffering, but that ultimately, they maintain an ongoing capacity for healthy functioning across time. Within community psychology, social work, and public health, studies of resilience and coping have long been centered on the individual personality attributes of children who thrive in contexts of abuse and urban poverty (Berkes and Ross 2013; Ungar 2011). Until recently, studies of resilience within psychology (Garmezy 1991) and those within ecology (Holling 1973) have been largely divorced from one another. Yet ecological concepts of resilience have become instrumental in founding new paradigms that consider "community resilience" (despite some incommensurate values in these approaches), which seek to understand how families and communities strengthen collective healing or resistance (Berliner, Larsen, and Soberón 2012; Carpenter 2013; Roche 2017).

Mental health researchers have also made efforts to differentiate "resilience" from "coping." Psychologists define coping as "cognitive and behavioral efforts to manage specific external and/or internal demands that are appraised as taxing or exceeding the resources of a person" (Lazarus and

Folkman 1984, 141). Coping styles are directly linked with stress appraisal, the interpretation of the severity and longevity of stress. Coping is not necessarily equated with good outcomes, however (Beasley, Thompson, and Davidson 2003). For instance, substance abuse, overeating, and other harmful behaviors can be effective ways of coping. But whereas coping can be understood as healthy or unhealthy, "resilience" always refers to positive and adaptive processes. A related concept is "cognitive hardiness," which describes the adaptive mind-set of resilient individuals who are not easily deterred by setbacks (Kobasa 1979; Beasley, Thompson, and Davidson 2003).

Within psychology and public health, resilience is largely understood as defying the odds with positive outcomes. Therefore, prevention and intervention have mostly targeted those presumed to be vulnerable and at risk in attempts to increase protective factors. Although resilience research is intended to explore the more adaptive sides of human behavior, in many cases, the upshot of typical study aims has "simply meant looking at the inverse of risk factors" (Kirmayer et al. 2011, 84). This separates people into two groups: those who are resilient and those who are not. Instead, resilience should be understood as a process that is dynamic, changing, nonlinear, and finely attuned to context. It is also deeply and complexly intertwined with harm, suffering, and oppression.

For instance, graduation from high school is often uniformly considered a positive outcome that is indicative of resilience. And yet, Lisa Wexler, DiFluvio, and Burke (2009) challenge researchers to be more finely attuned to cultural specificity by pointing out that in native North American communities where schools may be sites of colonization, graduation, while desirable, may also be synonymous with submitting to the dominant group. Likewise, schools can be dangerous for LGBTQ youth; in some cases, leaving school may actually reflect the extent to which one is empowered to make healthy choices (albeit not costless or necessarily heading for good outcomes in all areas). Researchers have long recognized the roles of discrimination, institutional structures, and unfair economic practices in health disparities. But it has largely missed the ways the interpretation of these structures can orient people in overcoming them and achieving positive outcomes in their lives (Wexler 2009; Wexler and Gone 2012). Lisa Stevenson's work in the Canadian Arctic (2014) reveals how even something like suicide cannot be regarded as a singularly undesirable outcome without attending the specificity of what it means for a culture to live a life that is worth living.

Anthropological studies of resilience tend to focus on how people continue to make meaning in the face of hardship. For example, Linda Green (1994) concludes that community-level discourses on suffering among Xe'caj have been instrumental in bolstering and rebuilding a robust community in a postwar Guatemalan society. In another Guatemalan village, Patricia Foxen (2010) shows how the K'iche, through the construction of collective memory, not only heal the contemporary and historic wounds of violence and social exclusion but also resist victimization through discourses of hope. Likewise, Carolyn Nordstrom argued that creativity and ritual can "unmake violence," as exemplified in Mozambican communities whose members, "by rebuilding and replanting in the face of repeated attacks, defied the war . . . [and] the assault on the present to construct their own future" (1997, 117). Studies like these challenge theoretical models that fail to capture how so-called vulnerable populations may be just as robust as they are "in need."

Compelling research on resilience must consider the transformational potential of deep suffering where resilience occurs not *in spite* of suffering, but actually *because of it*. In this regard, the Tibetan exile community is an instructive case study. For Tibetan Buddhists, compassion is considered a lamp that guides the way out of the darkness of samsara. The teachings say that compassion is difficult or impossible to learn without suffering, however. In fact, Buddhists believe that of the six realms of existence (gods, demigods, humans, animals, hungry ghosts, and hell beings), the human realm—not the god realm—is the most conducive for achieving enlightenment precisely because there is enough suffering to learn compassion for other sentient beings. The long lives of pleasure within the god realm do not provide enough motivation to want to get out of samsara. For human beings, Buddhist teachings focus on how suffering should be regarded as a great teacher.

Technologies of Compassion

Kaitlyn shrieked and gave Palden a little shove as they came screeching to a halt at the front of the Yak Café[1] where Palden, aged twenty-four, worked as a coffee barista. Nearly all of the guys who work there—early twenty-somethings—had Western girlfriends. Most had also come to Dharamsala as monks.

"*Acha* (older sister) Sara-La," Palden said, coming to my table when he spotted me. Kaitlyn went to sit with the other girlfriends sitting around a table with laptops, using the cafe's Wi-Fi. "I have a new list for you." *Northwestern University, Harvard University, University of Michigan*. Palden periodically presented me with lists of schools he hoped to attend in the United States. Having had no formal schooling outside of his monastery as a former monk back in Amdo (eastern Tibet), this seemed unlikely. But many of Palden's friends had gone to Canada, the United States, Australia, and Europe after meeting young women who were traveling in India. He wore jeans and sported a spikey haircut, which matched the bad-boy persona he cultivated with the motorcycle he shared with five or six friends. Once, after knowing me for a while, he showed me a small photograph of when he was a monk, laughing nervously and saying, "when I was humble."

Palden had not planned on disrobing as a monk. When he and his uncle were arrested by Chinese border police four years ago, he was taken into custody. There, he was interrogated for a week and made to denounce the Dalai Lama. At first, he tried bravely to resist. But the police showed him photographs of Tibetan "separatists" who had been beaten, and he cried, giving in and pledging allegiance to the People's Republic of China and calling the Dalai Lama a terrorist. Palden was also forced to consume alcohol and smoke cigarettes, which made him vomit.

"So at that moment, I was no longer a monk. I wore the robes, but I broke my vows.²" They also broke his spirit. After that, he was released, but his uncle was detained for another month. Palden, despondent, did not know what to do. He had come too far on his journey to turn back, so he called the abbot of his monastery back in Amdo and relayed what had happened. The abbot told him not to worry.

"You can do *puja* and *vajrasattva* [deity known for dispelling obstacles] mantra for purification," he said. "But it is not your fault. You did not break your *samaya* [vows] on purpose."

Despite these reassuring words, Palden did not feel better. He decided to push on and connected with some others from his county who were planning their escape into Nepal. He continued to wear his robes, "but in my heart, I was no longer a monk. When I came to Dharamsala, I changed," he said simply, meaning he disrobed. Having no way to make money, Palden enrolled in the Tibetan Transit School. When monks and nuns come to Dharamsala, they are taken into monasteries and nunneries, and any layperson under the age of eighteen goes to a Tibetan Children's Village boarding school. Lay adults are entitled to vocational training and a few months stipend issued by the Tibetan government-in-exile offices. At the Transit school, Palden was miserable. The damp monsoon weather and Indian food made him ill. And emotionally, he was consumed with anger.

"What else could I do?" he asked. "I made a friend there who was also previously a monk, so he understood my anger and my shame. Every day he reminded me that I should think about the karmic connection I had with the Chinese officers who made me break my vows. I should wish for their enlightenment, and I should think about all the others who just like me had been detained and harassed. Actually, many people had it much worse than me, and I should think about them." As Palden recounted this story, the advice given to him by his friend was familiar to me by now. When I had problems of my own, friends and neighbors encouraged me: *think about others.* This is a form of social connectedness, but it simultaneously helps people to drop the conviction that their problems are uniquely significant, and thus, massive and intractable. The imperative in healthy coping here—that is, behavioral or mental strategies used to mitigate taxing events—is, in fact, quite different from "self-care" ideology touted in the United States, which is aimed at soothing stress. The perspective in Dharamsala is much more radical in that it delegitimizes the utility of hanging on to stress (no matter how great) in the first place.

For members of the Tibetan diaspora, compassion is not merely an ethical value but is used as a practice or technology to work on the self, particularly in times of crisis. By "technology," I do not mean in the Foucaultian sense of self-regulation and discipline (Foucault 1980), but more simply as the understanding and application of particular knowledge to combat a problem. The techniques such as thinking of all the others in the world who are experiencing similar (or worse) problems and wishing happiness for all sentient beings are considered very skillful ways of working with distress. In this way, compassion is more utilitarian than moralistic.

Although in the West "compassion" is thought of as a nice personality attribute, it means something much deeper and more comprehensive in Buddhist contexts. And compassion is also an activity in which anyone can train. As with Tanya Luhrmann's (2012) ethnographic research among Evangelical Christians in the United States where she found that prayer and hearing the voice of God was considered to be a learned skill, the way that Tibetans talk about resilience and coping makes clear that cultivating compassion is not a moral accolade as much as an efficacious skill. It is both profound and pragmatic. Many Tibetans discussed how coping was more difficult when they were younger and had not yet learned how to "think broadly." For example, coping through talking about problems with others is acceptable when young, but not highly valued as one matures. This does not mean that people never share their worries and concerns with one another. But the idea of processing and talking at length about distress is frowned upon because it might solidify and churn up harmful negative emotions. Instead, more active approaches are used to transform distress, which create space and flexibility within the mind.

Lojong, Training the Mind

Lojong (mind training) are formal techniques that use Buddhist logic to deconstruct both the legitimacy and utility of negative emotions. When one is locked in suffering, *lojong* is a technology used to create space and flexibility. These teachings have become part of the very fabric of moral life for Tibetans, which, in turn, are important in strengthening resilience. Although not all Tibetans are particularly religious, Buddhist worldviews are a central force in cultural life and these techniques pervade everyday sensibilities. The teachings help one transform suffering by viewing any situation as workable.

Lojong (Tib: *blo sbyong*), was first brought to Tibet by Atisha, an eleventh-century Indian pandit who received the teachings from a meditation master in Indonesia. There is a story that when Atisha was preparing to visit Tibet, he brought along a particularly nasty Bengali tea servant because he heard that the Tibetans were so good natured he worried he would not have any difficulties to use in mind training. But as Tibetans love to joke—in fact, there were plenty of irritating people there, so his Benjali tea boy was there for naught.

The *lojong* teachings are also associated with the Kadampa master Chekawa Yeshe Dorje (1102–1176), who is said to have stumbled on the following lines of an open book:

> Give all victory to others;
> Take defeat for yourself

Chekawa later wrote what is considered one of the most important works in the Tibetan Buddhist cannon: *The Seven Points of Mind Training*, a set of teachings routinely taught to lay practitioners. In a decidedly "fake it, 'til you make it" style, the *lojong* practice coaches ordinary people to respond to adversity as if they were bodhisattvas, realized beings whose sole concern is the well-being of others (Kongtrul 2005). As I describe in more detail below, the fake-it-'til-you-make-it approach is central within Vajrayana Buddhism, known as a "resultant path" where practitioners visualize themselves as already enlightened beings to train their minds.

The teachings, despite their profundity, are written to appeal to common sense. *The Seven Points of Mind Training*, a root text, contains a set of fifty-nine "slogans": a pith instruction one can call upon in moments of discomfort. The slogans fall into two categories: those that help cultivate compassion and those to remind practitioners about emptiness (also referred to as wisdom, the correct view of reality). Buddhist sutras describe these qualities as two wings of a bird—without both wisdom and compassion, the bird cannot fly. Examples of slogans include: "be grateful to everyone"; "don't ponder others" (that is, don't overanalyze others' faults); "don't act with a twist" (don't do good deeds to get praise); "regard all dharmas as dreams—although they may seem solid, they are passing memories"; "in postmeditation, be a child of illusion" (see the illusory nature of reality). The *lojong* teachings show that putting others before self (like bodhisattvas) is not recommended just to be nice, but rather is seen as the most efficacious way to mitigate suffering.

Lojong is a broad category of teachings that center on using both compassion and emptiness to train the mind in combatting distress. Numerous traditions within Tibetan Buddhism have composed *lojong* texts, which are used not only in monasteries and nunneries but are also taught to laypeople. Below is an example of a short *lojong* text, composed by Kadampa Geshe Langritangpa (cited in Rinchen 2001).

EIGHT VERSES FOR TRAINING THE MIND
1. May I always cherish all beings
With the resolve to accomplish for them
The highest good that is more precious
Than any wish-fulfilling jewel.

2. Whenever I am in the company of others,
May I regard myself as inferior to all
And from the depths of my heart
Cherish others as supreme.

3. In all my actions, may I watch my mind,
And as soon as disturbing emotions arise,
May I forcefully stop them at once,
Since they will hurt both me and others.

4. When I see ill-natured people,
Overwhelmed by wrong deeds and pain,
May I cherish them as something rare,
As though I had found a treasure trove.

5. When someone does me wrong out of envy,
By insulting me and the like,
May I accept defeat
And offer the victory to them.

6. Even if someone whom I have helped
And in whom I have placed my hopes
Does great wrong by harming me,
May I see them as an excellent spiritual friend.

7. In brief, directly or indirectly,
May I give all help and joy to my mothers,
And may I take all their harm and pain
Secretly upon myself.

8. May none of this ever be sullied
By thoughts of the eight worldly concerns.
May I see all things as illusions
And, without attachment, gain freedom from bondage.

The text contains the core features of *lojong*: putting others before self; quelling negative emotions, which are harmful to self and others; and seeing worldly concerns[3] as a hindrance to realizing the illusory nature of samsara.

This mind-set of putting others before self is considered the supreme method for finding contentment (which is different from seeking out pleasure, self-confirmation, praise, and worldly gain). As one woman named

Tsekyi described it: "selflessness and taking care of others is the key to happiness. I think this really benefits self and others to think in this way. Then, if we practice contentment, this is really beneficial to the mind. We should always think that all human beings are the same—what I want, you also want. This is beneficial and helps you with any mental suffering." These phrases sound rather formulaic—and, indeed, they are, purposefully. I heard them repeated again and again by Tibetans who were dealing with great difficulty, to one another, to themselves, to me. At first glance, it might seem as if it is all too easy, or that people must be repressing their true feelings. But what I argue is that these stock phrases and *lojong*-style of thinking act as a sort of North Star principle to guide the way. Tibetans do not always think about others; they are not always content. But a cultural understanding of what one ought to do in the face of suffering (cultivate compassion, reflect on emptiness) guides their recovery.

Paradoxically, *lojong* coaches that to find happiness, we should "drive all blame into oneself." This does not really mean to "blame" ourselves for everything that goes wrong in the conventional sense but to recognize that ultimately a person's happiness or misery is up to them. At any moment, no matter what is going on, we can be miserable or we can try to shift our perspective to find contentment. This does not stem from ethical obligation; rather, it is utilitarian for those coping with difficulty and distress. Perhaps counterintuitively, Tibetans argue that by wishing happiness even for one's enemies, one is "liberated" from disturbing emotions. I often heard the Dalai Lama and other important lamas instruct community members to forgive the Chinese government—and not necessarily for the sake of the Chinese, but because anger and resentment are harmful to oneself. These negative emotions are not just psychologically unpleasant but can cause illness because of how they create imbalance in the body.

There is a meditation practice connected to *lojong* known as *tonglen*, the practice of "giving and taking," where one wishes to take on the suffering and misfortunes of others. The practitioner imagines breathing in illness, evil, and pain in the form of black tar or smoke, absorbing it into his or her heart and rejoicing that now others are free from misery. One then breathes out freshness, space, and light, which are absorbed by all sentient beings without discrimination. In fact, there is even particular emphasis on practicing for those one most dislikes as a form of "training." The *tonglen* practice is also used in particularly difficult situations, such as being with a dying relative. A young Tibetan woman who had done undergraduate-level training in psychology in New Delhi (the only mental health "professional" in Dharamsala) confided in me one afternoon: "When I don't know what else to do for people, sometimes I just silently practice *tonglen*." Others mentioned it as an ideal, or a practice that exemplifies the mind-set many wish to possess. Those who can put "others before self" are considered exceptionally resilient—indeed, this way of thinking is at the very pinnacle of emotional health for Tibetans.

The key feature of *lojong*-style advice is to shift from criticizing or changing the external situation; instead, one turns inward, seeing one's own mind as the root of suffering.

"Even if they don't know anything about Buddhist philosophy," explains Geshe Dawa, "when people begin to see their problems in terms of their own minds, and not [as something that is] out there somewhere, they develop a broad and vast view. And this reduces suffering." He offered the following as an example:

> I went to Portugal and met a girl who broke up with her boyfriend. I told her because you are young, you will find another boyfriend! I told her that she shouldn't contact the ex-boyfriend or try to meet him again; just let it go. Then she said that they work in the same office. I asked her if she could change her job. She said that it was the best office and she had an excellent salary. As they worked together in the same office, she would see him speaking with other girls and have even more suffering. Then I told her that I would teach her to practice *lojong*, which is something I used in prison. I explained that when I was very young in Tibet, I caught some flies and put them inside a jar. I played with the jar and listened to the jar as if it were a radio with the flies buzzing. I put many flies in the same bottle. When I think back to this time, it is the same as prison. A few flies even died in the jar. I thought that really, it is my karma to stay in prison. This helped me to deal with suffering because I realized that I created it myself. Actually, I had a great opportunity to experience a lot of suffering, which meant I was purifying obscurations [karma]. Thinking like this, my mental problems gradually diminished. Like this, in many past lives, you must have done something negative to your boyfriend. If you did negative actions, then this is the result. If you experience the result now, you won't get this suffering later. The best would be if you could wish happiness for your ex-boyfriend. You could even think, okay, just like me, the new girlfriend just wants to be happy. If you can think very deeply, then you will see it is not so difficult. One day, she told me she no longer had these problems, even working side-by-side with the ex-boyfriend.

This example is interesting because it contrasts conventional worldly advice with *lojong*.

Perhaps because she was a foreigner, he begins by making suggestions on how to change the external environment. When he switches to *lojong*, there is a shift from problematizing the situation's circumstances to the girl and how she creates her own suffering. The moment of success comes when she does not have to modify the situation because she has instead modified her thinking about the situation. This also shows how Tibetans use *lojong*-informed advice in a rather informal way. Certainly, most Tibetans do not walk around repeating *lojong* slogans to one another. Rather, this manner of thinking (to put others before self and to transform suffering) permeates cultural sensibilities.

Embodying Lojong

This book stumbles into a set of long-standing concerns within Buddhist studies and the anthropological study of religion, namely, the distinctions (and overlaps) between religious scripture and everyday practice. Many Tibetans living in Dharamsala do not consider themselves particularly religious, and yet cultural concepts of health and healing are shaped by Buddhist concepts to such a degree that it is impossible to divorce Tibetan medicine from religion (Adams 2001; Ozawa-de Silva and Ozawa-de Silva 2011). This false distinction between medicine and religion is typical cross-culturally, and likewise mirrors foundational theory on how religious values permeate societies in ways that feel more like common sense than religious ideology (Durkheim [1912] 1995; Weber [1930] 2004). When community members in Dharamsala use compassion as a method for cultivating resilience, they do not do so, necessarily, with the aim of being a good Buddhist. Rather, it is an efficacious way of managing suffering—something that one ought to do in the face of difficulty. Buddhist principles guide Tibetan action and thoughts regardless of whether or not one is religious.

The question of how Tibetans come to incorporate *lojong* into everyday beliefs is an important one. Anthropologists have long been interested in the question of internalization—that is, how and why a particular cultural ethos and associated beliefs are adopted by individuals (Carlisle 2008; Obeyesekere 1990; Spiro 1997; Throop 2003). Bradd Shore (1996) argues that through ritual and repetition, semantic codes are created to interpret events. Many Tibetans—monastic and lay alike—learn such codes and cultural values through anecdote and allegory. Religion scholars such as Hallisey and Hansen (1996) argue that stories and narratives are a typical means for shaping moral life across Buddhist cultures, revealing what matters most to the moral good. This style of teaching is found not only in Buddhist scriptures but also in everyday life. Many lamas with whom I visited answered my questions through storytelling.

Likewise, older people give younger generations advice through allegory. Many of these stories and anecdotes describe great bodhisattvas—realized beings who work only for the benefit of others. There is also a particular fondness for trickster yogis who act in seemingly outrageous ways, but through "skillful means" are actually working to benefit sentient beings. Such tales inspire courage, acknowledging that *it is* in some sense outrageous to put others wholly before self. But while most people do not meet the ideal of acting tirelessly for others (this would be to make the mistake of romanticizing Tibetans that Donald Lopez [1998] so wisely warned against), these stories show what Tibetans value most.

In the face of profound loss, many Tibetans, regardless of their overt religiosity conceptualized their experience in a way that Obeyesekere has argued is typical of many Buddhist laypeople across traditions; they automatically "generalize their despair from the self to the world at large" (1985, 140). Although these sentiments are linked undoubtedly with Buddhist values, they are not explicitly religious in nature. Many community members explained to me that just by virtue of "being Tibetan," they learn about compassion and mind training through their culture. Specifically, there was a sense that "good Tibetan families" teach their children to put others before self. In fact, the motto of the TCV schools is "Other before Self," which "appears on everything from the official website to textbooks to buildings and garbage cans on the TCV campus, [implying that] service" (Swank 2014, 83) is paramount to good citizenship. I often heard parents teaching their children the values of being humble and thinking about others. This goes further than the Golden Rule to do unto others as you would have them do unto you, because it foregrounds the concept that compassion without gain is the defining feature of the moral good.

A young man named Ngawang who recently finished high school in Dharamsala said the following:

When I was living in my village in Tibet, I didn't know that actually Tibetans are pretty kind. But when I went to many places in China and came to India, I saw many different people from all over the world. I realized that actually Tibetans are quite compassionate. Therefore, I think that these qualities are inherited from our ancestors. The real meaning of Buddhadharma is to use mind training to work with our minds for the benefit of others. Therefore, if we believe and practice Dharma, this creates peace. Moreover, it is beneficial to others. If we work for others with compassion and love, then whenever others see us, they will smile and respect us. Also, we don't need to worry that someone will harm us and want to hurt us.

Parents strive to teach their children that a meaningful life is centered around working for the benefit of others. An older monk spoke similar sentiments: "Some of my relatives came to me for help, but mostly they were very young and put into schools. However, from the bottom of my heart, I told them not to waste their time and to study hard to be a person who can help others. Other than that, I can't advise others very well." The idea of *studying hard* to become a compassionate person reflects the notion that one must train to put others before self.

Another important way the *lojong* teachings are learned in Dharamsala is more direct, through religious teachings—an integral part of community life. Nearly all community members attend the Dalai Lama's frequent teachings—if only to don one's finest clothing and have a picnic with family. *Lojong*-style teachings on emptiness and compassion are among the most common and were routinely referenced in interviews, certainly with monks and nuns, but with laypeople as well. For example, a seventeen-year-old student named Tenzin said: "We know from attending teachings by His Holiness [the Dalai Lama] that the best way to be happy is to put others before ourselves. But he knows this is hard to do, so we should start very small." It is common when giving advice for lay community members and monastics alike, to remind friends and family to hold the Dalai Lama as a model of decorum. More than just the spiritual leader of Tibet, the Dalai Lama is regarded as a realized being, the incarnation of Chenrezig (the bodhisattva of compassion). He is held as a point of reference and the devotion people have for him is not in the form of worship, but rather a sense that one should strive to emulate his behavior.

Emptiness

Lojong teachings are very pragmatic in nature. Since life is inevitably diffi-cult, the teachings show how adversity can be used as an opportunity to generate greater wisdom (realization of emptiness) and compassion. As one lama explains, there are different ways to work with suffering that bring the same result.

"All people want to have happiness," he said, "however, under the influ-ence of attachment and desire they are not happy. Some practice emptiness as an antidote to attachment and become happy; some practice compassion and cherishing others as a way to become happy." But while it is easy to imag-ine how practicing compassion helps one to be happy, what does it mean to practice emptiness?

Emptiness, or *shunyata* (Sanskrit), sometimes referred to as "voidness," is the Buddhist view of reality. Rather than seeing reality clearly, ordinary be-ings tend to view phenomena (and oneself) as permanent, unchanging, and independent. Not understanding emptiness is considered the very founda-tion of suffering. The *Buddhadharma* teaches that people suffer because they resist the nature of reality and wish to solidify their possessions, relationships, and health—we want to make them permanent and unchanging, and when we resist change, we suffer. Reflecting on emptiness as a way to cope with difficulty does not mean that people do not suffer. But they accept the Bud-dhist notion that suffering comes from the inside—from one's own mind—and not from the outside.

A practical way to reflect on emptiness is through recognizing imperma-nence: everything changes, and thus there is no solid existence. Tashi Dolma, a thirty-five-year-old woman who left Tibet ten years ago says:

> When my mother passed away, I tried to think about the no-self [doctrine] and emptiness. I thought how plants look beautiful, fresh, and alive in sum-mer. However, gradually seasons change and leaves fall on the ground. Like-wise, my mother was sixty-five years old and she had become old and reached the end of her life. There was nothing that could be done and I just ac-cepted it. I am a refugee and I was unable to see my mother before she died. I believe this is the result of previous karma. Thinking like this was of great benefit to me. Buddhist philosophy has influenced Tibetan habits, so people think about karma and impermanence, which helps them cope with problems.

Many people described that when they accept that things change and fall away, they relax and enjoy the beauty of life. It is not that things are meaningless. Rather, emptiness implies there is no *fixed* or *inherent* meaning. And in this view, there is freedom and a sense of possibility.

Another example comes from a lama from whom many community members seek help in times of difficulty. He explains that most people cannot look at their own faults and shortcomings, and this is why they suffer. He says:

> In society, if other people make us angry or unhappy we don't have to react very suddenly. We have to think that after coming into samsara, it is only natural that we would have problems! And it is better to react patiently and with compassion. Then all the causes and conditions of anger and unhappiness automatically diminish. If we can think about selflessness and emptiness, then when other people do something negative toward us, such as using harsh words, we don't need to react. There is no person to hate. We think that the person exists. But if we meditate on emptiness and selflessness, then we will realize that the person doesn't exist as we think they do. If thinking about emptiness is too difficult, then there is an easier way [practicing compassion].

The *lojong* teachings describe how the more one understands the relationship between emptiness and interdependence, the more compassion will naturally arise. If phenomena do not exist independently, this means that form can only arise in relation to other phenomena (known as *tendrel*, meaning "dependent arising" or "interdependence"). Although ultimately the world should be regarded as an illusion, the way that the world appears is fundamentally based on interconnectedness.

These philosophical concepts are not necessarily discussed in everyday life, and yet their influence is evident in an embodied understanding of healing and the body. In her ethnographic work, Nike-Ann Schröder asked a Tibetan lama what can be done to help with serious psychiatric illness. He said that those with mental illness often believe their suffering will be permanent; they "make the suffering bigger and will experience more suffering" (2011, 87). He goes on to say that another way of creating or increasing the problem is for people to think they are the only one suffering, or that their suffering is more severe than others.' The practice of compassion and thinking of others is not just a nice value, but a powerful method for mitigating suffering. As my interlocutors constantly reminded me, "it is only natural" to suffer in samsara.

Compassion

As exemplified in the bodhisattva vow,[4] the wish to continue taking rebirth until all sentient beings have attained enlightenment, compassion is the highest value among Tibetans and one must be continually trained in it, over and over, as a learned practice. Scientists in the West investigating the demonstrable health effects of compassion meditation also find this to be true; its positive effects are found to be mediated by gaining proficiency, suggesting that increased capacity for compassion is learned (Leung et al. 2012; Lutz et al. 2009; Pace et al. 2009). Indeed, there is a sense in the Tibetan community that people should train in building compassion, which monks and nuns accomplish through study and debate. The heart of many debates is to deduce logically why compassion is a natural response if one is in accordance with reality (emptiness). It is not necessarily about "being nice," but about "being real." If one understands the emptiness of self and phenomena, it is not a nihilistic view where nothing matters. Rather, through this realization of interdependence, connectedness and compassion are the logical result.

Many Buddhist teachings, and the allegories based on them, use a style of humorous logic to show why getting angry or harming others is illogical. It is not just morally wrong but is actually nonsensical. An older monk, Tashi Rabten, conveyed the following using an allegory from Buddhist scripture:

> Sometimes very close friends get angry with each other and use very harsh words as a result of afflictive emotions, even though they really love each other. If people can think of or understand the situation broadly, they will feel compassion and see that the nature of this person is really nice. But in this moment, the person doesn't have freedom because he or she is controlled by disturbing emotions. For example, if someone beat you with a stick, then you don't get angry with the stick or the hand of the person because the stick and hand cannot think for itself. You get angry with the person and not the stick! In the same way, you get angry with the disturbing emotions and not the per-

son himself. There are reasons to think about this. The person doesn't have freedom from their afflictive emotions. We see there is no reason to get angry. If we can distinguish between the subject and the action, then we don't get overly upset and can focus on solving the problem.

In other words, this kind of empathy is pragmatic. Tashi Rabten laughed and said, "Isn't it illogical to become upset with those who are impatient, or to become angry with someone else for being angry?" Rather than forcing oneself to be nice, he suggests that one should use logic and reason to develop compassion. But sometimes people do force themselves in that *fake it 'til you make it* way. These north star principles guide the way in moments of difficulty, which is linked fundamentally with physical and mental health. Even if it is not wholly genuine in the moment, Tibetans argue that one should look toward compassion as a way of training the mind.

The science of *sowa rigpa* is, in some sense, based on the healing properties of compassion. Within this medical practice and the everyday sense of health and healing, "the cultivation of compassion and empathy is seen as central to the logic of health itself, because such psycho-physical states are the very opposite of the negative emotions that give rise to the imbalances . . . that lead to disease" (Ozawa-de Silva and Ozawa-de Silva 2011, 99). In this way, a mind that is compassionate and calm is more highly valued than the capacity to express a range of emotion (which is highly valued in the West). Therefore, when people describe letting go of distress and thinking of others instead, their friends and neighbors applaud their skillfulness and do not think they are repressing their feelings.

A sense of compassion for others was present in nearly all the stories I collected about hardship and coping in Dharamsala. Many describe how talking too much about their problems and dwelling on negativity is not only harmful for oneself, but also creates problems for others. A young man named Tenzin explained:

When my best friend died on the journey to India, I was extremely sad. I was only around twenty-two years old, but I had studied in a monastery, so I was better equipped to deal with it. When I considered what had happened, I thought that he was the only one of forty people to have died. This was clearly the result of his karma. Therefore, I tried to deal by simply accepting it and I thought that crying and being unhappy would just make things difficult for others. If I cried loudly, my companions would have had difficulties. At this point, we were in mountain passes and hadn't had food for days, so we were exhausted. We were in a dangerous position. Second, Tibetans believe that if we make a lot of noise in desolate places, local deities and *nagas*[5] will harm us. For these reasons, I thought there was no benefit in crying.

While others would expect Tenzin to be sad after losing his best friend, he expresses concern that overt emotionality might harm his companions. Sometimes compassion was expressed directly like this, and at other times, it was more deferred and general, thinking of "all sentient beings" or those in one's same situation.

In fact, a key *lojong* strategy used to "train" in compassion entails thinking about others experiencing the same thing, all across the world. In Dharamsala, people coach friends going through difficult times to think "more broadly" about all the others in the world experiencing similar (or worse) problems. As one neighbor reminded me: "We can always learn about people who are worse off than us. It is good to remember those who are doing even worse than us. It helps us remember that we are not doing so badly. These are usual methods for coping with problems." Diminishing and downplaying adversity in life is not seen as repression, but rather as skillful and realistic. Remembering that others around you are also suffering seems to help Tibetan exile members cope even with severe events such as torture and imprisonment. Maggie Zraly and colleagues (2013) found something similar in their work on motherhood and resilience among genocide survivors in Rwanda. Women described how thinking about how others lost their children reminded them that things could always be worse. It was the sense of gratitude that comes from such realizations that seemed to bolster resilience and strength.

When talking with Pema, a forty-five-year-old woman who has lived in Dharamsala for twenty years, she described how coping with her mother's death prepared her for when she was imprisoned. Having been arrested by border police when trying to leave Tibet, she was sentenced to nine months in a Chinese prison. During that time, she was raped (along with a group of nuns) by the prison guards. She explained:

> When my mother died, I didn't really have the same coping methods, or way of thinking, that I do now. During that time, I was small, so I didn't under-

stand Buddhism, although I was influenced by it. However, after thinking carefully, I understood that when someone dies, there is no way to bring them back. I understood that no matter how much I cried or called my mother, she wouldn't come back, so I thought there was no benefit in doing so. Thinking like this, I consoled myself. Also, I wasn't the only motherless child, there were others in the same situation. I thought we were the same, and gradually the suffering decreased. Likewise, when I was violated and raped in prison, I just tried to think about the poor nuns. And also all the other women in the world who have been raped. It was the only thing that helped me—trying to send good prayers to all the others.

Some go a step beyond acknowledging that others are also suffering by making aspirations to take on the pain of others, particularly those who are even worse off. Thubten is a fifty-eight-year-old street vendor who sells sweaters in a small stall on the side of the road. He left Tibet as a monk in the 1980s. He says:

> I joined a monastery in Lhasa after being in school. But because I knew how to read and write in Chinese, I had to work in the monastery office, meaning I could not attend classes with the other new monks. I had finally made up my mind to become a monk, but it almost didn't matter because I just had to sit in the office. I was very depressed. But one day, I realized that if it wasn't me here, another monk would be sitting here in my place. Thinking that doing this work allowed someone else to practice the precious Dharma filled me with joy. My mind suddenly felt very spacious and I was very happy to remain in the office on behalf of the others.

The *lojong* teachings advise people to look at irritating or upsetting situations in life as precious opportunities. As one lama told me: "discomfort should be regarded as a great teacher. It shows you the work you need to do—where your mind is still obscured by ignorance."

The "Six Perfections"

When a person takes a bodhisattva vow, the wish to continue taking rebirth until all other sentient beings have attained enlightenment, they vow to train in the six *pāramitās* (Sanskrit; *pha rol tu phyin pa drug* in Tibetan), which translates as "the six perfections." The six *pāramitās* are generosity, discipline, patience, exertion, meditation, and *prajñā*. The first five help to generate merit (good karma) and culminate in the last one, *prajñā*, which is wisdom that comes through realizing emptiness. The idea is that practitioners train in the six perfections to become bodhisattvas; while this may take many, many lives to accomplish, Mahayana Buddhists believe that those who train in the six perfections will eventually become a realized being on the path to enlightenment. The training in the six perfections is meant to take place "on the ground," so to speak, meaning in everyday situations. This is what people mean when they talk about taking adversity onto the path. Tibetan lamas often joke that you don't have to "look around for problems in order to practice"; because there are always difficulties in life, there are innumerable opportunities to practice the *pāramitās*. Monks and nuns in Dharamsala talk explicitly about using the six *pāramitās* to cope with adversity. Laypeople do not necessarily use this term by name (although some do), but many of the "perfections" such as generosity and discipline form the bedrock of how Tibetans cope with adversity in life.

An older man, Dundrup, who was somewhat rough in appearance although dignified just the same, explains how patience can be used even in severe circumstances such as torture and imprisonment:

> We have to talk about two factors for being able to cope with problems. The first is people who have knowledge about *Buddhadharma* and those who really practice. This kind of person, whatever the experience—beatings, torture, imprisonment—the suffering is only temporary. They might get angry temporarily, but then they will think that those who are beating them, probably they have families and need money for their children. Maybe they have to work in the prison to help their children. This helps them to cope with problems. Also, if we can practice Buddhism and meditate on compassion and patience, it is very beneficial for our minds when we have problems and difficulties. Those who can practice, when they have problems, they can think that even if they have problems this means that maybe others won't have the problem. And also, we all have problems, so it is only natural. If we can think like this, it really benefits our minds.

The values (generosity, patience, and so forth) are important to maintaining a harmonious social world, but these values are not particularly moralistic as in Judeo-Christian virtue.

In general, Tibetans tend to think of emotions not as bad or good, but as helpful or useful (or not). A young man named Rigzin says: "Because my parents are my dearest relatives and they were not friendly to one another, this made me very unhappy. If someone is angry and it is beneficial to be angry, as with fighting for political justice, then it is okay to be angry. But if it doesn't benefit anyone, then it is not useful to be angry." Those who are stingy and impatient are seen as not very bright or skillful. There are countless Tibetan Buddhist texts dedicated to the six *pāramitās* and their usefulness in developing compassion and a view of emptiness. Such ideas also permeate everyday cultural sensibilities. An abbot of a small monastery in Dharamsala says:

> The Dalai Lama always says that we can meditate on love and compassion in order to see all people as equal. From the practices of bodhisattvas, we see that we can stop negative actions. We all have this capacity, but we have to train. For example, some children behave very badly. There are constructive ways for parents to advise their children. Sometimes parents need to speak sweetly and sometimes they need to speak more wrathfully. Sometimes it is skillful to lightly beat them. But parents never look at their children as an enemy. Parents always wish for the best for their children; they want them to become good people. Mainly we need to avoid being angry very directly with someone, even if they perform very negative actions toward us. We must remember that the source of their behavior is afflictive emotions. If we remember this, then this would be very beneficial. This practice can be done by all people, not only monks and nuns. It is very possible for ordinary people to practice this. *Lojong* (mind training) is a practice of a bodhisattva and all people can take bodhisattva vows. We need to try to generate *bodhichitta*. There is no distinction in capacity among people who are rich, poor, old, young, and so forth.

Within Tibetan Buddhist sensibilities, there is often a juxtaposition between the bodhisattva ideal and ordinary human beings. People reflect on how bodhisattvas, realized beings, would approach a situation and then remember that all sentient beings have the same potential because of inherent buddhanature.

Many classic texts draw on humor to teach these lessons, showing how illogical it is to be impatient and selfish. The great eighth-century Buddhist master Santideva, for example, instructs people who struggle with generosity to spend their lives taking a piece of fruit in one hand and giving it to the other hand. Until the practitioner sees being stingy with others as just as absurd as a reluctance to pass the fruit from one hand to the other, they are advised to continue this practice. This is an example of *lojong*, which is all about going against the grain; it is swimming upstream. Jetsunma Tenzin Palmo, an important female abbot, once told me that *lojong* is like going to the gym. She said, "You don't just keep lifting the three-pound weight all the time. That's not good for training; it's too easy. To develop your capacity, it's good to strain just a little bit. That is how you develop your muscles. Developing greater compassion and the realization of emptiness is like that. You just train in both; little by little."

Help Seeking in Dharamsala

As with many places across the globe, there is no mental health system in Dharamsala. In fact, the concept of "mental health"—that is, a specialized set of quasi-medical practices and clinical experts devoted to treating discrete mental problems—makes little sense in this context. In part, this is because problems that manifest within the mind are generally connected to broader systemic distress within the body. The practice of *sowa rigpa* takes into account how the weather, social environment, spirit harm, karma, and humoral imbalances lead to disturbances that manifest simultaneously in the body and mind (Craig 2012a). From the viewpoint of *sowa rigpa*, which is based on the science of Buddhist philosophy, disease and illness are fundamentally a result of the three roots of samsara, or "the three poisons": ignorance, passion, and aggression. Unlike in biomedicine where science and religion are diametrically opposed, in this system, they are fundamentally intertwined. Practitioners of *sowa rigpa* and Buddhist lamas routinely make "referrals" back and forth to one another and work in tandem to treat illness, particularly if there is a suspicion of spirit harm or karmically based disorders.

Lamas, Doctors, and Yogis

Tibetans lay claim to a long-established body of medical practice knowledge known as *sowa rigpa*, dating back at least to the eleventh or twelfth centuries. Physicians who practice *sowa rigpa* are known commonly as *amchi* (a Mongolian word); the Tibetan word for doctor is *men pa*. They are degreed specialists who study traditional Tibetan medicine for around seven years at a *mentsikhang* (traditional Tibetan hospital) training institute. The classical Tibetan medical text, "The Four Tantras" (*rgyud bshi*) describes many syndromes that include psychological symptoms such as anger, sadness, delirium, and anxiety, but in general, problems of the mind are just one part of general systemic imbalances. Equilibrium is related to harmony within the three humors of *rlung* (pronounced *loong*, translated as "wind"), *mkhris-pa* (pronounced *tree-pa*, translated as "bile"), and *bad-kan* (pronounced *pay-gen*, translated as "phlegm"). In this way, *amchi* must treat physical and mental dis-ease together.

When patients visit *amchis*, they do not begin their consultation by telling the doctor what is wrong. Rather, the doctor tells the patient what is wrong, or merely prescribes treatment without the patient being too concerned about a discrete diagnosis. Instead, they might be made aware of an imbalance within particular organs or humors (e.g., "kidney problems," or *rlung* imbalance). *Amchi* make their diagnosis by feeling a patient's pulse, through urinalysis (traditionally assessing the color, appearance, and smell), and by examining the tongue. Patients are often prescribed herbal medicines and given lists of foods to avoid or other behavioral changes they should implement. For example, I once visited an *amchi* who after feeling my pulse for a few seconds told me that my blood was deficient and taught me a series of breathing exercises I was to do immediately upon waking to better circulate oxygen to my organs. Sometimes acupuncture and moxibustion[6] are used to treat patients, often in conjunction with herbal medicines. Increasingly, *sowa rigpa* has entered the global marketplace of so-called alternative medicine (Adams, Schrempf, and Craig 2013; Craig 2012a; Kloos 2016), and anthropologists have studied the ways that it introduces new forms of knowledge, which may clash with ontological assumptions in biomedicine related to cause and effect (Craig 2013), and what counts as evidence and efficacy (Adams et al. 2005).

The practices and techniques of *sowa rigpa* are highly systematic and rigorous. But while medical systems such as biomedicine are often considered to be in opposition to religion, the science of healing in Tibetan medicine actually stems from Buddhist philosophy. For example, Tibetans often visit lamas for a *mo* (divination) before seeking medical treatment to find out which hospital to visit, which doctor to see, on which date to go, and whether the medicine will even be effective (Schröder 2011). It is not assumed that medicines will work on all people, at all times. It is important to note that the question of efficacy relates not just to the quality or potency of the medicine, but whether a person has the karma for it to work.

Amchi work alongside lamas, *ngakpas* (yogis), and other religious specialists, such as *lha pa* and *lha ma*, also known as *kundun* (oracles). Oracles become possessed by deities who diagnose and treat illnesses, among their other spiritual duties; often particular monasteries are associated with one or more specific oracles who have historically "worked" with them, such as the *lha* (spirit), Pehar, and the Nechung Oracle who advises the Dalai Lama. The term "lama" is a broad name for highly regarded Buddhist practitioners who could be either monastic or a householder who is married. Women lamas are often known as *khandro* (*dakini*, translated literally as, "sky dancer"). Some lamas are known for their abilities to treat mental distress through prayers, blessings, advice, and protection cords/amulets; some are known to have particularly strong connections to their personal *yidams* (meditation deities) (Schröder 2011), such as White Tara or Vajrayogini. *Yidams* represent aspects of an enlightened mind that are depicted in human form so that practitioners can better envision themselves transforming into these deities. During a time when, inexplicably, I was having difficulty sleeping, some Tibetan friends suggested I visit a reputable lama known for a *mo* (divination). People seek a *mo* for many reasons, including illness and other disturbances, or to obtain answers related to important decisions such as marriage, a new job, or applying to university. They are practiced by lay and monastic lamas alike, and even the Dalai Lama is known to do the occasional *mo* (Proust 2008). My friends thought that getting a *mo* would be a logical first step in that it might reveal the cause of my insomnia and what I could do to find a cure.

As I prepared to visit Denma Locho Rinpoche during his weekly office hours, I gathered a *khatag* (silk ceremonial offering scarf), some fruit and juice to offer, and five hundred rupees—about eight U.S. dollars. As I sat on the floor in front of him, I launched into my story about the insomnia in the way one does when visiting a specialist in the United States. But Rinpoche cut me off as my interpretation of the problem was not relevant. After accepting my offerings, he rolled a pair of dice, noting the results before holding up a coin pendant for a few moments, watching it swing. He nodded and then wrote some notes as if writing on a prescription pad. Denma Locho Rinpoche explained, "Okay, you probably have some problems with *rlung* (wind), so you should visit Dr. Dorjee at the Upper Mentsikhang Office. And then," he paused. "There's a small *gdon 'dre* (malevolent spirit) problem." "A *dön?*" I asked with alarm. But the issue of spirit harm and the exorcism ritual he recommended was not seen as a big deal, and in fact, people see this as rather commonplace and easily treatable. Rinpoche sent me down the street to the Ganden Monastery *puja*[7] house. Many larger monasteries have small *puja* houses in town for the sole purpose of conducting rituals for community members.

I presented the slip of paper to one of the monks at the *puja* house who wrote in a notebook what was "ordered": a specific protector deity practice with *torma* (a homemade cake of barley flour and butter used for appeasing spirits and clearing obstacles), and a series of sutras, scripture from the Buddha, that were to be read aloud by a group of monks. "This will take about eight hours, and we ask for a donation of RS five hundred (eight U.S. dollars)," he said, simply. I asked him when I should come back, assuming I needed to be there for the rituals, but he looked at me with some amusement. "No, it is not necessary for you to be there. We will do them for you." He told me they would be done within two days and sent me on my way. Unsurprisingly, my sleep improved. Next, I visited Dr. Dorjee, where I explained the results of the *mo*. After taking my pulse for a few minutes, he gave me a prescription for *rinchen rilbu* (precious pills), an herbal medicine blessed with prayers. The precious pills—meant to be crushed and taken with warm water three times a day—would correct the *rlung* imbalance that was causing insomnia. My case was fairly typical in that the fundamental causes of my ailment were simultaneously and synergistically physical, psychological, and spiritual. Spirit harm is both a cause and result of a weakened psychophysical system and thus treatment is often multipronged, with a mix of medicine and ritual. The problem, as it was diagnosed, was caused both by a *rlung* imbalance and subtle spirit harm.

A Mind Unsettled

A number of studies investigate the incidence of *srog-rlung*, a diagnostic category that means literally "life-wind" imbalance (Clifford 1994; Millard 2003 Samuel 2005, which is a specific cultural idiom of distress in Tibetan communities. The term "idioms of distress" (Hollan 2004; Kirmayer 1989; Nichter 1981, 2010) is used to describe the ways that particular cultures articulate, understand, and experience distress. It is important to note that these idioms can be religious, medical, or political in nature and have shared meaning within a cultural group. This approach recognizes that idioms are dynamic and contextual, and does not automatically place suffering within a medical model. Exploring cultural idioms of distress also reveals generational, regional, and other kinds of diversity *within* cultures.

Several anthropologists have written on *rlung* disorders (Adams 1998; Janes 1995; Proust 2006), suggesting that traumatic distress becomes subsumed into this culturally constituted category of illness. Of the three humors that must remain in balance, *rlung* is associated with *sems* (heart-mind) (Adams 1998; Clifford 1994; Janes 1995; Millard 2003), and an imbalance may result in dizziness, insomnia, chest pain, syncope, vertigo, sadness, disorganized thinking, and psychosis. One is said to be at risk for developing *rlung* disorders if negative emotions are strong; some inherit a propensity for the disorder in past lives, putting them at higher risk (Adams 1998). There are a variety of rlung-related illnesses and not all of them are associated with mental illness.

Not all community members cope easily with stress, and indeed, many struggle with chronic psychological problems. Within many Tibetan communities, overt mental illness (*sems kyi na tsha*) is often attributed to various types of spirit harm from *gdon*, *btsan*, *rgyal po*, or *mamo* (different types of malevolent spirits), for which one needs the help of a lama (Clifford 1994; Samuel 2005. As Schröder found in her work among Tibetan healers in Ladakh, "neither the term 'illness' nor the term 'mental' serves to cover" the interpretations of mental distress (2011, 26). There are not clear distinctions between illness that is "mental," illness that is "physical," and illness that is "spiritual." If *rlung* (wind), as well as the other two humors, *mkhrispa* (bile) and *badken* (phlegm), become unstable, a variety of physical and mental disturbances can arise.

Political prisoners are thought to be at higher risk for *rlung* imbalance; as a result, some researchers equate *rlung* disorders with PTSD.[8] Indeed, some symptoms of *rlung*, such as insomnia, irritability, and anxiety, are also part of the cluster of symptoms that characterize PTSD. Researchers such as Benedict, Mancini, and Grodin therefore deduce that because "the *srog-rlung* diagnosis is nosologically similar to PTSD comorbid with MDD [Major Depressive Disorder] or GAD [Generalized Anxiety Disorder]" (2009, 489), it must be a unique cultural presentation of PTSD (i.e., what is "really" going on). And yet I assert that *rlung* imbalance is not a "trauma" disease. For instance, although political prisoners are at increased risk, so are students studying for exams and practitioners engaged in intensive religious practices. What all share in common is excessive activity within the mind: mental exertion from studying or strong emotions from witnessing torture are equally plausible conditions for developing a *rlung* disorder. There are also key symptoms of PTSD that would likely not be attributed to *rlung* problems. A patient experiencing bad dreams, intrusive thoughts, and nervousness might be more likely diagnosed as a victim of *gdon* (spirits) affecting the *bla* (life essence). This could be true even among those who had been exposed to a traumatic event. A traumatic experience can make the mind unstable, which puts one at increased risk for spirit harm. Whereas investigating the universality of psychiatric categories is a topic that is of great concern for researchers within global mental health, my inquiry is not aimed at resolving this quandary.

Rather than debating whether *rlung* disorders are the same or different from PTSD, a more fruitful investigation might be to consider the ways that conditions for developing *rlung* disorders may be present in exile culture. For example, might excessive crying, worry, thinking, or talking too much and overexertion (Jacobson 2007; Janes 1999a, 1999b) be more prevalent in exile? Because *rlung* is associated with both intellectual exertion and disturbing emotions, it makes little sense to characterize the disorder as one linked only to trauma (as is the case for PTSD). Anthropologist Audrey Proust (2006) points out that it is often very "high profile" scholarly monks who leave Tibet and come to Dharamsala in the first place. The increased risk factors for *rlung* disorders in exile might have just as much to do with the intensive debate and study staged within schools and monasteries as it does with refugee experiences. On the other hand, one *amchi* told me that Western expats are more prone to problems with *rlung* than local Tibetans, which she ascribed to the overactivity foreigners seem to have within their minds. She added, "*injis* [foreigners]) also do not learn basic techniques to train their minds."

When *rlung* imbalance is described as *snying tsha*, or a "heart illness," it is important to remember that for Tibetans the location of the *sems* (mind) is in the heart, not inside the head. Richard Davidson (2017) tells a story about a neuroscience experiment his research team conducted among Tibetan monks in long retreats in northern India. The experiments were conducted with an audience of fellow monks standing by and when one of the subjects emerged with electrodes covering his head, the monks roared with laughter. Davidson said to them, "yes, he does look pretty funny!" But the monks were laughing at the foreign researchers who put electrodes on the head when claiming to conduct an experiment on the mind. The notion that the heart (not the brain) is the major center for emotion is found across the world and has been explored extensively by cultural psychiatry researchers (e.g., Good 1977; Hinton, Um, and Ba 2001; Kohrt 2005). That emotions, and indeed, the mind itself, sit within the spatial region of the heart and not the brain, shapes the embodied experience of distress.

As with *rlung* disorders, a common perception across many cultures is that such imbalance within the heart might present increased risk for other kinds of problems. Mental distress can be both a cause and a result of these disorders of the heart. For example, as Devon Hinton and colleagues explain: "Cambodians worry that heart weakness may cause strong reactivity to various stimuli, for example, to sounds and to smells, and predispose to experiencing certain negative emotional states such as being easily frightened, frequently becoming angry, and both engaging in worry and not being able to stop worrying" (2012, 395). Among Khmer trauma survivors, Hinton et al. (2002) found a high prevalence of complaints related to a "weak heart," which seemed to be worsened by anger, worry, or other psychological disturbances. Similarly, Good (1977) found that "heart distress" or heart illness in Iran, known as "malaise of the heart" (*narahatiye*) causes a variety of negative symptoms. These comparisons show how commonplace it is for the heart to be the nexus of embodied emotion.

Many medical anthropologists have explored the inherent difficulty of classifying mental distress within cultures that do not make clear separations between body and mind. For example, rural Nepalis experience a kind of distress known as *jhum-jhum*, which tends to be conflated with depression by researchers. As with the case of *rlung* disorders among Tibetans, there are no specific etiological agents or events associated with the development of *jhum-jhum*—it is often attributed to spirit harm, but equally plausible causal factors include chronic tension and overworking (Kohrt et al. 2005). In both the Nepali and Tibetan cases, the forces that cause humoral imbalance may yield problems in both the body and mind, and they are often intimately connected.

Many Tibetans explain how negative emotions can cause illness—particularly if they are pervasive and long-standing. For example, Dechen, a sixty-year-old mother of four explained: "This back pain, my kidney problems. It comes from too much worry and crying. When my husband died back in Tibet, I had to care for my children by myself. We did not have enough food. I worried and worried for many years, so now I am sick a lot." The notion that worry and prolonged distress can itself lead to mental illness is a common belief across cultural contexts.

Soon after my arrival in Dharamsala, people around town learned that I was interested in understanding mental distress. From time to time, people would say, "Oh, you are interested in mental illness? You should talk to Ani Dawa." *Ani*, being the colloquial term for "nun," is a seventy-one-year-old Tibetan nun who has been living in Dharamsala for almost twenty years. "She has problems," people told me. It was not immediately clear what kinds of problems she was known to have; it seemed to be a mix of physical illness, mental illness, and spiritually based concerns. I went to see Ani Dawa, a plump woman whose cropped hair was a bit long and unruly for a nun. She spoke very openly about her problems. She did not live in the nunnery but rather stayed in a small rented room with another nun who helped care for her. This is somewhat unusual, but not unheard of. Most monastics stay in the monastery and nunnery for the convenience of housing and food, but it is not a requirement. She explains that she often "blacks out and has many problems," which disturb the other nuns. Unlike other Tibetans I interviewed, the details of Ani Dawa's life were disorganized and vague as if she was not quite sure how she ended up in Dharamsala. Her young caretaker sat nearby nodding, as if to confirm that no one quite knows where she came from.

I asked them what kind of treatments she has tried over the years and what she thinks she needs to recover. To this, Ani Dawa replied, "Gradually, I started to think that everyone [doctors, lamas, and others inside the nunnery] had helped me as much as they could, but with no real benefit. I thought that my illness and suffering in this life were the result of negative actions committed in previous lives. Right now, I make aspiration prayers and practice *gewa* [virtue] with the view of helping clear the suffering and *nyöndrib* [obscurations] of others. This makes me mentally happy."

She went on to explain that if someone has problems, they should not pray for oneself, alone. Instead, it is better to make healing aspirations for all those in the world with the same problem. Focusing on yourself, she reiterated, makes you miserable.

Some of the narratives I collected are, in a certain sense, extraordinary. It is difficult to understand how someone develops aspirations to take on the suffering of others. But rather than deducing that these must be extraordinary people who simply possess these traits, Tibetans themselves argue that these capacities can be learned by anyone. The training can be intentional, as in *lojong* practice, or can be developed through exposure to the culture of resilience engineered in exile culture. Although my interlocutors do not transcend from "broken" to "whole" through aligning with God, as in Judeo-Christian traditions (Lester 2005; Luhrmann 2012), Tibetans do look to spiritual guides for support and inspiration. These highly regarded practitioners share something in common: they never solidify and hold on to suffering. In fact, those who are seen as exceptionally resilient seem to avoid thinking much at all about their problems.

Thinking Too Much

Research elsewhere describes how "excessive thinking" is a local idiom of distress across a number of cultural contexts (Hinton et al. 2015 Kaiser et al. 2015; Yang and Singla 2011; Yarris 2014). Across these various cultural contexts, the idioms associated with excessive thinking are both a symptom and cause of mental illness, as with the Malagasy, where *miasa loha* (overworked mind, worry) is deemed a primary cause of madness as well as a symptom of spirit possession (Sharp 1993). To avoid churning up excessive emotions that can lead to dangerous psychological states, people understand that avoidance of upsetting topics is adaptive. For example, in Cambodia, Devon Hinton and colleagues argue that "excessive thinking" is a complaint that "describes a mental state that has the following characteristics: one thinks of upsetting topics such as current problems (e.g., difficulties with money or children), past traumatic events (e.g., during the Pol Pot period), and separation from loved ones owing to their having died or living at a distance; one has a hard time not thinking about these things; and one thinks about these things to the point that it induces symptoms like headache and dizziness and potentially brings about various physiological disasters" (2012, 395). Anyone may develop this kind of problem, although across cultures that have "excessive thinking" idioms, there are certain kinds of people who may be at increased risk.

In Dharamsala, young monks and nuns studying for philosophy exams are thought to be at high risk for *rlung* disorders because of thinking too much. For this reason, my research assistant became very concerned when I decided to study philosophy at one of the monasteries. "But, Sara-la, you already do too much thinking!" he cried. "You cannot study debate philosophy. You will become ill." There is a strong sense that one needs to maintain a calm inner and outer environment to stay healthy. Overthinking, excessive emotionality, and volatile environmental conditions can all lead to *rlung* problems.

For instance, many Tibetans describe how much difficulty they experienced with food and weather upon arrival to India. These difficulties are more extensive than a mere distaste for new food and monsoon rains. As Vincanne Adams explains: "Winds outside the body are the winds inside the body; they are of the same substance and potentiality—effects outside are effects inside. . . . For example, when Tibetans talk about food and job frustrations as similar disruptions to their winds, they are telling us that, in terms of bodily experience, these two things are in the same category" (1998, 88–89). While imprisonment, torture, and displacement are more severe in degree, they are understood to be just like any other potential disturbance (e.g., bad food, bad weather), which can make it difficult to control the mind. The extent to which one experiences mental distress depends on the reaction to the event; in other words, suffering can only come from within. As my elderly neighbor told me, a Tibetan proverb says: "Self is the protector of itself." Because losing control of one's emotions is thought to lead to illness and the generation of negative karma, Tibetans have great motivation to recover quickly in the face of adversity. This recovery can be spurred by spiritual practices as well as medical treatment.

Thinking as Cure

Whereas uncontrolled thinking and excessive emotionality can cause illness, Tibetans in Dharamsala assert that thinking in the right way can orient a person toward recovery. In fact, thinking in ways that enhance compassion, in particular, is essential for making other kinds of treatment more effective. When I visited Dr. Dorjee at the *mentsikhang* (traditional Tibetan clinic) after arranging my practices at the *puja* house, I asked him for more explanation about *rlung*. Though his demeanor was not particularly warm and inviting, he took a keen interest in my questions. He drew me small diagrams on the back of a prescription pad, depicting the movement of internal "winds," which if not in balance can cause both physical and mental illness, often in tandem.

He systematically pointed to jars of herbal medicine lining the shelves behind him, citing examples of how to correct imbalance. The pills (*men tsa*), are usually crushed and taken with hot water several times a day. Tibetans consider their traditional medicine to be highly effective, although it is known to work slowly (unlike Western medicine that is quick acting but may not address fundamental underlying causes of illness). Dr. Dorjee gave me some examples of common diseases (e.g., liver problems, diabetes, and gastrointestinal issues) and showed me the pills that he might prescribe for each one. "But how much these work," he said, "depends on the mind of the patient." He elaborated, stating:

> Actually, there are three different ways of coping with disease (best, middle, and least desirable). The best is when someone is sick, they make a wish for this disease to affect them and not others; they wish to experience the disease, so others don't have to. This is a Buddhist practice. The next best is when they have these problems they wish, *after I recover, I will help others and wish to do something beneficial for others*. With this motivation, they recover. The third method is not as broad and spacious. They just feel very encouraged to get better, but they don't think about others. Some people who cannot practice any of these three methods become damaged or discouraged—even *nyönpa* (crazy). They can take many pills, but it will be difficult for them to recover without broad thinking.

His colleague, a young Tibetan woman who recently finished her physician training, said, "Each person has a unique presentation of the illness. If people come to *mentsikhang*, they cannot solve their problems through medicine alone. We also have to give them advice. It is important for us to analyze the person's state of mind and we need to try and experience what they are feeling." She went on to explain that if doctors speak with great compassion, it will greatly benefit the patient by making the medicine powerful. Within Tibetan medical science, compassion has tangible effects.

The importance of compassion is reflected in medical and religious practices, alike. After doing any Buddhist practice, Tibetans "dedicate the merit" of the practice to all sentient beings. This dedication of merit (good karma) is thought to have a ripple effect; it benefits others and the generosity of giving good karma away creates an abundance of merit for oneself. Lamas and teachers emphasize that practitioners should not have selfish motivation but feel good in knowing their generosity and compassionate acts will come back to them. By wishing happiness for others and not for oneself, paradoxically, this brings happiness. These ideals, which stem from Buddhism, are reflected in Tibetan medical practices.

On another visit to the *mentsikhang*, I arrived around 7:30 a.m., right as the doors were opening. A young Tibetan woman who worked behind the reception desk asked me to have a seat. "The doctor will see you after the morning prayers," she said, gesturing to a wooden bench where I was to wait. Shortly thereafter, all the staff, including pharmacists, receptionists, doctors, and even a young girl employed as a cleaner, gathered together in one of the exam rooms and shut the door. Sitting outside, I was able to hear a string of prayers in Tibetan—the refuge prayer to the Buddha, a long-life prayer for the Dalai Lama, several recitations of the Medicine Buddha mantra, and a dedication of merit. After about fifteen minutes, the staff filed out and returned to their stations.

The doctor gestured for me to come in. Dr. Norbu knew I had come to conduct an interview, but perhaps out of habit, he reached for my wrists to take my pulse on both hands, jotting down notes on a prescription pad. He began listing off the health problems he was able to discern through my pulse—low blood pressure, frequent colds and congestion—he said, "this weather in India is not good for you." He started to compose a list of foods I should avoid, such as cold drinks and milk products.

"Can you tell me about the prayers you were doing before?" I asked. He raised his eyebrows, surprised by my question. "Oh," he said casually, "it is important that we have good motivation." I nodded, hoping he would elaborate. "And the prayers, to the Medicine Buddha, makes the medicine more effective. The blessings from the Medicine Buddha," he added. I asked what happens when Tibetan clinicians do not have a good motivation. He explained that their treatments will have limited efficacy.

"Actually, the most skilled physicians," he said, "are those who can with great confidence visualize themselves as the Medicine Buddha." It is evident here that compassion is not merely a moral value, but an important causal factor in Tibetan science and medicine. Great compassion is not only an indicator of resilience but is also used as a method to train and learn resilience. To develop greater compassion, Tibetans argue it is important to develop devotion for lamas and other cultural heroes they can emulate as examples of people with *sems pa chen po*.

Faith and Devotion

Ani Dawa, the nun who is known around town as mentally ill lives in a small room that is decorated similarly to that of other Tibetans in exile, lay and monastic alike—that is, covered with posters and postcards of deities and the Dalai Lama, butter lamps neatly aligned on a small shrine shelf, and a *khatag* (silk scarf for offering) draped ceremoniously across a larger photograph of the Dalai Lama. Tibetan deities are colorful, rich, spirited, and may be peaceful or wrathful in their compassionate activity. The humble dwellings of Tibetans in Dharamsala are often stylized like monasteries, with offerings of candles, fake flowers, and colorful iconography from floor to ceiling.

The colorful display within Tibetan *lhakang* (temples) are noticeably different from more austere Zen and Theraveda places of worship, reflecting the distinct approach within the Vajrayana tradition. Here, the rich array of human experience, including negative emotions, sexuality, and relationships are not renounced, but instead are subjugated and transformed into opportunities for "waking up" and helping others. Deities, such as Drolma (Green Tara), a female Buddha depicted with one foot outstretched and ready to leap into compassionate action at any moment, and Vajrasattva, whose mantra purifies negative karma, are not worshipped but emulated. Practitioners do not merely pray to deities, but actually visualize themselves becoming the deity.

As with other religious traditions, the Buddhist faith seems to help people manage difficulty in life. But unlike in theistic religions, there is no external figure dictating one's fate; practitioners must work with their own minds to achieve enlightenment. "It is up to you," they say. And while daunting, in another sense it is very empowering because every sentient being has the inherent potential to become enlightened. Because ultimately all beings have buddhanature, they can rely on buddhas, not just the historical Buddha, Siddartha Guatama, but all those who have "gone beyond" to show the path. These religious teachings argue that no matter how many blessings one may have, ultimately each being needs to work with his or her own mind to become enlightened. Faith and devotion to lamas and gurus is a method for revealing one's own realized mind and seeing that ultimately one has the same enlightened mind and his or her teacher who one should visualize as a buddha. The notion of *mogu* (devotion) is notably distinct from worship in this context in that devotion comes from realizing that ultimately one's mind is the same as one's enlightened teacher.

What does it mean to be a buddha? A buddha is a being who has purified all of their karma; with all obscurations gone, only a stainless mind remains. Within Mahayana and Vajrayana traditions, an *arhat* (who has extinguished his or her negative karma) must also continue to purify more subtle obscurations and achieve *bodhichitta*, the mind of awakened compassion. The Buddhist teachings posit that anger and other disturbing emotions are based on misperceiving reality—that actually, a mind free from negativity is what is most natural. By looking to teachers, lamas, and examples of realized beings, Tibetans feel inspired that they, too, can learn to purify their negative karma. The framework of karma is a fundamental way for Tibetans to orient personal experiences, more so than a grand metaphysical claim (Cho 2014) because it provides an ordered sense of what to do with negative emotions and how to think about misfortune.

Someone once asked the Dalai Lama at a teaching in Dharamsala if it is ever beneficial to become angry. He thought for some time and then explained that if anger was used to fuel something righteous, such as fighting inequality, it is good. But hatred is never acceptable. The problem with hatred, he explained, is that it is based on a misperception; hatred causes us to see a person as completely negative. It is also said that when a practitioner becomes an *arya* being, someone who has had a direct perception of emptiness, he or she will never again experience anger. Like many negative emotions, Tibetan Buddhists argue that those who see reality clearly will see no reason to become angry. Instead, they will feel compassion for those who struggle with their minds.

Mind Training and Resilience

In this chapter, I argued that *sems pa chen po*, a vast, flexible, and spacious mind, is the way that Tibetans practice resilience in times of turmoil. *Lojong*, both as a formal Buddhist practice and as a culturally embodied technology for working with distress that is embedded in everyday wisdom, helps people to strive for a spacious mind. The reason I refer to *sems pa chen po* as a north star principle is because most Tibetans are just like any other human being: fallible, imperfect, and unable to quell emotions simply through positive thinking.

And yet this is precisely why *lojong* and other practices are referred to as "training." Using compassion and emptiness to train the mind is a way to orient and look toward the horizon of resilience and recovery. In a certain sense, the entire Vajrayana path of Tibetan Buddhist takes this resultant or fruitional approach: practitioners are trained little by little to start from a place as if they were already enlightened. Whereas scholars in the Global North—particularly those who are invested in social justice—may see a purposeful downplaying of oppression and even a willingness to take on the suffering of others as internalized oppression, Tibetans understand this approach as *sems pa chen po*.

Sems (heart-mind) is involved in thinking, the emotions, and sense perception. It is also highly volatile and susceptible to negative and external influence, such as disappointments, interpersonal problems, spirit harm, and even bad food or weather. But there is another kind of mind known as *rigpa*, which cannot be swayed by external forces and factors. *Rigpa* (known as insight or knowledge) is inherent to all sentient beings—the traditional metaphor for *rigpa* is the brilliant blue sky that always exists behind the changing weather. There is a saying in Tibetan: "*sems tang tralwe rigpa*, or *rigpa* free from *sems*," which means trying to rest in the vast open sky rather than dwelling in the minutia of ordinary samsaric life. From this viewpoint, it does not matter how justified a person may be in feeling anger and resentment—it will not bring contentment. And thus, mind training helps ordinary people align with *rigpa*, their natural state of awakenment.

In the next chapter, I explore further why becoming stuck in past suffering is psychologically dangerous and moves a person further and further from the spaciousness of *rigpa*. I argue that people in Dharamala who have faced sociopolitical hardship in Tibet, and subsequently in exile, "resist chronicity" by disrupting and transmuting negative emotion. Whereas healthy trauma work in many cultures involves finding, reworking, and sometimes publicly telling one's narrative, for members of the Tibetan diaspora, abandoning the entire narrative insofar as it perpetuates self-clinging or self-cherishing is an important part of cultivating a spacious mind.

Chapter 3

Resisting Chronicity

There is a Tibetan Buddhist concept known as *shenpa*, which the contemporary lama Dzigar Kongtrul Rinpoche (2013) translates as "the juice of self-centered emotions." Shenpa is not a specific emotion but rather the energy behind emotions that lead to ego clinging and the suffering it produces. Teachings on *shenpa* explain that when a person feels wronged, negative emotions such as fear, anger, and resentment arise almost simultaneously, making it seem as though external forces *cause* suffering. Kongtrul Rinpoche argues: "Shenpa comes alive whenever there is a strong sense of self-importance. We think of everything in terms of what we want in or out of our lives, what will help or hinder us, and what we hope and fear. We struggle to fix and maintain the world according to our preferences" (2013, 1). *Shenpa* is also sometimes described as the experience of being hooked—that is, trapped and caught in a cycle of suffering in which we just cannot let something go.

An important aspect of Buddhist practice is to recognize that whereas it seems that emotions arise simultaneously with difficult situations, if one trains in creating spaciousness, one begins to notice a "gap" before emotions enflame. This training to perceive the gap and to make it longer and longer, is why people should learn to meditate. With some space around emotions, one can resist becoming swept away; that is, meditation practitioners talk about having more of a choice and more freedom. They are not imprisoned by strong emotion.

But whereas fewer Tibetans engage in meditation (that is, in the form of sitting and watching the breath) as foreigners might expect, this cultural truism about the way emotions work and the space one should seek permeates commonsense notions of what one ought to do in the face of adversity. When Tibetans in Dharamsala talk about how important it is to let go of suffering, what they mean is that they seek to unhook themselves from churning up more and more emotion that can only lead to revving up the ego clinging of *shenpa*. Therefore, no matter how righteous the cause and how much a person is wronged, from this perspective it is ultimately the juice of self-centeredness that causes distress and not external circumstances.

The argument I seek to make in this chapter—that Tibetans actively "resist chronicity"—is a temporal one. As I will explore below, Buddhist concepts of time shape the ways that people in Dharamsala understand the properties of emotion, and thus, what it takes to recover. Although it may seem self-evident that working with trauma narratives is a necessary step in the recovery process, here I argue how *mi rtag pa nyid* (impermanence)—*annica* in Sanskrit—frames why Tibetans are reticent to solidify their experience into fixed narratives. Instead, as I described previously, Tibetans in Dharamsala seek to develop *sems pa chen po*—a vast or spacious mind that resists settling on one true and fixed story about what happened. As Cheryl Mattingly argues, moral becoming and aspirations can "travel backward and forward in time, shaping the way any particular moment or event is experienced. Even the past becomes different as the present and future change shape" (2014, 18). What is unique about the Tibetan case is their cultural and religious training in seeing the flexible nature of memory. With an ongoing project of striving to disrupt harmful emotions that endure over time, Tibetan Buddhists resist fixating on a singular story framed by trauma.

The north star principle of *sems pa chen po* acts as a horizon in times of stress, helping people navigate their way through difficult emotions, which one should think of as illusory and impermanent. Recovery for members of the Tibetan diaspora is not a project based on processing past events. Instead, people encourage one another to remember that they have now purified negative karma by living through difficulty. As one often says, "Feel at ease—you won't have to experience it again in your next life." Recovery, then, has a temporal orientation toward the future and not a looping back to reexperience past pain and suffering. Debriefing and sharing with others is not seen as particularly helpful but focusing on one's future—including future lifetimes—is part of how a person keeps a "big mind" perspective.

Dolma

As she did every morning, Dolma, my eighty-year-old neighbor, rose to the clang, crash, and bang of bells and drums in morning *puja* at nearby monasteries and nunneries. Pulling herself out of bed, she stepped onto the small rug and carefully avoided touching the cold cement floor with her bare feet as she pulled on woolen stockings. Dolma fastens her *chuba* (wrap dress) over a blouse and ties a piece of fabric with sheep's wool stitched inside around her waist to protect her kidneys from the cold, which could cause illness. Bad weather like cold, dampness, and wind is not just an annoyance but can directly influence a person's *inner winds* and make one sick. She switches on a small electric kettle and prepares a light breakfast of *bhod cha* (Tibetan butter tea) mixed with *tsampa* (or, barley flour) before starting her walk down to the main temple, known as the *tsuklhakhang*.

"*Tashi delek* [hello]," she greets others, mostly older people, heading down the steep short-cut path. "*Sab sab che-a* [be careful], Sara-la," Dolma warns, greeting me as I see her along the path. Most of my interactions with Dolma begin with a good-natured scolding: *Don't be lazy! Why aren't you wearing socks? Don't talk to those rough Amdo boys!*

Some people veer off to head to the *khora* (circumambulation) path around the Dalai Lama's residence. The Jampaling old-age home is nestled right alongside the *khora*. "What else would we do?" says Dolma. "Old people need to get serious about preparing for death. It is the time to accumulate more virtue, more merit." We walk straight into the gates of the Dalai Lama's temple and do just one *khora*, circling around the inside of the inner-most area where Gyalwa Rinpoche's, that is, the Dalai Lama's teaching throne is located, before heading to the prostration boards. I help her pull out an old wooden plank and lug it to where others have already taken all the newer ones. It is already 6:30 a.m. We are late today. Prostrations are done by bringing hands in prayer to the forehead, paying homage and taking refuge in the Buddha's (or one's root lama's) enlightened body, and then to the throat, for enlightened speech, and to the heart, taking refuge in enlightened mind, *bodhichitta*, before lowering completely prone with arms outstretched on the board. The practitioner gets up as quickly as possible to begin the next prostration, so they are a highly aerobic exercise known to be as good for the physical body as they are for the mind. Many of my discussions with older Tibetans inside the *tsuklakhang* happened during short breaks between prostration sessions or walking the *khora* before or after practice.

Dolma did not see much use in talking to others about the difficulties she has experienced as a refugee from Tibet. Others had it much worse, she explains, and besides, it is only natural that people face difficulty in their lives. But Dolma's life had not been easy. Before she left Kham with the group of families from her county, she had endured a lot, including the disappearance of her husband.

"When the *tulku* (incarnate lama) went missing from our monastery, my husband and his brothers went to help. They never came back."

Once Dolma's family made it to India in 1960, her suffering was far from over. They had survived starvation on their journey across the Himalayas, traveling in bitter cold temperatures at night. People helped one another as best they could once they safely crossed the border into India from Nepal, often huddling together with others from their region of Tibet. At that time an abandoned military cantonment, Dharamsala had very little in terms of services or infrastructure. The landscape, food, and weather were not easy to manage. Food insecurity was commonplace in those early days, not only because of extreme poverty but because typical Tibetan food made from barley flour and yak milk products could not be acquired. As her three children grew up and Dharamsala became more heavily populated by Tibetans fleeing their homeland, schools were built. Unlike Dolma who could not read, her children learned to read and write in their native Tibetan language; they also began to pick up some Hindi and English words. But life was never easy for them. In the mid-1990s, Jamphal, her oldest son, started consuming large amounts of alcohol and a cheap form of heroin that had made its way into town from New Delhi.

As with any community, there are some Tibetan youth who abuse alcohol and drugs, perhaps out of boredom or despair (Yankey and Biswas 2012). Once students age out of the Tibetan Children's Village schools and boarding houses, there is often nothing for them to do and nowhere to go. Jamphal went into liver failure at the age of twenty from consuming too much *raksi* (cheaply distilled liquor). "There was nothing that could be done," said Dolma, flatly. "He died." Her two remaining children, Dekyi and Thubten, were good students and seemed to be on a better track. But Dekyi contracted tuberculosis and died a few years later before her twenty-fifth birthday, leaving behind a young daughter of her own. Thubten had gone to live in New Delhi in the Tibetan enclave, Majnukatilla, where he works at a hotel. He sends money to Dolma when he can, but she has struggled to pay rent and buy food. "But you see," she explains, "it is good to have all this suffering in this lifetime because in my next life I won't bring this with me. It is over now, this karma is purified." As I explain below, karma should not be misunderstood as fatalism, or passive victimhood. Rather, karma is an explanatory feature of human interconnection, where all sentient beings are paying debts that they, themselves, created in past lives. Therefore, karma is a just system and one where negative karma can be purified through Buddhist practices of merit making and devotion.

Karma

Karma is a central aspect of the social imaginary (Taylor 2007) in Dharamsala and it readily structures Tibetans' basic concepts of reality. Because karma is better understood as a pervasive epistemic and ontological framing than a "belief," Pierre Bourdieu's concept of *doxa* is a useful way to understand the ubiquity and unarticulated nature of karma in the Tibetan worldview. Bourdieu's concept of *doxa* extends beyond his commonly cited concept of *habitus* (encultured habits and norms) in that *doxa* refers to ideas that are assumed to be universal or those that are not even articulated because they seem so natural (Bourdieu 1977, 1994). Whereas karma is considered (by outsiders) to be a religious belief, it is more so a basic and fundamental ordering principle of reality in Dharamsala and something taken for granted even among Tibetans who are not particularly religious.

Naturally, with exposure to other cultural ideals and practices, Tibetans (especially those in exile) come to recognize that people of other faiths do not believe in karma. But until they meet someone who does not "believe" in karma, many do not think to question it. Kirmayer and Sartorius (2007) note that implicit cultural beliefs may be difficult to identify not only because they are second nature but because such knowledge is "distributed, that is, not held by any single individual but parceled out among many actors and emergent from their cooperative interaction" (2007, 833). There may also be something about Buddhist faiths in particular that make the question of "belief" different from other religions.

In Julia Cassaniti's comparative work in northern Thailand among Buddhists and Christians, she noticed something curious. She observed that while the notion of "belief" is paramount for Christians, for Buddhists, they seem not to "conceptualize their relationship to their religious ideas as one of belief" (2012, 297). She explains that "in the Buddhist context agency is constructed by accessing what is conceptualized as a cosmologically natural self, and belief is hence rendered unnecessary" (2012, 297). Thai Buddhists may talk about practicing their religion or having respect for Buddhist teachings. But "whatever will happen will happen, you don't have to believe," explains Cassaniti (2012, 301). She gives examples from a popularly cited sutra (*Kalama Sutra*) where the Buddha instructs his disciples to adhere only to what is experienced directly, rather than believing in something told to them by others: "Jesus said you have to believe in God," one Thai interlocutor explained. "The Buddha didn't say anything like that" (2012, 302). In this worldview, karma and other Buddhist laws simply articulate the workings of reality.

Concepts of causality have long been fruitful sites of inquiry for cultural and medical anthropologists. In Evans-Prichard's (1937) classic research among the Azande, he notes that while Westerners often ask, "Why me?" for the Azande, the most important question is "Why now?" When Tibetans evoke concepts of karma to explain causality in illness and misfortune, it is not in the fatalistic sense. Although someone can have the karma to get sick, they might also have the karma to get better. At the same time, unlike illness caused by spirits, or an imbalance in the wind humor, illnesses that are caused largely by negative karma are known for being particularly intractable and long-lasting. Until the heavy negative karma is purified through religious rituals or is exhausted by running its course, the patient will not recover no matter how potent the medicine.

Many community members in Dharamsala understand after a difficult life event that they have purified a karmic debt. Negative actions of body, speech, or mind create karmic seeds in the mindstream; if not purified, the imprints of this seed will eventually ripen. For example, the experience of anger creates a *bija* (seed) for anger. Later on, usually in future lifetimes, an event happens (say, someone cuts a queue) and because that seed for anger is present in the mindstream, the imprint of that seed ripens and anger is experienced again, perpetuating more karmic seeds. Therefore, from this perspective, when a negative event occurs, Buddhist logic teaches that one should try one's hardest to avoid reacting negatively. If someone cuts in front of you in line and you do not react with anger, that particular seed is purified and will not be experienced again. The *lojong* approaches discussed in chapter 2 give people pragmatic strategies for making sure negative karma is purified—for example, if someone cuts you off, you could generously think in your mind that you allowed them intentionally to pass.

One may struggle with what happens in one's life, but ultimately, reflecting on karma seems to soothe people and bring about acceptance rather than internalized self-blame. Anthropologist and psychotherapist Rebecca Lester (2013) raises a complex issue that she has encountered working with trauma survivors in the United States. Although she is compelled to help patients see that they are not at fault for traumatic events that have happened in their lives, she notes that there is often some ambivalence in doing so. Her clients seem to have difficulty "accepting that they did nothing at all to provoke or elicit what happened to them, that their participation, such as it was, was entirely 'innocent.' They often strain against the notion that they were powerless and at the utter mercy of someone or something outside themselves" (2013, 757). In contrast, Tibetans are rarely encouraged to think of themselves as victims or "survivors" (an imported idea from the West), even in cases of imprisonment and torture. "Maybe it is because of my karma," is a common idiom, and one that brings a sense of order and reason to a terribly fraught experience. Most Tibetans do not necessarily think about karma in technical terms such as *bijas* and imprints. Rather, there is a built-in sense of reality that dictates that one could feel relief when something negative happens. This formulation is metaphysical rather than moralistic.

A number of Tibetans living in Dharamsala lost friends and family members in a major earthquake in Tibet in 2010. As one soft-spoken young man, Tashi, age twenty-four, explains:

> Most of my family died; seven of us died. Only me and my younger brother survived. This is karma. It was their karma to die and it was our karma to live. There were also many Chinese killed. The Chinese were frantic and wail-

ing in the streets. Tibetans were much calmer. I don't think we were any less sad, but we accept death as a part of life. We also believe that it does not help the situation to become very upset. This can prevent those who died from moving on through the *bardo* [intermediate state between death and rebirth], and it doesn't help us either. My brother and I joined some others from our county and made prostrations to Lhasa [some 750 miles away]. We made offerings along the way and dedicated the merit [good karma], to our family. I felt at peace knowing that we were doing something to help our deceased loved ones.

In turn, life circumstances are earned; that is, negative events in the present are understood as the result of negative actions in the past. To fully understand how Tibetans in exile cope with suffering, it is essential to recognize that their view extends much wider than the present; what happens in this lifetime is only one small piece of a much larger picture of past and future lives.

A Russian colleague working in Dharamsala, Kuba Bobrzynski, once explained to me that he met a Tibetan man in his seventies who had his arms and legs bound while being held at a Chinese prison. With time, he learned to pull his hands out of the binds. But after some time, he rebound his own hands thinking that otherwise he would not be able to "repay his karma" if he found a way to suffer less (letter to author, July 3, 2012). Naturally, Tibetans do not seek out pain to purify karma, but many maintain daily practices aimed at purifying negative karma and generating merit (e.g., circumambulating *stupas* and temples, prostrations, reciting mantras, making offerings), and as they draw nearer to death older generations often devote the remainder of their lives to these practices. They also view difficult life events as an opportunity for purification. Friends and relatives console one another with reminders that karmic seeds or imprints have been purified. "It is over now," they say. The seeds are extinguished and one is advised not to ruminate or cling to negative emotions. Disturbing emotions that lead to negative actions only reproduce suffering by strengthening karmic imprints. Karmic seeds are held in a kind of storehouse within the consciousness, ready to ripen in future lives. But once that seed ripens, it is vanished forever.

Life's difficulties are painful, but in a sense, they are not wholly unwelcome. Once my wallet was stolen in New Delhi; when I mentioned it to my friend Yangzom, she replied cheerfully: "Oh, that's good! You purified the negative karma you had with the thief." This perspective stems in part from the Buddhist ideal of achieving enlightenment, which is more a process of clearing away than needing to acquire something. Even among Tibetans who cannot explain the metaphysical workings of karma, most seem to have a built-in sense that difficulties in life also contain great potential and can be weathered to benefit.

The (Im)persistence of Memory

The laws and interworkings of karma are an important feature within the architecture of Tibetan concepts of time, and thus, traumatic memory. Although people tend to assume that the things that happen in their lives are due to negative karma, they do not dwell on karmic retribution or feel they are being punished. If anything, it seems to allow them to more quickly let go of what might be called traumatic memory. The lingering of traumatic memory has become the hallmark of modern-day suffering after extreme life events (Fassin 2009; Luhrmann 2010) to the extent that it is assumed that the cluster of symptoms that make up PTSD, such as flashbacks, trigger points, and nightmares, are wholly natural (and not cultural) occurrences. However, anthropologists working across the globe write against the universality of PTSD for many reasons, including because trauma symptoms cluster differently across cultures (Hinton and Lewis-Fernandez 2011), and because in severe conflict areas there is often no "prior" and "post" demarcation of suffering (James 2008). In addition to these claims, I argue that different cultural systems of *time* render the category of PTSD potentially incommensurate with local norms across the globe.

As Allen Young has explained: "The *DSM* theory of PTSD is simple . . . it is simply taken for granted that time and causality move *from* the traumatic event *to* the other criterial features and that the event inscribes itself on the symptoms. Because the traumatic event is the cause of the syndromal feelings and behaviors, it is logical to say that it precedes them. If this were not true, if it were acceptable for syndromal features to occur *before* the traumatic event, then the term 'reexperience' would lose its accepted meaning" (1995, 115–16). Among my Tibetan interlocutors in Dharamsala, it was not typical for those exposed to political violence to struggle with persistent triggering and "reexperiencing" trauma. This does not mean that Tibetans never have nightmares or flashbacks; some certainly do. But this feature of traumatic memory that is commonplace in Euro-American contexts is not prominent among Tibetans in Dharamsala and there is no mental disorder that may be glossed as PTSD.

Although there are Tibetans who struggle with nightmares and intrusive thoughts following stressful events, they still framed their experience with phrases such as it is "over now" and "I have purified this negative karma," as a way of orienting themselves toward recovery. As I described in the previous chapter, sometimes these statements had a definitively fake-it-'til-you-make-it feel to them. Whereas war veterans returning home in the Unites States support one another by normalizing the reoccurrence of trauma through PTSD as an illness that anyone can develop (Finley 2011), Tibetan survivors of political violence normalize a sense of relief that karmic seeds have been purified. For those still struggling to move past traumatic memory, the north star ideal of *sems pa chen po* guides the way. *Bzod-pa gom che-a* (be patient), people say to one another. "Keep building a spacious mind; it will be easier in time," they say.

Enduring Memory

Across disciplines, scholars have become particularly concerned with memory—understood to hold important keys for mechanistic understandings of the brain, as well as cultural studies of violence, trauma, and war. Because of time's intrinsic connection to everyday reality (Berger and Luckmann 1966; Husserl 1970), memory becomes a core aspect of what constitutes experience. Humanistic studies of memory tend to focus on the ways that bodies remember and forget, and show that memory itself is highly flexible, interpretive, and socially defined. That memory is a flexible category is reinforced by neuroscience where its plasticity can be shown in experimental settings. Cultural framings of memory are directly related to cultural concepts of time, and many scholars have emphasized the ways that historical epochs, including modernity, shape such framings.

For instance, the very defining features of globalization and late modernity are temporal ones—rapid pace, forward momentum (Appadurai 1990), and anticipation (Adams, Murphy, and Clarke 2009a). Within postcolonial contexts, scholars call for an "ontology of the present" (Stoler 2009) and a reading of culture through the lens of alterity (Povinelli 2002; Simpson 2014; Taussig 1992) to consider what happens when present-day knowledge confronts racialized beliefs from the past. Others seek to ground ethnographic interpretation within the "everyday" (Das 2015), where the work of temporality is in the creation of the subject. These perspectives reveal the fluidity of memory and the impact of structural factors such as racism and inequality on personhood.

Ethnographic studies of collective trauma and what has been called "historical trauma" are necessarily linked with temporal concerns through investigating how structural violence permeates lived realities across generations. Groups such as Holocaust descendant support groups (Kidron 2010) and Native communities in North America (Csordas 1999; Gone 2013) have identified as survivors of historical trauma to reclaim their social agency. As Angela Garcia (2008, 2010) articulates in her work on multigenerational heroin addiction in New Mexico, pain that is diffuse—even atmospheric—causes conditions such as addiction, poverty, and violence to take on temporal registers of "permanence" and "chronicity." This is the trauma of everyday life (Das 2007; James 2008), what US clinicians rather opaquely call "complex trauma," delineating it from one specific and catastrophic event characteristic of PTSD.

Indeed, those who endure chronic suffering often grapple with unpredictable temporal as well as material certainties, including housing, medical care, and employment (Mendenhall 2012; Weaver and Mendenhall 2014). The synergistic impact of marginalization across multiple domains may be a hallmark of symbolic and structural violence, what Jonathan Wolff (2009) calls "clustered disadvantage," the way that deprivation in one area has a cascading effect across other domains (e.g., unemployment leading to social isolation, which leads to depression and cardiovascular disease). Individuals in privileged positions tend to experience suffering as isolated and episodic—that is, a temporary misfortune or momentary setback.

Those who face uncertain spatial realities, including refugees, migrants, and the homeless live within insecure temporalities that further entrench social suffering. For example, in her ethnography of Iraqi refugees in Egypt, Nadia El-Shaarawi (2015) considers the effects of waiting among those caught between places, neither able to return home nor to resettle. Those forced by structural forces to remain in transit for months or years face simultaneous spatial and temporal uncertainty, which for El-Shaarawi's Iraqi interlocutors, is the fundamental cause of new forms of mental and bodily illness (2015, 46). Similarly, Amy Cooper (2015) observes the impact of navigating confusing and inconsistent "empty time" and "over-scheduled time" among homeless women, where institutional waiting exacerbates psychiatric illness and further yields marginalization. In reading these scholarly accounts, it is intuitive that secure housing and predictable temporalities such as the capacity to plan, would yield good health.

And yet, Tibetan refugees—a group that is also facing severe spatial and temporal uncertainties—have offered alternative perspectives with their emphasis on impermanence and the meaning of instability. Those who come from Tibet in search of a better life lament that they are not granted asylum or permanent residency in India. Moreover, traditional Tibetan medicine portends that disruption to the outer environment can yield inner disruption in the form of illness (Craig 2012a). However, many temper their dissatisfaction by pointing out that *life itself* is insecure, unstable, and impermanent. In fact, their Buddhist beliefs teach them that resisting this "fact of life" is the root cause of suffering. When something upsetting and difficult occurs in life, Tibetans remind one another—"remember what the Buddha said"— that is, everything is impermanent and always changing.

Many canonical works on oppression (Fanon 1963, 1967; Farmer 2001; Fassin 2009) demonstrate how the temporality of trauma extends far beyond the present and is embodied within the social landscape of marginalized communities. And while the plight of Tibetans within the People's Republic of China could be understood through the theoretical lens of structural violence,[1] the Tibetan exile community itself works to actively resist becoming entrenched in trauma legacy when it comes to individual healing.[2] To do this, *they resist chronicity.* Tibetan exile members support one another not through debriefing about trauma narratives, but by helping one another to remember that emotions are changing, shifting, and merely illusory. Then, using Buddhist beliefs on impermanence and compassion as support, one knows that difficulties in life—no matter how great—are inherently workable.

Chronicity and the Return

The meaning of emotions themselves—and what to do about difficult ones— in Dharamsala are incommensurate with basic assumptions in the Global

North about concepts of mind. The assumptions about how the mind works in North America and Europe harken back to the late nineteenth century with Freudian psychoanalysis and the advent of the concept of the unconscious. Sigmund Freud's works, such as his essay "The Uncanny" (1919), explicates the "return of the repressed": the psyche's obsession with continually reliving and recreating its most disturbing traumas as a way to master them. Since then, the emotions occasioned by distressing life events—known as psychic trauma—are thought to necessarily become trapped in the mind. The project of psychotherapy, then, is to perform retrospective excavation work to liberate the psyche from traumas lodged deep within the recesses of the mind. Such assumptions about what the mind does in response to adverse events have become built in to commonsense understandings of recovery and healing.

But whereas contemporary psychiatry in the Global North has entered a paradigm shift that privileges cognitive behavioral and psychopharmacological interventions over trying to understand one's past, the conviction that past trauma must be cathartically expelled in the present has not been wholly abandoned. Indeed, as Tanya Luhrmann (2000) argues in her ethnography of American psychiatry, biomedical treatments seem to hang awkwardly alongside psychoanalytic understandings of mind, where good psychiatrists must master both pharmacological treatment and psychotherapy techniques. Although many argue that we have moved beyond psychoanalysis in North America and Europe, it is still the case that if those exposed to traumatic events do not talk about them, friends and relatives worry they must be repressing their feelings. It appears self-evident that if people do not talk about it, trauma will remain lodged deep within the psyche. An important lineage of trauma clinicians have pushed back against this assumption, arguing that talk therapy is not sufficient to heal and may even make things worse. Instead, somatic and neurobiological approaches aim to help individuals exposed to traumatic events decouple the fight, flight, freeze or fold response from triggers that trick the body into thinking it is in danger (Levine 2010; van der Kolk 2014).

This taken-for-granted notion that trauma must be excavated through talk therapy was central to the formulation of theories on Post-Traumatic Stress Disorder in the twentieth century (Finley 2011; Young 1995). There are long-standing debates within anthropology, transcultural psychiatry, and other fields about whether PTSD is a universal response or one that is culturally and historically bound (see Hinton and Lewis-Fernandez 2011).

Rather than arguing for or against this biomedical construct, I follow Jean Langford's approach (2013) to thinking of violent memories as "traces," which may indeed find narrative homes in diagnostic categories such as PTSD, although not necessarily. Many Tibetans exposed to political violence take great care to think of such "traces" as fundamentally illusory and impermanent. The reticence to talk about personal trauma narratives is not based on a propensity to repress emotion, but rather on a refusal to solidify suffering into fixed narrative. This constitutes a highly adaptive practice of flexibility (Lewis 2013) that is emblematic of *sems pa chen po*. It is recognized that solidifying and holding tightly to negative experiences—perhaps crystallizing the traces of violent memories—only makes things worse.

Regardless of overt religiosity, Tibetans embroiled in hardship often call to mind the Buddha's First Noble Truth: *the truth of suffering.* This truth is regarded as "natural," rendering belief in it unnecessary (Cassaniti 2012); many Buddhist cultures reflect on it, however, and indeed are soothed by this core religious tenet in times of duress. Many of my Tibetan friends teased me good-heartedly for being a Westerner—that is, a "big complainer" who has not known a difficult life. Wangdor, a young man who came from a nomadic family explains that because he was accustomed to hardship such as severe cold and scarce food, this helped him traverse the Himalayas to make his escape into exile. "Many *injis* [foreigners] cannot even walk thirty minutes uphill from the market in lower Dharamsala," he says, emphatically. It was not uncommon in my interviews for people to argue that Tibetans are more resilient than other cultural groups simply because they do not expect life to be easy.

In fact, it is a common idiom across the Himalayas that early hardship in life can be beneficial because it serves as preparation for inevitable suffering later on (Desjarlais 2003; McHugh 2001). The point is not to avoid misfortune and pain (it would be impossible anyhow), but to learn to cultivate inner resourcefulness. Time and time again, Tibetans remind one another that suffering in life is "only natural." While events from the past play an intimate role in the present and future (specifically in terms of karma), solidifying descriptions of what has happened is not seen as a particularly skillful way of managing traumatic events. When the Indian psychologist Honey

Oberoi Vahali asked older people in Dharamsala to talk about their past, many said: "The past is past, why unravel it now?" (2009, 6).

There's No True Story

Dekyi, age sixty, cried her way through much of our interview at the reception center for newly arrived refugees in Dharamsala. After waiting for two months at another refugee camp on the Nepal/Tibet border, a bus finally arrived to take her and forty other Tibetans to Dharamsala, where they were received at the center for medical treatment and rest. "Next week, we have our audience with Gyalwa Rinpoche [the Dalai Lama]," she said, tears still brimming. I asked whether she wanted to stop the interview, as it might be too upsetting to discuss her recent ordeal. But she wanted to press on, explaining, "we are human beings, so it is only natural to have this suffering." In other words, crying and feeling sad was natural given her situation. She went on to tell her story:

> In Lhasa, Tibetans can go to *khora* in the Bharkor, but not peacefully. They are asked for their identity card and hassled by the police. When I go to *khora*, sometimes I think, "Today, I will remain very peaceful and be kind to all others." But if I am interrogated during my *khora*, it is difficult not to become angry and unhappy. The Chinese government does not allow Tibetan employees to go to *khora*. Some Chinese government service people (who are Tibetans) believe in the *Buddhadharma* and have great faith; these people go at night to *khora* and cover their heads with a scarf. Or they go silently from their cars to *khora*. Sometimes in the street, if a Chinese man and a Tibetan man have an argument, the police automatically make a phone call and service people will come from the army or police. If the Tibetan guy tries to explain himself, the Chinese will accuse him of doing something political even if the argument was just a personal one. The Tibetan will always be arrested over the Chinese. These days, many Tibetan young people are arrested in the street and taken to the police station. They are kept alone and beaten without due cause. Also, when Tibetan people go to make offerings, most cannot outwardly pray for the Dalai Lama. Really, it is like this. We don't have any freedom. [She begins to cry] In Lhasa, there is a place called Moru. If Tibetans get permission, they go every year for a prayer festival in Moru. But these days, only old people can attend. Young people will never get permission to

go. During the *mani* prayer festival [*om mani padme hum*, the mantra of compassion], the police and army circle around the place, intimidating Tibetans. The Chinese government says that Tibetans have freedom of religion and speech. But we don't have these freedoms in reality. For these reasons, I have come to India. Those who finish high school cannot get jobs in the Chinese government. Some Tibetan people finish studies but just hang around Lhasa without jobs, so they have no choice but to escape into exile.

The next time I saw Dekyi was a few months later over tea in a small and neatly decorated room she shared with a cousin. Having recovered from her journey and the obstacles she encountered to get to India, she was no longer tearful. Typical research perspectives might seek to investigate the sources of resilience Dekyi found as she resettled in exile. Before she was crying and fearful, and now she was not. But such perspectives that view resilience as a mere absence of distress are not in sync with how Tibetans understand things. In fact, a person can be resilient at the height of distress. One might be resiliently sad, or resiliently angry, or fearful. Through her tears at the reception center a few months prior, Dekyi recounted the many atrocities she witnessed: her nephew was arrested and tortured, religious temples were destroyed before her eyes during the Cultural Revolution period, and she was plagued by severe hunger and frostbite while traversing the Himalayas. She was not untouched, unharmed, or stoic. Her resilience was not marked by the capacity to withstand or resist impact. In fact, she was deeply touched and affected.

"We Tibetans have suffered so much," said Dekyi during our initial meeting.

But it is also good to remember that many people have suffered. There was one *inji* lady [foreigner] I met in Nepal who was a Jew, and she told me about the Holocaust and how her people still face a lot of persecution today. We had a lot in common and I tried to explain that the way Tibetans deal with oppression is through compassion, and also thinking more broadly. My sister's son was arrested for peaceful protest and treated very badly in a Chinese prison. So the whole family tried to make aspirations not just for my nephew, but for the police and the prison guards. A very wise elder reminded us that maybe the guard was also a father who loves his children. He was not just a guard. We try to think in this way, to think about things more broadly and spaciously.

This kind of flexible thinking is emblematic of resilience among Tibetans.

Resilience is not to defy or resist suffering; rather, it is to become softened by it. Compassion opens new doorways, helping people to cope. The aversion to creating fixed narratives and instead looking at things more flexibly (e.g., seeing that prison guards may also be loving people with families) is a cultural approach that is consistent with Tibetan Buddhist framings of emptiness, where there is no "true" or "real" interpretation to be found. Seeing that there is no fixed and solid view of reality promotes recovery, and a unique kind of resilience. Although this style of resilience is particular to this community because of its Buddhist orientation, there are many clinicians in North America and Europe who have become interested in investigating how practices such as meditation and mindfulness may enhance psychotherapeutic intervention.

For example, psychiatrist Daniel Stern writes in *The Present Moment*: "As each new present moment takes form, it rewires the actual neural recording of the past and rewrites the possible memories of the past. The originals are changed and no longer exist in the way they were initially laid down" (2004, 200–201). This notion that there was never a "true original" is already taken for granted by Tibetans. Even at the sociopolitical level, the Dalai Lama's political approach, "The Middle Way," is based on dialectical logic, which suggests there is never ultimate truth to be found in one perspective. Buddhist notions of "emptiness" are not easily articulated among average Tibetans, but such ontological underpinnings are deeply embedded in everyday notions of reality.

Like Dekyi, another refugee, Tashi, a forty-three-year-old torture survivor, used nearly identical tactics to work with traumatic memory. He explains: "In my memory, I only know the prison guard who beat me as a torturer. But that is just one view, and one perspective. Maybe he is also a loving father and a good friend. If I look at this situation more flexibly and see that my interpretation of this person should not be so solid, it helps me let go of hatred, which the Dalai Lama tells us is self-poison." Managing traumatic memory effectively does not involve finding an accurate narrative, but rather finding ways to let go of fixed interpretation.

Haunting Past, Looming Future

Anthropological understandings of suffering have become increasingly concerned with how memory and interpretation of the past revisits, loops, and (re)creates embodied distress (Good 2012, 2015; Langford 2013). For Tibetans whose temporal engagement stretches not just to the past but to future reincarnations, orienting oneself to a looming future extending beyond current lifetimes may serve to enhance agency and empowerment in the present.

The confidence that Dolma and others found from their conviction that they would find a better life in their next rebirth is a strategy that many women, in particular, used to cope with present-day distress. Within Tibetan Buddhism, the continuity of personhood beyond death is a topic that plays out in intriguing ways. Whereas all sentient beings (humans, insects, animals, gods, demons) take rebirth, there are certain individuals known as *tulkus* whose incarnations are carefully tracked, such as the Dalai Lama (currently the fourteenth), the seventeenth Gyalwa Karmapa, head of the Kagyu school, and many lesser known lamas who skillfully choose where to take rebirth. Enlightened beings defy spatiotemporal conventions by manifesting emanations (countless "copies" of oneself sent to help sentient beings) and hiding *terma* ("treasure" teachings that can be transferred and downloaded to the minds of qualified future students, sometimes centuries later). Through their relics gathered in cremation grounds where any fraction "contains the potency of the whole" (Gayley 2007, 473), students have tremendous devotion to the enlightened bodies and minds of great teachers they strive to emulate. The interconnected web of karma that links the deep past with both present and future incarnations means that death marks the end of the present incarnation—but not the totality of existence. In fact, death is not merely an end but the beginning of one's next life.

With this framework in mind, Charlene Makley (2015) urges readers to consider the "sociopolitical lives of dead bodies" in her investigation of self-immolation in Tibet. At the time of this book's publication, more than 150 people have set themselves on fire to protest the Chinese occupation of Tibet. Here, the dead are "active and changeful subjects—they speak, gesture, haunt, yearn, suffer and demand" (2015, 453). As Makley observed townspeople in Ngaba (China's Sichuan Province) mourning, organizing, and praying collectively in response to self-immolations, I was at this same time in

Dharamsala, joining the community in vigil after candlelight vigil. But while my Tibetan interlocutors assumed that the global community would surely spring to action, the immolations have had little demonstrable impact on the issue of Tibetan autonomy in China.

The lack of global impact communicates a grave silence. Susan Sontag writes that for voyeurs of mass violence, "compassion is an unstable emotion. It needs to be translated into action, or it withers" (2003, 101). While there are many forms of suicide-protest across the globe, for those who believe there are many more lives to come, death takes on a different register in that one's current life is only a tiny blip in a stream of countless lives within samsara. Buddhist cultures tend to see suicide as something that could lead a person to a hell realm—not because it is a "sin," but because one's state of mind at death impacts rebirth. Suicide is dangerous because the anguish a person feels at the moment of death may lead them to be reborn in that state of mind. When I asked people in Dharamsala about this, many had the same stock and largely unquestioned response: it is not suicide, but rather a supreme act of generosity that generates tremendous merit (see chapter 4 for more on self-immolation and political protest).

Questions about karma and rebirth among Tibetans may also be social, for those with whom they share "collective karma." Ethical slogans such as "Don't lose self-determination. Don't agitate the minds of others," words spoken by the great Tibetan lama Khenpo Jigme Phuntsok, appear in pool hall posters and pop songs (Gayley 2013, 259), urging young people not to contaminate Tibetan culture with fighting, drinking, and other immoral behavior. Such calls to action run very deep as older generations worry that youth think only about satisfying present-day urges and do little to prepare for their rebirth.

Because negative karma can be purified, even in dire situations people feel empowered to change future outcomes—if not in this lifetime, in the next. Negative things in life occur because of past wrongful actions. And yet when this occurs, many Tibetans reflect on how they have purified and exhausted that karmic debt. The way someone responds to negativity is important because it dictates whether suffering will be merely recapitulated over and over again in a pattern of negativity. Because the Tibetan moral praxis is one that extends beyond this lifetime, both backward into past lives and forward in future lives, a sense of personal agency and self-efficacy may well be extended beyond the present moment.

This kind of "planning for the future," what Buddhists think of as planting good karmic seeds, is shared in other spiritual traditions. In China Scherz's (2013) ethnographic research among Catholic nuns running an orphanage in Uganda, rather than making budgets, spreadsheets, and applying for grants, the sisters prayed: they saw this as active planning for generous donors and other "little miracles" that would support financial needs. Their good deeds are thus "simultaneously focused on the immediate present and eternity" (2013, 632). In the United States, Christians in the Vineyard Church learn to see every mishap, setback, and crisis as part of God's plan for their learning and salvation (Luhrmann 2012). Similarly, many Tibetans exposed to political violence tend to avoid processing specific details of trauma, as would be done in counseling and debriefing sessions, focusing instead on activities such as prostrations and reciting mantras of compassion, which they believe create more positive life circumstances in future lives.

Practices of Un-Remarking

In the West, healthy coping is considered to be highly active and process oriented. Psychologists are ambivalent about what they call "suppression," a decision made to defer paying attention to difficult feelings. However, Tibetans argue that choosing not to focus on difficult feelings is not the same as denying their existence. Many interventions that fall within the sphere of global mental health, a growing field that seeks to enhance "mental health literacy"—that is, familiarity with biomedical concepts and treatments for psychiatric disorders—often provides what is hoped to be culturally sensitive training and many interventions take great care to train local health care workers or lay peers in how to provide counseling. The problem with these approaches is that psychotherapy and counseling are themselves highly culturally bound within a Eurocentric tradition.

This is evident in the ways that some researchers wonder whether Tibetans who do not meet criteria for mental disorders are merely avoiding their feelings or failing to report them in clinical interviews. Researchers note that Tibetans often do not express much of their physical and emotional pain even when asked directly, which served as a warning that better mental health services were needed (Servan-Schreiber et al. 1998). Indeed, researchers have spent a number of years attempting to scale up a mental health programs in

Dharamsala that ultimately failed. Other scholars are skeptical about studies that report low levels of psychological distress among Tibetan refugees, arguing there is response bias (Sachs et al. 2008)—seen as the only logical explanation for calm and cool recounting of severe adversity, such as torture and imprisonment. As I discuss more in chapter 4, the tendency for Tibetans to avoid talking about distress becomes problematic when they seek asylum in Europe and the United States where clinicians and human rights lawyers need to document sustained and chronic psychological distress to authenticate the need for political asylum. But this practice of "un-remarking" about the past runs deep.

In her account of why Tibetans in Labrang avoid "speaking bitterness" in relation to the Chinese occupation of Tibet, anthropologist Charlene Makley (2005) asserts that purposeful omission or nondisclosure of traumatic experiences should be viewed as an "alternative practice of time" where a reshaping of cultural memory is at once an act of self-protection and political resistance. Makley argues that to view a Tibetan propensity to avoid recounting stories of political violence as "repression" is to grossly misrepresent cultural values and the function of memory.

Here, too, rather than ascribing to binary reasoning (e.g., either Tibetans are extremely resilient and "bounce back" in the face of difficulty or they repress emotions and deny pain), I take a more nuanced look at processes of coping and resilience, seeing resilience as a learned process and moral practice characterized by flexibility. Tibetans actively deploy shared cultural understandings, often infused with Buddhist doctrine, to reframe the mental distress associated with loss, violence, and other distressing experiences. The nature of reality within Tibetan ontologies is that all phenomena are ultimately empty of inherent existence. Seeing things with an attitude of flexibility also means recognizing that people, objects, situations, and emotions are constantly changing and in flux. The Tibetan attitude of resilience appreciates that clinging or wanting things to remain static can only yield disappointment and suffering. When things are described as ultimately empty of inherent meaning this does not mean that they do not exist, but they do not exist in the way that we perceive them—as solid, as independent, and as permanent.

The stance of flexibility within *sems pa chen po* is a way of appreciating the illusory nature of things and, at the same time, living pragmatically in the world. It is appreciating a certain kind of paradox. From an ultimate per-

spective, when a traumatic event occurs, there is nothing solid that happened and there is no solid self to which the acts were done. Even at the time
of death, one is advised to take comfort in knowing that ultimately there is
nothing to worry about—there is no death and no self to die. The Tibetan
yogi Gotsangpa says:

> When it's time to leave this body, this illusionary tangle,
> Don't cause yourself anxiety and grief;
> The thing that you should train in and clear up for yourself
> There's no such thing as dying to be done
> It's just clear light, the mother, and child clear light uniting
> When mind forsakes the body, sheer delight! (cited in Holecek 2013, 94)

Such an orientation might seem at first glance to produce a lack of "ontological security" (Giddens 1991), a feeling that there is nothing solid to hold
on to, and nothing on which to rely. Why would this Buddhist view of emptiness bolster resilience?

As argued in chapter 2, cultural wisdom dictates that the more one lets
go of a conventional hold on things and sees the self as "empty," the more
content one becomes. This is also known as abandoning fixation—hope that
things will turn out a certain way, and conversely, fear that things will not
turn out the way we planned. There are many Tibetan Buddhist teachings
on the dangers of hope and fear, seen as different sides of the same problematic coin. Seeing reality clearly, which means seeing everything as changing,
impermanent, and not solid, leads to a mind-set that is free from the trap of
hope and fear. Seeing the illusory nature of things does not lead to despon-
dency. Actually, the opposite happens; people are more in the present moment because they are not attached to particular outcomes and not swept
away in fruitless ego clinging. The point is not to be dull and devoid of emotion, but to avoid becoming overly fixated and attached.

Richard Davidson, a neuroscientist at the University of Wisconsin–
Madison, tells an anecdote about the Dalai Lama to illustrate this point.
Apparently, the Dalai Lama is known to burst into tears when hearing about
a sad event and then in the next moment he is laughing and joking. In other
words, he feels the full range of emotions—sadness, happiness, grief—but
then quickly lets them go. Davidson's neuroscientific studies on meditation
(2000) have led him to believe that people who learn to meditate recover from

negative emotions faster than control groups. This is true among adept meditators and has also been observed among people who spend only ten to twelve weeks learning to meditate; this result has even been found among preschoolers who learn mindfulness techniques. They do not have fewer negative emotions, but the duration is shorter, the persistence is less, and the chronic fixation on negative emotions is reduced. This concept of "emotional plasticity" may be a significant factor in managing stress (Davidson, Jackson, and Kalin 2000; Davidson and McEwen 2012) and is emblematic of the Tibetan approach to resilience. From this perspective, negative or difficult emotions are not bad in and of themselves; they become problematic only when their duration and intensity become fixed in time.

Emerging research on emotions and the brain challenges what psychologist Lisa Feldman Barrett (2017) calls "the classical view." The classical view, which harkens back to Plato, Descartes, Freud, and Darwin, sees emotions as a fixed and universal product of our basic biology. Emotions are seen as at odds with the rationality of the mind, which fights against the brutish and more base drives and feelings that may overtake us. Barrett argues that modern science has assumed that "sadness circuits" or "anger circuits" are biologically based, connecting a complex web of hormones, neurotransmitters, and physiological changes in blood pressure and heart rate. No evidence for universal circuits have been found, however. "They are not universal but vary from culture to culture," she argues.

> They [emotions] are not triggered; you create them. They emerge as a combination of the physical properties of your body, a flexible brain that wires itself to whatever environment it develops in, and your culture and upbringing, which provide that environment. Emotions are real, but not in the objective sense that molecules or neurons are real. They are real in the same sense that money is real—that is, hardly an illusion, but a product of human agreement. (Barrett 2017, xii–xiii)

Barrett calls this view, in opposition to the classical view, the "theory of constructed emotion." Cultural anthropologists have long argued for this perspective based on observations that the experience of emotions seemed to differ from culture to culture. Some emotions that are recognized in the anthropologists' home culture seem missing in the places where they study, whereas others seem wholly new, emotions the researchers had never heard of before (see Rosaldo 1989). The question of whether emotions are biological and universal—but perhaps expressed and managed differently—or wholly culturally constructed, has been a long-standing debate in the social sciences (see Lutz 1988; Wikan 1990). What Barrett and her colleagues propose is that emotions are *both* biological and culturally constructed. That is, our biology is much more plastic and flexible than we previously thought. If these theories about the nature of emotions are true, then actually relating to one's own mental state as flexible may prove therapeutic and more in line with somatic realities.

Freedom from Fixation

Recent studies in psychiatry have shown that mental health interventions that focus on promoting greater flexibility within the mind are effective in helping patients manage anxiety and trauma (Hinton and Kirmayer 2017; Kashdan 2010). Kashdan (2010) defines psychological flexibility as the ability to distance from current or habitual mind-sets and consider other possibilities; he also argues that flexibility is absent or diminished in many forms of psychopathology. Hoping to test these observations clinically, Devon Hinton and colleagues (2011) developed what they call "Culturally Adapted Cognitive Behavioral Theory (CA-CBT)," which asks patients diagnosed with PTSD to replace distressing thoughts with culturally relevant images while making "self-statements of flexibility" (e.g., "May I flexibly adjust to each situation just as the lotus flower is able to adjust to each new breeze") (2011, 349). Among college students in the United States, research suggests that the ability to move flexibly from one coping strategy to the next may be an important feature of resilience (Galatzer-Levy et al. 2012). The common theme in these studies is that a flexible mind—one that accommodates change, openness, and new possibilities—allows one to more quickly let go of, or transform, suffering.

In Dharamsala, when I asked Tibetans to identify the characteristics of a resilient person—that is, I asked, "How would you know that in the face of difficulty a person was doing okay, and what does 'doing okay' mean to you?"—they describe someone who is compassionate, humble (does not exaggerate their problems), and has a flexible, vast, and spacious mind. Not exaggerating problems was important because making a problem seem very large defied cultural values such as humility and may also solidify negative emotions. As Dekyi explained: "Some think, 'oh, this is a small problem and it is only natural to experience some difficulties in life.' Then they just ignore the problem and move on. These people are very skillful because they don't disturb others with their many problems. It doesn't mean they are like cows who feel nothing! But they don't disturb or harm others when trying to cope. Anyway, whether people can cope well or not depends on individual ways of thinking." Comments such as "just ignore it," "try to move on," or "it's not a big problem" are not about repressing the problem; instead, there is a strong sense of not taking oneself or the situation too seriously.

While there is fervent and passionate political activism at the social level (see chapter 4), when speaking about personal distress and difficulties in life, many Tibetans in Dharamsala can seem somewhat detached at times in their descriptions of difficult life events. Often downplaying the severity of their plight, many seemed to hold rather lightly (or not at all) to their past and current struggles without resentment. The north star perspective of *sems pa chen po* encourages a big mind that looks at things flexibly, taking a wider view. Just as forgiveness is more about the person who was wronged letting go of resentment (Tutu 2000), an important feature of resilience and recovery among Tibetans is to become free of negative emotions, or free from fixation. In this way, one important method for letting go was humor.

Perhaps best exemplified in the Dalai Lama's exuberant, joking demeanor—many religious teachings and cultural sensibilities emphasize that a certain lightness and sense of humor is required for effective coping. A well-known high lama, Dzigar Kongtrul, states: "Having a sense of humor doesn't mean laughing or being cheerful all the time. It means seeing the illusory nature of things—and seeing how, in this illusory life, we are always bumping into the very things we meticulously try to avoid. Humor allows us to see that ultimately things don't make sense. The only thing that makes sense is letting go of anything we continue to hold on to" (2009, 131). With a relaxed, or even humorous, stance toward suffering, *resistance* to the feelings lessen—the difficult situation may remain but a flexible attitude helps one cope.

Ian Hacking (1998) argues that a survivor's experience of trauma (also called the "trauma loop") is fueled by feedback from the social world. But in Dharamsala, the loop seems to lose rather than gain momentum. When Tibetans minimize their pain, others do not accuse them of repressing their feelings. Rather, they applaud their humility and broad-mindedness. As Lisa

Feldman Barrett's (2017) psychological experiments on emotion have shown, emotions are made and not triggered. This is an important distinction in that it suggests that the brain constructs meaning based on how we interpret bodily sensations; there are no inherent emotions to be found and the way we interpret the body and our thoughts is culturally constructed and conditioned. This recognition of flexibility can help to show that the way we interpret our mental states means we may have much more freedom within the mind than we imagine.

A common theme among those coping with difficulty was the notion of maintaining mental stability or equilibrium, often more highly valued than expressing emotions. But cultivating equilibrium takes work and is not something that a person achieves easily. Instead, it is a continual practice of mind training over and over again. In Schröder's (2011) study of post-traumatic stress in another Tibetan refugee community, she gives an account of talking with a ritual healer, or *onpo*, about depression and sadness following a traumatic event. She described a woman who was imprisoned in Tibet and now living in exile; she is sad, not interested in anything, and does not care for her children even when they are crying. The healer explained that this happens when someone loses control of the mind. He emphasized that the imprisonment is not the cause of the woman's problems. In a similar vein, when Schröder asked another monk-healer to discuss a checklist of PTSD symptoms, he explained that the major problem among those with fear and fright is that they cannot control their mind (*sems ma dzin pa*). This is also the way ordinary people talk about mental distress. As Pema, a young woman who washes dishes at a hotel restaurant, explained:

> In 2008, the Tibetans staged a large protest against Chinese rule. We were detained and couldn't go outside for one month. If we fought the Chinese, we would be defeated; they wouldn't listen to us. We were locked inside our house and I became almost like a crazy person. Both me and my friend became so upset that we couldn't control our minds. Many times, I would even become so upset I would faint and lose consciousness. At this time, any monks and nuns who were outside would be arrested. So we hid eight monks inside our home. If the monks wore their robes, then they could tell very easily who was a monastic. So we tried to clothe the monks in laypersons' clothes. My brothers didn't have enough clothes for all of them, so we borrowed some men's clothing from our neighbors. It was very difficult to find *btang snyom* (equanimity) during this time.

Again, the primary problem is not necessarily considered to be the fright itself, but rather the "no-control" that results from an unstable mind.

Many Tibetan contemplative practices aim to help people to develop their capacity to tolerate the stress that comes from unstable outer (and inner) environments. Psychological health in this context is not "positive thinking" or being happy all the time. Indeed, it is also ill advised to be too exuberant when something good happens, getting swept away in elation. Rather, emotional health is marked by the capacity to remain stable no matter the external circumstance. In Dharamsala, I observed many such moments of equanimity in action.

For instance, it is not uncommon for Tibetans living in India to be badly treated by Indian visa offices and government officials—never knowing if their documents will be renewed or denied. On a few occasions, I witnessed such discrimination. But rather than becoming very upset or hostile, Tibetans remarked how important it was to maintain equanimity. "It is not worth it, getting upset," a woman named Drolkar explained. "It does not help. It only hurts one's own mind—we are the ones who lose out if we become upset." Many community members (lay and monastic alike) would be told to wait on a wooden bench outside the visa office, often waiting six or seven hours for a single visa stamp.[3] As a foreigner myself, I had to do the same.

Waiting hours on end while the visa officers drank chai and sat around gossiping among themselves and blatantly ignoring those sitting outside, I found it difficult not to become upset. Several times I could not resist going up to the window and pointing at my passport just sitting idly on the desk. *Please sir! Can you just give me the signature?* My Tibetan neighbors teased me for my impatience. "Sara-la," they would say. "If we get angry, it doesn't hurt *them*. We just make ourselves upset." While my own cultural ideals tend to value things like "justice" and "fairness" (not to mention feeling entitled to efficient service), Tibetans value putting equanimity above other concerns.

But certainly not all Tibetans maintain calm equilibrium in the face of difficulty. During interviews, I asked participants to describe why some people do better than others in difficult situations. A fifty-four-year-old man named Wangdu who came to India six years ago said the following:

> Two people may have the same problem, yet feel very differently. Some people even if they have many problems, say nothing, but they are very stable and cope easily with their problems. I think the people who don't say anything

are happy inside. It is not important to express every problem you have. It is more important to remain stable no matter what is happening. The reason people cannot deal well with problems is that they don't have the quality of spaciousness or vastness in their minds. When that person encounters any problem, it exhausts everything and they have no space to deal. They become unhappy and sick. The person who is ready to face difficulties will not have many problems even if they are a political prisoner sentenced to seventeen or eighteen years, or even a death sentence. They can deal with these problems because they have the patience to cope with anything. If Tibetans are compared with people from other countries, they can deal with things much better. Around here, there are many ex–political prisoners. Their bodies are very weak and exhausted because they were tortured and beaten severely in prison. But mentally they maintain a sense of dignity and confidence. Others would become upset very easily.

Still, I wondered why it seemed important not to talk about problems with others. Why is there such an emphasis on keeping negativity to oneself?

Perplexed, I asked my neighbor, Tashi Wangyal, a fifty-two-year-old mother of four to help me understand, though she seemed equally perplexed as to why I seemed to think that talking about problems might be helpful. Patiently, she explained: "Coping depends on individual thinking. If someone has good thinking, then if they have problems with finances or health or legal issues, it is not important for them to go around making trouble. It is best to keep your problems to yourself and instead think very widely and spaciously. Bothering many people with your problems will also bring others difficulty. It is best to cope with it on your own, through making your mind spacious and open. It depends on one's thinking." Not liberally expressing one's problems is commonplace, and this was coupled with the notion that coping through changing the way you think is effective in making the mind more spacious, open, and flexible.

To cultivate this flexibility, instead of resisting the situation one works to transform one's relationship to what is happening, even in the face of severe outer and inner chaos. As Sonam Tashi explains:

> I was arrested in 1988. Those in prison have great suffering because they have no freedom and are put in small cells. The guards use harsh words and torture inmates relentlessly. After we die, some become hungry ghosts and hell beings. We don't know their suffering, but here on earth, the worst suffering

is prison. When the youth couldn't tolerate their hunger and thirst, I would give them advice according to Buddhism. Many masters of the past made great efforts to become bodhisattvas despite many hardships. When I think of this, I didn't feel my suffering in prison was very great. When I went to prison, I had one small *mala* [prayer beads] around my wrist. The guards asked me what I would do with it. I told them I would recite mantras. I had to stay as a prisoner, but I just thought of it as a retreat house. I was given food, and other than that, all I had to do was practice. If we have too much food, we feel sleepy; since I only had a little food, actually this was much better for practice! I was there one year and was able to recite one hundred thousand mantras each of Guru Rinpoche and Chenrezig. There were many monks there like me, using it positively as an opportunity to practice. Some said: 'Since we are monks, if we have to stay our whole lives here and die in prison, then it is not really prison because we are here practicing the Dharma.' It is good to have all this suffering now in this life because then it is purified and we won't experience much later.

This passage foregrounds a number of typical coping strategies among Tibetans. He acknowledges, "I have to be here anyway," so he tries to accept the situation and transform his mind to think more broadly.

In Dharamsala, people often recite the Dalai Lama's perhaps favorite piece of advice: "If you can't change the situation, why worry? And if you can change the situation, why worry?" The monk does not deny pain and hardship. Yet he changes his attitude or the way he relates to the situation, using his time in prison as a "retreat house." While at first glance, stories such as these may seem like internalized oppression or merely accepting one's fate. The difference seems to be the location of agency and exercise of reflection. With enough space in the mind to accommodate such thinking, one maintains his or her power even in unthinkable situations. These ways of building resilience are also collective and inherently social. Whereas stress is often seen as an individual problem that must be overcome, in this context, suffering is a foundational aspect of the human condition. It actually defines what it means to exist in samsara, and thus, the entire Buddhist path is structured around liberating oneself from suffering. As human beings, it is impossible to avoid pain, but suffering comes with resistance to that pain rather than letting it pass by and accepting the ebb and flow of favorable outcomes. The idea is to find equanimity in a troubled world. Perhaps paradoxically, Tibetan Buddhist masters claim that the more one accepts and sees the illusory nature of reality, the more compassion for others trapped in a samsaric view one develops. This is an important aspect of developing *sems pa chen po*.

Past Is Past

The commonly used phrase "past is past" is a pith aphorism that indexes the cultural wisdom and skillful approach to managing difficult emotions that I described in this chapter. For on the ultimate level, every event, and even the person experiencing the event, is in reality, illusory and empty of inherent existence. This ultimate view may seem bewildering to outsiders—how would such a view promote resilience? And yet this view helps Tibetans in Dharamsala to experience and think about memory as plastic, fluid, and flexible. This orientation is highly pragmatic in that trying to solidify past events is an unreliable way to find contentment, particularly insofar as it churns up *shenpa*, the "juice" of the emotions and ego clinging. Instead of debriefing and sharing stories, or even launching public truth commissions (which seem to bring about healing in other cultural contexts), Tibetans in Dharamsala strive for freedom from fixation.

And yet this story of resilience and recovery in Dharamsala would not be complete without examining an intriguing paradox with which the community must wrestle, namely, that "past is past" will not fuel a human rights campaign. Based on Buddhist sensibilities of what one ought to do in the face of suffering, Tibetans tend to reflect on how all living beings are suffering, on how suffering can be used to generate compassion, and ultimately, on how we should resist taking ourselves and our problems too seriously. And yet— such interior maneuvers that promote resolution and acceptance do not produce narratives that strengthen collective claims of human rights abuses and oppression. Indeed, Tibetan activists worry that signs of strength, resilience, and recovery may weaken their political campaign. In the next chapter, I explore this paradox and suggest that rather than attempting to resolve this contradiction, Tibetans in exile employ a flexible stance, which promotes inner resolution through *sems pa chen po*, while simultaneously insisting that they are a vulnerable population in need. Rather than becoming postcolonial victims of Western trauma concepts, Tibetan political activists have appropriated foreign ideas and fashioned them not for psychological healing—

indeed, they reject foreign mental health services—but as a political device to fuel their human rights campaign. With a keen awareness of how evidence of chronic and intractable suffering provides legitimacy on the global stage, Tibetan activists have revamped local sensibilities of "telling trauma" by encouraging their countrymates to disseminate their stories of violence to the world.

Chapter 4

The Paradox of Testimony

"Are you writing this down?" asks Palden. "Is your tape recorder working?"

"Yes, I have it," I say. He continues speaking.

As I told you already, my parents were farmers. My sisters and brothers are nomads today. I went to school for only two years because our livelihood depended on us working. In our county, women cannot have more than two children; if they have three or four children, then the children will not be given citizenship and they need to pay a fine of twenty thousand Chinese yuan. As for my family, two of my brothers were not given citizenship. Also, the Chinese government ordered us to plant bramble bushes in our fields, which hurts our animals. If we don't plant them, we are heavily fined by the Chinese. An additional problem is that they create fences and boundaries between families and neighbors, so when the animals cross the fences it creates problems among Tibetan families. We don't want to create these fences; Tibet used to be very open and free. Maybe . . . if you could write about this. You said you could write books and articles about us. I think this is a very good motivation you have.

Palden was eager to share stories of life back in Tibet and often volunteered to recruit his friends and family members to participate in my study. "I'll tell them *you are publishing a book,* and that this will help us."

Like many researchers engaged in international work, I often struggled to describe the enterprise of anthropology to people in Dharamsala and what they might have to gain from speaking with me. In IRB consent forms, social scientists write vague and deferred statements such as "this research may help us better understand your community," but it often remains unclear how ethnographic research may benefit (or harm) the people who generously give their time and willingly share intimate details of their lives. I felt an ethical obligation to explain that my book might be read by students, other academics, and possibly by people interested in Tibet or Buddhism, but that it is not an exposé aimed at exposing human rights abuses or publicizing the Free Tibet campaign. But still, people in Dharamsala assumed that once foreigners read about the plight of Tibetan people, they would understand and be called to action. They would help.

Each semester when Sonam Tashi meets with American study abroad students living in Dharamsala, he begins his talk with a life history narrative. He explains that he was born to humble nomad parents in eastern Tibet and that life was peaceful and simple. He was the oldest boy and made his parents happy by becoming a monk when he was around seven or eight years old. In his monastery, he learned to read and write, and he studied hard. Life was decent and good before the Chinese Cultural Revolution in the 1970s, he explained to his student audience; then, stupas and monasteries were destroyed before his eyes. Chinese police and military personnel stormed his monastery and required the *khenpos* (abbott or teachers) and *ge-ku* (discipline master) in the *shedra* (monastic college) to publicly denounce the Dalai Lama in front of their young pupils. Those who refused were detained and dragged away, causing a riot inside the monastery. Days later, Sonam Tashi and some others around the county posted political posters around town leading to their arrest and imprisonment. The American college students sit transfixed as he tells his story. Some wipe away tears. But they have been prepped for this conversation—the faculty issue trigger warnings before the talk, telling students that Sonam Tashi may discuss being tortured in prison.

Study abroad programs, service learning opportunities, and NGOs (nongovernmental organizations) have become woven into the social service landscape in Dharamsala, where foreigners act as donors and hopeful providers of care. This is similar to what Johanna Crane (2013) details in her ethnography of HIV programs in Uganda, where global health opportunities for students who want to travel abroad creates new and reciprocally beneficial opportunities for locals "in need," and their foreign visitors wanting to help. Indeed, travelers and students in Dharamsala are a willing audience for whom Tibetans perform as refugees and survivors of political violence (Diehl 2002; Kloos 2012). Through these engagements, Tibetans have learned something important over the past fifty years: human rights campaigns are predicated on the trauma narrative (Adams 1998)—something that on the personal level is seen as antithetical to healthy coping. Resilience is built on letting go of suffering, on refusing to create solid stories, and of taking a wider view based on emptiness and compassion. But such a stance will not fuel a human rights campaign.

Testimony in the Diaspora

For diaspora communities, legacies from the past necessarily shape public and private identities of the present. The acts of reparation, nostalgia, and reclaiming (Hirsch and Miller 2011) are central to navigating what might be called "social memory," in culturally specified ways. Scholars concerned with memory have articulated the ways that interpretations of past events are crystallized through testimony and narrative (Antze and Lambek 1996; Connerton 1989). In many cases, truth commissions and other forms of public testimony become powerful vehicles within social movements to expand the range of voices that may otherwise have been silenced (Stephen 2013; Weine 2006), including those of perpetrators and offenders (Theidon 2015). In these contexts, testimony is used both to reveal and to repair injustice.

And yet testimony itself may not be a universal genre of discourse (Makley 2015), which for Tibetans is related to notions of a flexible past where letting go is more highly valued than crafting solid narrative. When asked about past events (both personal and political), it is not uncommon for those in Dharamsala to seem unsure of specific details and rather unconcerned with recalling them. As anthropologists of Tibet such as Carole McGranahan (2010a) argue, forgetting in this context is not a mere absence of memory but an active process mediated by social praxis. Likewise, when Charlene Makley's Tibetan interlocutors skirted her questions about the past: "I don't know anything! I'm too young, you know!" (Tib: Ngas shes ni ma red, nga lo chung gi mo) (2005, 40), at first she interpreted these utterances to mean that as uneducated laywomen, they were not legitimate narrators of history. It was not until later that she realized these moments exposed something crucial about the category of history itself. She argues that a "vigorous alternative historiography" (2005, 41) flourishes among Tibetans as an act of political resistance. Rather than seeing the Tibetan tendency not to reveal too much about the past as repression, these scholars interpret the reluctance to create narratives of past suffering as a form of refusal imbued with agency.

Often downplaying the severity of their plight, I was initially skeptical of the ways that many Tibetans with whom I spoke describe their violent encounters in Tibet very matter-of-factly, seemingly without resentment. For example, a thirty-four-year old monk named Lhundrup said:

> When the Chinese authorities came to the monastery and tried to harm the monks, first I felt very angry. I even felt hatred for them. But when they came again, I tried to be a little more patient. I prayed and wished the Chinese leaders' wrong views and negative motivations would be purified. I also tried to think that we have these problems as a result of previous lives. Therefore, we have to accumulate virtue to purify our negative karma causing these problems. Also, I pray and wish that all the problems between Chinese and Tibetans will soon be resolved and we can all enjoy our lives. Really, I feel compassion because the Chinese are accumulating so much negative karma.

Knowing Lhundrup to be a survivor of torture, I wondered if maybe he was repressing his rage. His narrative—"it is because of karma, I am generating compassion"—displays a characteristic coolness that flavors testimony in Dharamsala.

Given his religious conviction, it is possible that, indeed, Lhundrup no longer experiences anger. There is another possibility, however: one that does not presuppose that *either* Lhundrup is not admitting his true feelings *or* that he is no longer impacted by his imprisonment. As I argued in the first half of the book, Tibetans purposefully aim for *sems pa chen po* as a north star principle—a horizon guiding the way even if they are struggling (and perhaps especially if they are still struggling). Like religious mantras, known as "mind protection" that keep the mind from wandering into negativity, the imperative to try to cultivate big mind that accommodates compassion and emptiness helps people know what to do in times of difficulty. In his statement, Lhundrup takes a wider view beyond his own situation and acknowledges that everyone in the situation (including the Chinese) is suffering. This flexible stance both acknowledges his own suffering and provides enough "space" such that he resists identifying too strongly with negative emotions.

Reflecting on multiple views and vantage points is a common strategy for helping people to remember that in any situation people are biased by their own "self-cherishing." The reluctance to describe one's traumatic past is reflected in the ways that many stories of resistance are told "quietly, humbly, and infrequently, if at all" (McGranahan 2010b, 770). Humility is an important cultural value and to speak openly about withstanding great suffering can be seen as brash and aggrandizing. Becoming self-righteous and overly assertive, insisting that your own perspective is more righteous than others is considered to be arrogant (it is not understood as assertive "self-care" as in the West). And yet these values are not easy to live by.

Within the sociopolitical realm, Tibetans identify strongly with their small counties yet struggle to articulate loyalty to a monolithic Tibet where they experience vast diversity in language, culture, and custom (Yeh 2013). However, they keenly understand that articulating a cohesive narrative about Tibetan political autonomy is paramount to meeting their aims for political autonomy or independence from the PRC. Strong and unchallenged discourse on political sovereignty is important for fueling a successful campaign, and yet, another ingredient holds even more persuasive power on the global stage: the trauma narrative. As I describe in more detail below, the genre of testimony that features the trauma narrative has become a core component of human rights discourse that Tibetan political activists increasingly seek to cultivate.

The Paradox of Testimony

Many works in anthropology detail the ways that biomedical practices spread across the globe, usually usurping local practices (Jenkins 2015; Kleinman and Good 1985; Kohrt and Mendenhall 2015). And yet in this community, something unusual has transpired. Rather than becoming postcolonial victims of Western trauma concepts, Tibetan political activists have appropriated foreign ideas and fashioned them not for psychological healing—indeed, they reject foreign mental health services—but as a political device to fuel their human rights campaign. With a keen awareness of how testimony and narrative give legitimacy to politics, Tibetan activists have revamped local sensibilities of "telling trauma" by encouraging their countrymates to disseminate their stories of violence to the world. While on the personal level Tibetans do not see much therapeutic utility in recounting details of torture and imprisonment, they readily distribute bloodied photographs and trauma narratives to journalists and foreign researchers with hopes of garnering international support. They carefully link names and personal stories with statistics, often emphasizing how peaceful and humble individuals are brutally treated within China's Tibet.

The processes of individual and collective recovery in Dharamsala have taken a paradoxical turn. On the one hand, there is purposeful refusal to craft trauma narratives, which is seen as antithetical to healthy coping. Indeed, elaborating and talking about past suffering is considered highly ineffective and even harmful. Yet simultaneously, Tibetans in exile understand that human rights campaigns are predicated on testimony that recounts and elaborates trauma (Adams 1998; Lewis 2013). While solidifying interpretations of past events will only make a person's suffering more real and solid, letting go of suffering does not fuel a human rights campaign. And thus, these competing ideologies remain unresolved.

Trauma Stories

World War I marks an important time period in the genealogy of trauma as a psychiatric category. Anthropologist and captain in the Royal Army Medical Corps W. H. R. Rivers served during this time as a psychiatrist specializing in "nerve regeneration." War neuroses, as they were called, came in four related but distinct forms: shell shock, hysteria, neurasthenia, and disordered action of the heart (Young 1995). Shell shock, as the name suggests, was a condition associated with the shock waves from explosions. The forms of hysteria that were common among soldiers (e.g., mutism, paralysis, fugue states) are similar to conditions articulated by Freud in the Victorian era where repressed ladies swooned and fainted on couches. Nerve exhaustion, or neurasthenia, in soldiers often took the form of chronic fatigue, headache, loss of appetite, and difficulty sleeping. Some veterans were diagnosed with a condition known as "disordered action of the heart," a more diffuse anxiety disorder characterized by weakness, palpitations, and problems concentrating, harkening back to what was called "soldier's heart" during the American Civil War (Levine 2010). Disordered action of the heart was often found among those not on the front lines or exposed to direct combat (Young 1995)—those who were seen as too weak to handle the atrocities of war. Since this period, "trauma" as a psychiatric category has been linked with survivors of war and political violence (Finley 2011), where specific symptoms appear inevitable and self-evident.

The syndrome known as PTSD first appeared in DSM-III (1980). Ongoing and pervasive distress following a traumatic event was known as a "gross stress reaction" in DSM-I and "transient situational disturbance" in DSM-II. Since the term PTSD was coined in 1980, its symptomatology has remained relatively stable: persistent and distressing reexperiences of the traumatic event in dreams, flashbacks, and intrusive images; symptomatic numbing, such as emotional amnesia or loss of interest in activities previously found pleasurable; a tendency to avoid situations that might trigger recollections of the traumatic experience; and increased physiological arousal, evidenced in sleep disorders, difficulty concentrating, and irritability.

Historicizing these categories is instructive to understand how culture shapes our understanding of mental illness—it may also be a fruitful way to "read" culture itself. For example, DSM-II was revised during the relatively tranquil interlude between World War II and the Vietnam War (Andreasen 1980), so it was not until DSM-III committees convened in the late 1970s that transient situational disturbances became post-traumatic stress disorder. At this time in the United States, the stereotype of the angry, violent, and drunk Vietnam Vet also emerged (Young 1995), further reinforcing this disorder as one marked by unpredictability. In the mid-1970s, clinicians merged what was known as "rape trauma syndrome" with PTSD (Ozer et al. 2003). That trauma has now become synonymous with a mental disorder is an important fact. As clinician Peter Levine, who takes a decidedly non-pathological approach to understanding and treating traumatized individuals argues, it is a mistake not to view trauma as a healthy and appropriate response to atrocity and instead as "simply a disorder, an objectified collection of concrete and measurable symptoms; a diagnosis amenable to vested research protocols, detached insurance companies and behavioral treatment strategies" (2010, 33–34). PTSD remains entrenched within the Euro-American imaginary as a disordered response to atrocity and violence.

Looping Effects

To better understand how particular idioms such as PTSD come about in particular places at particular moments (and to show why such idioms are used by Tibetans only as a political device, but not a therapeutic one), I draw on Ian Hacking's concept of "looping." In his essay, "Making Up People," Hacking argues that as people come to identify as new kinds—such as heterosexuals, teenagers, or someone with multiple personality disorder, all fairly recent inventions—categories are reified, further perpetuating the ontological status of the category. Hacking (1999) refers to this interplay between self and society as "looping," a reciprocal process whereby individuals change their behavior to match a culturally constituted category, and vice versa. Psychiatric categories are not sufficiently perpetuated merely by labeling; rather, individuals are disciplined (Foucault 1965; Goffman [1968] 1990) to identify with being and phenomenologically experience oneself as a depressed, psychotic, traumatized, or otherwise-categorized person. The self is shaped largely by the responses of others; the more the category is recognized in oneself (by others), the more one identifies with the category, strengthening its salience.

The effects of looping are not merely philosophical, but rather can directly influence the phenomenology (Kirmayer and Sartorius 2007), and even epidemiology of local biologies (Krieger 1994; Lock 2001). Without feedback and reinforcement from the social world, categories of mental disorders do not remain prominent (Seligman and Kirmayer 2008). Such was the case of multiple personality disorder in the 1980s, a disorder designation that has since fallen out of fashion (see Hacking 1998). In Emily Martin's ethnographic account (2007) of how the prevalence of bipolar disorder rose in the United States, she writes about what people did when they found out they were bipolar. In many cases, she describes patients who felt relieved there was a name for their cascading problems and instability. As the disorder gained familiarity within the popular imagination, people began to self-diagnose—a telltale sign a category has taken hold.

Similarly, when American soldiers or survivors of sexual assault struggle to move on, they are not surprised to "find out" that they have PTSD. In fact, some expect to get PTSD before it even happens (Finley 2011; Wool 2015). The culturally embedded notion of what happens to a person psychologically when they are exposed to violence and the horrors of war is already pre-scribed. Soldiers see how others around them respond; in fact, it is likely they already know someone with PTSD and are taught to watch out for signs such as irritability, nightmares, and flashbacks. The looping between self and society involves institutions, experts, popular media, public policy, insurance companies, clinical training programs, and therapeutic practices, reinforc-ing the perceived naturalness of the disorder. At a basic level, it reinforces the notion that difficulty after a traumatic event is a psychiatric problem, as opposed to some other kind of occurrence, which could be religious, social, moral, or interpersonal. Here, I am not suggesting that mental health programs and disability benefits *cause* PTSD, but rather that reciprocal reinforcement of trauma behavior reifies the category. The language empha-sizing the chronicity of the disorder is reflected within these institutions (and in fact, chronicity is required to qualify for services in a managed care system). Understanding PTSD as a chronic mental disorder is also lived experientially, by patients and their families.

Hacking refers to this mutual reinforcing between individuals and the so-cial world as dynamic nominalism (1999, 165). He understands psychiatric categories such as PTSD as "interactive kinds," distinct from the "indifferent kinds" or natural kinds of the natural sciences. Quarks are quarks, for exam-ple, in spite of us naming them as such or learning of their existence. In other words, their existence is indifferent to social influence. Interactive kinds are shaped by a dynamic relationship between selves and society. In this way, cat-egories of persons can be read as objects of knowledge (Foucault 1965), which Hacking also understands as "new possibilities for human choice and action" (2002, 4). With regard to trauma, it is only through dynamic nominalism that kinds of persons (trauma victims), the study of trauma (traumatology), and psychosocial treatment programs such as Wounded Warriors in the Ameri-can VA system arise. American soldiers returning from war become experts in navigating complex benefits paperwork, carefully explained in docu-ments such as the *Hero Handbook* (Wool and Messinger 2012) and other materials given to veterans and their families; documents such as these also "teach" people how to perform their illness through codified language.

Recovering from PTSD in the context of a VA takes different forms than it does among survivors of sexual assault, for instance. And yet there are commonalities for all who are diagnosed with this disorder in the United States, namely, that the work to be done in counseling and psychotherapy involves helping people to work retrospectively on psychic injury from the past. In her book *Trauma and Recovery*, Judith Herman articulates how it is the therapist's job to help the patient reconstruct traumatic memory from "the fragmented components of frozen imagery and sensation . . . and to slowly assemble an organized, detailed, verbal account, oriented in time and historical context" (1992, 177). Patients are encouraged to locate and uncover the site of psychic trauma; "every patient conceals a narrative, his pathogenic secret" (Young 1995, 227)—therefore, articulating this narrative is paramount for recovery. When the narrative emerges, it is expected to be cathartic; it is also the moment that Hacking's loop comes full circle. The once painfully hidden narrative that is now exposed to the light and uncovered serves as evidence of the disorder's veracity and existence in the first place.

But is this always the case that traumatized people must necessarily find ways to reconfigure their stories? Clinicians today do not all agree that going back is beneficial. For example, in her ethnographic study of therapists and their attempts to provide help during and after 9/11, anthropologist Karen Seeley (2008) describes how clinicians who descended on lower Manhattan began to wonder whether debriefings and the retelling of the horrors people witnessed were actually cathartic. As time went on, they too, began to struggle with the atrocities around them, sparking a wave of recovered traumatic memories among providers—what Seeley (2008) understands as trauma contagion. This dilemma rings true of Rebecca Lester's assertion: "When we conflate trauma-as-moment-of-injury and trauma-as-ongoing-lived-experience, we forever loop present-day experience back into the past, affixing it to the original insult or injury and severely constraining our interpretive and therapeutic horizons" (2013, 755). By connecting all present forms of suffering again and again back to the same narrative, opportunities for having a different kind of experience are foreclosed.

This space of possibility—to imagine something new—is what Tibetans refer to as "freedom from fixation." Recognizing that moment to moment everything changes creates the potential for a kind of radical freedom where no possibilities are foreclosed. In this way, silence may prove more therapeutic in some contexts than testimony and narration (Back et al. 2009). My Tibetan interlocutors argue that by clinging tightly to something that has already passed, we limit the capacity for authentic experiences of the present moment. The more one clings to traumatic memory, they argue, the more one is trapped in misery. Therefore, the response to coping with trauma is not to work with its narrative but to drop the narrative project altogether.

Helping Institutions

Why do Tibetans find it rather natural to "hold lightly" to traumatic memory, whereas Euro-Americans tend to believe that it is helpful to focus on and work with trauma narratives? One important reason may be because Tibetan Buddhists are raised with cultural understandings of impermanence, karma, and the naturalness of suffering. Growing up in a world that is understood to be imperfect seems to help later in life when confronted with difficulty. A stressful or adverse life event—although potentially devastating—might at the same time be understood as a natural part of life. Karma as an ordering principle of reality mitigates the feeling of senselessness that might be felt in other cultural contexts when disaster occurs. Even when overwhelmed with pain, there remains a silver lining: the negative karma that has ripened is something that will not be experienced again. There is comfort in knowing they will take rebirth without this heavy karmic burden now that its imprint has ripened.

But what is the difference between this perspective and internalized oppression? Unlike in contexts where people may come to feel that they somehow deserve maltreatment, here it seems that accepting suffering as a natural part of life lends itself to compassion—we are all human, and thus we all experience both happiness and loss. People are "told" by the environment if their behavior is appropriate or problematic (Bateson 1972), and thus in Dharamsala there are sharp distinctions between self-compassion and self-pity. If a person focuses too much on his or her own misfortune, they receive feedback from the social world that they are only making things worse by seeing their plight as special. Excessive self-pity, depression, or self-deprecation is considered a form of arrogance among Tibetans because it suggests people are taking themselves and their problems too seriously. This was how Ani Dawa explained living outside the nunnery. "I live on my own with help from neighbors and other nuns. *Nying-je* [compassion]," she explains with a sigh.

"People are very kind to me. I couldn't keep to the schedule in the *ani gompa* [nunnery], so it is better that I don't cause problems for the other nuns."

"But," I ask, with some skepticism, "do you feel bad that they cannot accommodate your needs and disabilities?"

"Feeling bad about our situations just makes us feel worse. We shouldn't think that we are so special; nor should we think, *oh no, my problems are so bad!!*" she emphasized. "I need to be patient and one day, either in this lifetime or in my next lifetime, my karma will be purified. This is part of samsara." Having problems—in Ani Dawa's case, a seizure disorder and mental illness—is deemed something that makes people human. For Tibetans, resilience is not a mere absence of problems but relating to problems with compassion and a big mind. The sense that one's problems are a result of past karma is not at all like a neoliberal system of personal responsibility or blame. There are many formal and informal care structures in Dharamsala to help in times of need. Support for ex–political prisoners and torture survivors, however, is not clinical in nature, but rather comes from community-based organizations that provide material and social support. Therefore, "contact zones" (Martin 2007), places where violence, distress, and resettlement are framed, are done so in terms that are not automatically medicalized.

The prominent center for Tibetan political ex–political prisoners, GuChuSum, started by Tibetan ex–political prisoners themselves features material support for housing, employment, and educational training. The organization is a registered NGO with the Indian government that is funded through local and international donations; its executive staff are local Tibetans, including a young woman born in Dharamsala, a *tulku* (incarnate lama), and a monk and two lay Tibetans who are themselves ex–political prisoners. As I explore in more detail below, foreigners tend to view Dharamsala as a resource-poor community that lacks mental health services (thus requiring intervention from global mental health experts). However, the kind of care local Tibetans create reveals what they understand to be most helpful for political refugees rebuilding their lives in India.

Unlike GuChuSum, which does not feature Western-style mental health services, another place to seek services in town is the Tibetan Torture Survivors Program (TTSP) within the Dharamsala Department of Health, which explicitly draws on biomedical language and psychiatric terminology to describe its approach to care. This program was started by a foreign NGO interested in improving mental health literacy and worked to train local Tibetan health workers in how to provide counseling. And yet in 2012 when I asked the director of the program how many Tibetans they had treated within the last year, she sheepishly explained that only two had come.

Since then, there has been increased interest among foreigners in revamping the underutilized counseling program, where its lack of clientele further reinforces the need to promote mental health literacy. The Department of Health in Dharamsala has readily accepted the foreign aid associated with its scaling up. Since 2016, USAID and an NGO called Les Amis DU Tibet, LUXEMBOURG, have begun funding the Tibetan Torture Survivors Program. A "plans" section on the website states:

> The TTSP plans to take care of at least forty torture survivors each year and is working towards gradually integrating this new system into a Community based Health Care System. Early efforts concentrated mainly on the treatment process, but it has now become increasingly evident that efforts must also focus on raising funds and providing social support. We are also planning for our Indigenous Treatment Method or Spiritual Healing session to have greater role to play [*sic*] in seeking to address the psychological problems of torture survivors along with religious or spiritual intervention. To this effect, the team has already established contact with one of the senior Buddhist monks to participate in the Group therapy. (http://tibet.net/health/#code0slide1, accessed May 1, 2017)

The plans to implement the "indigenous treatment method" reflect a trend among global health programs, which rather feebly gesture to cultural sensitivity while ignoring the ways that counseling itself may not be universally comportable across the globe (Calabrese 2008; Summerfield 2012). The word "indigenous" is a particularly odd word choice, for Tibetan political activists have long rejected being characterized with terminology they understand to refer to people fighting for their own rights but incorporated into another state (Coulthard 2014; McGranahan 2016b). One feels immediately that this language was written by outsiders who have come to Dharamsala to help. Here, USAID and their international NGO partners acknowledge that "spiritual healing" is an important aspect of how locals in Dharamsala cope with mental distress. The attempt to integrate these perspectives is perhaps laudable, but it remains to be seen to what extent Tibetans will appreciate mental health services and counseling as a worthwhile enterprise. Thus far, many are skeptical that this form of treatment, which involves processing details of past trauma, could help. And yet as I argue below, they willingly interact with foreign entities not for psychological healing but as a political device.

Circulating Trauma Narratives

Tibetan notions of recovery based on compassion, emptiness, and a big-mind view are largely incommensurate with biomedically based forms of treatment, which often begin by working with trauma narratives. Globalized discourse on refugees has become fused with trauma narrative where the personal story counts as evidence (often depicted in evocative photographs and videos that go viral) where the personal becomes political. International human rights campaigns across the world are dependent on exposing trauma as evidence for why political, legal, or humanitarian intervention is needed; indeed, Tibetans in exile are eager to gain support from the international community, which may question the veracity of human rights violations at the hands of the Chinese government.

Performing bodily, psychological, and social harm signals worthiness in a resource-scarce humanitarian landscape (Fassin 2012; Ticktin 2011a, 2014), where psychiatric expertise confirms or denies a would-be refugee's claim to assistance. Miriam Ticktin's work reveals how demonstrating harm as the best way to get papers as an undocumented immigrant as compared to, say, selling one's labor power (Ticktin 2011b) is a rather new kind of discourse within the politics of immigration. And yet the imposition (and play of possibility) of new psychiatric concepts into myriad local worlds has long been a form of social control (Foucault 1965; Goffman [1968] 1990). Psychiatry within postcolonial contexts (Fanon 1967; Pandolfo 2008a, 2008b) becomes even more insidious as an instrument of control when locals seek out care for not conforming to colonial mores, newly labeled as mentally ill. Biomedicine within humanitarian and global health apparatuses restrict forms of suffering, producing victims whose trauma verifies and authenticates their deservingness of help (Fassin 2009; Redfield 2013). And yet as I will describe below, the flexible thinking that is emblematic of Tibetan notions of resilience may help to explain why there is little motivation to resolve the paradox at work where on the one hand, generating trauma narratives is ill advised for recovery, and on the other, they are created and circulated for political power.

Volunteers and NGOs

The influx of volunteers, global health programs, and foreign aid in the Global South is strongly connected with the ways that particular illnesses come to the forefront, often eclipsing other concerns. This has been shown most prominently with how global HIV/AIDS programs help to provide care and yet simultaneously mask local priorities such as exploitation and gender-based violence (Kenworthy 2014), or other chronic illness including, diabetes (Mendenhall and Norris 2015) and cancer (Livingston 2012). Likewise, the enterprise of global mental health and its conglomerate of NGO assistance, gap year programs for premedical students and residents, and interests of pharmaceutical companies all implicitly fuel the production and circulation of psychiatric categories across South Asia. Those who come to Dharamsala to help Tibetans assume this refugee population will necessarily be a traumatized community and the lack of mental health services justifies why foreign help to enhance mental health literacy is needed.

The vast array of studies investigating rates of PTSD among Tibetans in exile (Benedict, Mancini, and Grodin 2009; Evans 2008; Holtz 1998; Hooberman 2007; Hussain and Bhushan 2011; Keller 2006; Ketzer and Crescenzi 2002; Lhewa 2007; Sachs 2008) take great care to discuss cultural sensitivity. Many of these studies note that PTSD is not recognized among locals and they largely acknowledge that Buddhist forms of healing are prominent in how Tibetans cope with mental distress. Yet the presence of these studies alone draws attention to the ways that PTSD is being introduced to Dharamsala residents. As Allen Young writes:

> To say that traumatic memory and PTSD are constituted through a researcher's techno-phenomena and styles of scientific reasoning does not deny the pain that is suffered by people who are diagnosed or diagnosable with PTSD. Nothing . . . should be construed as trivializing the acts of violence and the terrible losses that stand behind many traumatic memories. The suffering of

PTSD is real. But can one also say that the facts now attached to PTSD are *true* (timeless) as well as real? Can questions about truth be divorced from the social, cognitive, and technological conditions through which researchers and clinicians come to know their facts and the meaning of facticity? (1995, 10)

As NGO and foreign-funded mental health centers are formed in Dharamsala, it remains to be seen whether or not the category of PTSD will take root. As I describe in more detail below, to date, foreign efforts to implement mental health services in Dharamsala have been largely unrealized. This is not because people do not suffer, but because they do not suffer in the way that the psychiatric apparatus of "trauma" asks of them.

Counseling in Dharamsala

As I discussed in the previous chapter, excessive thinking and emotionality puts one at risk for developing *snying rlung* (heart-wind illness), and thus, students studying for exams, practitioners engaged in intensive meditation, and circumstances that evoke strong emotions are potentially dangerous. Among Tibetans living in Dharamsala, many seemed to think that counseling that is comprised of talking about past traumatic events could *cause* illness.

In the West, a highly bound, discrete, and intact "self" is one of the hallmarks of emotional health (Scheper-Hughes and Lock 1987). Traumatic memories that threaten to disrupt the cohesion or continuity of self are considered to be indicative of psychopathology and thus require repair. But from a Tibetan Buddhist perspective, clinging to the notion that there *is* a fundamentally cohesive self is actually a foundational cause of ill health and suffering. While psychotherapy patients in the Global North are largely coached to see mental illness as "just another illness" such as diabetes or heart disease, Tibetans encourage one another to see mental distress as no big deal. This approach is purposeful in that Tibetans believe a person will recover much faster if they do not see their distress as insurmountable.

Inklings of this way of thinking can be found within pockets of biomedical researchers and clinicians, who question whether thinking about mental illness as chronic is helpful. For example, proponents of recovery-oriented mental health argue that contrary to common belief, it is possible to recover from schizophrenia and other serious mental illnesses. Tanya Luhrmann and colleagues (2015) demonstrate how Americans, in particular, understand experiences such as hearing voices as symptoms of an intractable and lifelong brain disease from which they could not recover. Some studies suggest that communicating to people (particularly youth) that they face lifelong disability will be deeply disempowering (Lewis, Hopper, and Healion 2012; Whitley and Siantz 2012), perhaps stalling recovery.

In this way, clinicians who believe their patients' distress results from chronic mental illness may give subtle cues that reinforce disability rather than promoting recovery (Von Peter 2010). Although a compelling argument is made that under the recovery rubric those who do not recover may experience a kind of neoliberal moral blaming (Myers 2015), those who expect their distress to be chronic may indeed come to live out this prophecy. This is partly why the Tibetan case is compelling, in that they very purposefully strive to prevent mental distress from solidifying into chronic illness. Letting go, cultivating flexibility, and thinking that others are even worse off are skillful and purposeful ways of resisting chronicity.

Counseling and other talk therapies are ubiquitous within biomedicine. Many NGOs and other organizations developing international interventions aim to integrate so-called traditional or local medicine with biomedical approaches (Ager 1997). As shown above with the USAID-funded torture survivor's program and their pledge to incorporate "indigenous treatment methods" and "spiritual healing sessions" into mental health treatment programs, this kind of synergy may look innovative from the perspective of global health programs. Yet Tibetans in Dharamsala do not need spiritual healing sessions at foreign-run medical centers. The presumption that incorporating "indigenous methods" into biomedical forms of treatment will make them relevant is commonplace across the global health landscape, revealing deep ethnocentrism.

The problem is that these approaches fail to appreciate that sometimes the practice of counseling *itself* may have only limited cultural utility. As within other contexts, family members, friends, and other loved ones are usually involved in healing rituals; therefore, the sterile and "professional" clinical practices of psychotherapy may be unnerving (see Calabrese 2008 and Del Vecchio Good et al. 1994 for discussion on Euro-American bias toward one-to-one clinical dyads). Many mental health programs that are developed for (not by) Tibetans seem to view culture as a vexing variable that needs to be moderated and accounted for.

Anthropologists have described similar phenomena elsewhere. For example, in his study of international mental health aid in Kobe, Japan, following the earthquake, Breslau (2000) describes how foreign mental health professionals encouraged the practices of testimony and debriefing, despite the dissonance with local concepts of recovery. Likewise, McKinney (2007) found that among mental health services in the United States and Denmark aimed at helping survivors of political violence from around the world, the dominate form of therapeutics seemed to be helping people find their "trauma story." It is assumed, she argues, "that every client holds some sort of traumatic memory, a memory that by definition disrupts the continuity of identity or self" (2007, 270). While biomedical perspectives portray the acts of telling, processing, debriefing, and testifying as inherently therapeutic, they are antithetical to Tibetan notions of healthy coping.

An example of a project that took great care to think through local cultural concepts, and yet ultimately dismantled, was the Transcultural Psychosocial Organisation (TPO), established in Dharamsala in 1995. The TPO (now known as HealthNet TPO) is a Dutch organization that has worked across the world (in Nepal, Uganda, Cambodia, Lesotho, Thailand) to help train and empower people to set up mental health systems in settings where they do not yet exist. Their mission is to merge evidence-based interventions with "local knowledge." Indeed, they spent four years engaging various stakeholders in Dharamsala with the intention to work collaboratively to plan and implement a mental health program. The group conducted a needs assessment by interviewing community members about whether or not they thought mental health services would be beneficial for those with mental illness (Ketzer and Crescenzi 2002). An immediate limitation is that depending on how the researchers conveyed it, the term *sems kyi na tsa* (mental illness) might have been understood by interview participants to refer to psychosis. Other less severe problems are not necessarily categorized as mental illness (Mercer, Ager, and Ruwanpura 2005). Whereas many Tibetans in Dharamsala responded to the needs assessment indicating that people with mental illness could benefit from services, it remains unclear if they were responding to the questions that the researchers assumed they were asking. Culturally, Tibetans sometimes find it rude to say "no," further complicating the reliability of interviews (something I also had to contend with as a qualitative researcher).

The objective of the TPO project in Dharamsala was to integrate Tibetan cultural beliefs into Western-style counseling, using a complimentary approach. They spent approximately two years translating and back-translating the Harvard Trauma Questionnaire into Tibetan so they could assess symptoms of PTSD. The idea was that this instrument could be used at the refugee reception center in Dharamsala so those in need of mental health services could be identified on arrival. The TPO trained a number of Tibetan nurses, health outreach workers, and other community leaders (Ketzer and Crescenzi 2002). Before the foreign team left Dharamsala, they conducted more community interviews and reported that locals found the initiative very helpful. The program did not continue, however. During my time in the field, I located some of the Tibetan individuals who had been involved in the project. They identified two major problems: (1) the foreign researchers did not take seriously enough their assertions that many people visit lamas and would not think to visit the Department of Health for problems with mental distress; and (2) psychotherapy itself, that is, sitting one-on-one with a professional talking about one's problems was not seen as helpful.

The failure with the TPO and similar programs is not merely a problem of East versus West. In Dharamsala, many people quite happily and without conflict utilize the Delek Hospital (a biomedical clinic) and the *mentsikhang* (Tibetan medicine clinic), often in tandem. "*Bod smen* [Tibetan medicine]) is good"; "foreign *smen* is good!" many say. The issue here is not with Western clinical practice per se, but with categorization. There are some kinds of mental distress for which Tibetans seek the help of a lama and might be concurrent with a medical problem, such as a *rlung* disorder. In these instances, Tibetans visit both lamas and Tibetan medicine practitioners without problem. However, no one would think to visit the Delek Hospital, where they go for antibiotics, obstetric care, and chest X-rays.[1] When I asked Tibetan friends and neighbors if anyone ever goes to the Delek Hospital for *sems kyi na tsa* (mental illness) I received strange looks. "No, you should visit a lama first, and maybe an *amchi*," was the standard answer. "Why would they go to the hospital for pills?" asked a young woman named Lhamo. "The problem is the mind."

At this time, psychotropic drugs are not being used in Dharamsala. However, a Canadian physician who was volunteering at the Delek Hospital for three months revealed that the hospital pharmacy contained several dozen boxes of expired medication, including antipsychotics and SSRIs (selective serotonin reuptake inhibitor). For some years, the hospital has been a recipient of aid from a nonprofit organization, which included medical supplies, such as bandages and stethoscopes, along with discarded medications of various sorts. The medications that were not stocked at the pharmacy were put into a back storage room. The Canadian physician discovered several boxes containing Haldol, Prozac, and Paxil; *but we don't use those*, he was told with a shrug. It seems that there was not a strong ideological opposition, but rather a sense of indifference among the Tibetan clinicians (including Tibetan clinicians with Western medical degrees). With time, it will be important to investigate whether programs like the USAID-funded torture survivor's program and other NGO-funded programs introduce psychiatric concepts and practices with any long-lasting effect.

The Veracity of Suffering

A prominent feature of the cultural landscape in Dharamsala is the Tibetan resistance movement—one that has become diverse in its ideology since it began in 1959. Political posters are strewn around town and local cafes host talks with ex–political prisoners aimed at educating foreign travelers. At these talks, Tibetans give graphic accounts of their imprisonment, rallying support for the Tibetan cause. As Vincanne Adams asserts, "firsthand accounts 'count' for everything in human rights discourse" (1998, 82). But the Tibetan experience of suffering is in many cases inconsistent with human rights discourse (Adams 1998; Lewis 2013), particularly insofar as cultural beliefs such as karma shape the experience of difficult life events. The newly garnered testimony practices that feature the trauma narrative among Tibetan political activists appear in stark contrast with the customs of everyday life.

Inside of GuChuSum, the community organization started by and for ex–political prisoners, one finds the walls covered by gruesome photographs of torture victims and corpses—bloodied and disfigured. These images displayed as proof for visitors ask them to bear witness to the bloodshed; they also galvanize political sensibilities within the community. Many who run the organization and hang the photos are themselves former political prisoners. Similar photographs are displayed at the new arrivals center where the

Tibetan government-in-exile provides medical services and housing for newly arrived refugees. With ongoing protest marches, candlelight vigils, and political signs plastered around town, Tibetans arrive to Dharamsala already marked as political refugees. This identity is both elaborated and confirmed by human rights paradigms.

And yet it is not self-evident how to define a political refugee: by others or for oneself. As in slums where residents described as squatters do not identify themselves as such—squatters are those who are much worse off (Walker 2013)—many Tibetans do not self-identify as political refugees and survivors of trauma. In general, people emphasize a traumatic past only when speaking in a politicized forum. Because political prisoners, activists, and those who self-immolate for Tibet are seen as heroic, it is somewhat arrogant to claim that one has survived severe torture or imprisonment. The utterance of "it wasn't so bad for me, others had it much worse" was a common idiom among those with histories of imprisonment. However, some of the same individuals who warned me about the psychological dangers of talking about past suffering and identifying too strongly with mental distress, elaborated lengthy narratives in other contexts for political aims. Talking at length and debriefing about suffering may not be of much therapeutic use; however, activists realize the potential power of affect within political spheres.

Although the veracity of torture and human rights abuses need not be questioned, there are some researchers who find evidence of exaggeration within the exile community. For example, Shannon Ward (2013) in her study of discourses of reproductive practices found that Tibetans in exile have not shifted their actual practices but rather their narratives about reproduction. She describes how many young women discussed reproduction in terms of their "right" to bear children, which is seen as resistance to Chinese control of their bodies. While forced abortions and sterilization are not typical, discourses circulate within the exile community (reciprocally perpetuated by exile members and foreign human rights activists), which suggest that such practices are commonplace (Ward 2013). Such studies on exaggeration do not necessarily diminish the severity of the Tibetan political situation; rather, they reveal how exile members use their newfound political citizenship.

Narrative and cinematic representations of traumatic events—what Pandolfo calls "biographical artifacts" (2008a)—are integral to the construction of evidence. Such evidence is important because there is so much at stake, not only in terms of "enabling, or disabling idioms within larger logics of the state, as grounds of appeal, compensation, recognition, or inclusion" (Pandolfo 2008a, 65), but in deploying strategies of power. When sharing my work with other academics, they often want to know: are Tibetans *really* resilient, or are they *really* suffering? The tendency to search for the authentic story, what is *really* going on, reveals not only an unwillingness to appreciate the multiplicity of concerns people may have on personal and political levels; it also reveals something unique about Tibetan forms of resilience themselves. The tendency among Tibetans to focus personal recovery on quickly letting go of past hardship and not dwelling on the past, and to simultaneously elaborate chronic and intractable suffering for global consumption, presents a certain conundrum to researchers in how to make sense of seeming contradiction.

In ethnography, translation is always a practice of alterity (Gardiner 1996; Taussig 1992). To take seriously the voices of my interlocutors and to practice an ethical sort of writing, I allow for multiple kinds of truths to exist simultaneously. I recognize that my position as a researcher shaped the stories people shared (and those they did not). A middle-aged Tibetan man once told me that his "greatest suffering in life" was in his youth. He was born to a nomad family in Amdo and early in the morning before sunrise, he and his two older brothers had to begin herding the family's yaks. Because he was the youngest, his brothers made him walk in front so he would get all the morning dew and they would stay dry. "Every day," he said forlornly, "my *chupa* [Tibetan garment] would be so wet. It was very uncomfortable." He went on to tell me that he came to Dharamsala to "study the precious Dharma." I found this interview to be quite sweet. But later, my research assistant said: "Maybe that guy did not want to tell you about his life. Everyone knows that he left Tibet because he killed someone."

The question of truth is a concern for both qualitative and quantitative researchers across disciplines. There are numerous forms of reliability and validity tests as well as methodological procedures for managing social desirability bias. But ethnographers take a complex stance on such concerns (Yanos and Hopper 2008). We tend to be curious and view it as useful data when people say different things to different audiences. Sometimes people who are interviewed find the experience to be therapeutic; do such instances make those data any more or less reliable than instances when interviewees feel uncomfortable? This "peripheral vision and peripheral listening" (Pandolfo 2008a) may reveal important details of study participants' inner worlds as well as how certain kinds of discourse are used intentionally for particular social aims.

In a psychiatric ward in Morocco, a woman who has been admitted asks Stefania Pandolfo (2008a) to interview her. Although she is a known "mad woman," she proclaims that she wants to be married and have a normal life. By stating her intention, tape recorded by a foreign researcher, this somehow solidifies and authenticates the desire. It becomes public and official. Elsewhere, in Brazil, a woman named Catarina used her (now well-known) notebook, and subsequently Biehl's critical ethnography (2005) to empower her own (disempowered) voice. I found something similar. Whereas I assumed it would make Tibetans in Dharamsala nervous to learn that my work may be published, I found that instead it made people more likely to speak with me.

Many Tibetans, and particularly women, were somewhat shy and reticent to be interviewed. The major source of hesitation was that they were "not an expert." I explained that I was interested in the lived experiences of everyday people; however, this was rarely convincing. My fieldwork in this regard paralleled Charlene Makley's (2005), whose interlocutors in Tibet spoke to her about the past at great length, over meals and on walks in the village; and yet they vehemently declined her requests for formal interviews. It was not because they did not want to speak to her, but because they resisted formalized testimony.

Unlike what I anticipated, when I explained what I would do with the information, specifically that it would be published, many changed their minds about participating in formal interviews. There were two reasons for their eagerness. Many Tibetans believe that they are, in fact, more resilient than other refugee communities. When I explained that the articles or books I intended to write might be read by researchers working with other refugee groups around the world, many became enthusiastic about sharing their experiences and seemed to drop earlier concerns about expertise. Second, some saw participation in the study as an opportunity to testify—to express publicly "what is really happening in Tibet." Their desire to act as political subjects seemed to supersede their usual resistance to testimony.

Dekyi

In my first interaction with Dekyi, the mother of the *tulku* (incarnate lama) who cried during much of our first meeting, she asked about my parents and whether they were worried about me living in India. I said that they were, but that my mother had recently come to visit and we had the chance to meet the Dalai Lama together at his residence. I opened my laptop computer to show her a photograph of our meeting. She was overcome with emotion. In seeing the photograph of my mother, she remarked, "Very clean, bright face. Very white! *Sonam chenpo dug* [great merit, very fortunate]." Dekyi was not referring to the actual whiteness of my mother's skin. Rather, many Tibetans explain that a person who is suffering tends to have a very dark appearance. It is also said that a dark tongue or darkened face is an ominous sign of death. A bright or white appearance is not as much about the color of one's face, but rather a comment about its radiance and vitality. "Very good virtue. Very good merit," she repeated.

I asked Dekyi why she decided to come to India. Her eyes again filled with tears. She had not let go of my hand. Back in Tibet, she was diagnosed with kidney problems and had been in and out of the hospital. In addition, she has many problems with *rlung* (inner winds) that seems to exacerbate her poor health. Dekyi describes flatly that she is not expected to live a long life. *What can I do?* she asks, rhetorically. She tells me that she had had a very difficult life. She came from a farming family and as a child they never had enough money. As a young woman, she had lost two children, one in childbirth and one to illness. But she did have some fortune in her life. Her youngest son was recognized as a *tulku*, and once he was enthroned at their small monastery, she did not have to worry about putting food on the table. She attributes all of this to her karma. Dekyi left Tibet to be closer to her son and wants to spend the remainder of her life making religious pilgrimages to Buddhist sites in India. She also came to meet the Dalai Lama. "It is okay that I suffered so much in this life," she says. "Going into my next life will be better because those karmic seeds have burned. It is the same with people who are imprisoned. Not everyone gets caught, you know. It is also their karma, so it makes sense [why some people face misfortune]." It may be difficult to accept, but there is a sense of order behind what happens. Very little is considered "unfair," let alone inexplicable or baffling.

One might then ask: How is it that Tibetans can at once believe that something is *unjust* but not *unfair*? The system of karma does not lead Tibetans to believe that they deserve their suffering in a punitive sense, but that no one comes to their life's circumstances by chance. In this way, oppressors and those they oppress are enmeshed in an intimate karmic entanglement. As Vincanne Adams describes, Tibetan political prisoners are "as concerned with the effects of karma on their oppressors, their actions on all living beings, their next lives, turning their enemy into their greatest teacher, and freeing all living beings from suffering, as they are with making sense of their experience in the terms of the United Nations or Geneva Convention" (1998, 93). The conviction that what happens in one's life—even torture and imprisonment—is spiritually justified presents somewhat of an epistemological dilemma for Tibetan political activists who need to demonstrate that human rights abuses have led to chronic suffering. Despite the ways that global human rights discourses may come into conflict with Tibetan understandings of violence, they have used a newfound technocratic savvy to enter the global stage.

Tibetan political activists create and circulate particular narratives that emphasize trauma and the violation of human rights in a variety of ways. They create political pop music lyrics and videos, produce YouTube videos, post on Twitter, and participate in formal international human rights forums such as Amnesty International and Human Rights Watch. Grassroots organizations such as Students for a Free Tibet have been instrumental in documenting arrests and prison sentences, naming and making public those who are convicted.

Music, Media, and "Telling Trauma"

Organizations such as the International Campaign for Tibet maintain a celebrity support base, which is an important aspect of successful human rights–based campaigns; this one in particular has been supported by the Beastie Boys and the actor Richard Gere, who converted to Tibetan Buddhism. The nonprofits that depend on foreign donations raise money for education, health care, and infrastructure support (many locals in Dharamsala told me that Richard Gere had personally financed the community dumpsters and garbage trucks that came through town on a weekly basis). Justification for fund-raising is necessarily linked with rendering this population as a group of political refugees escaping human rights abuses. As Nora Kenworthy (2014) has argued in another context, the global Product RED campaign is predicated on snazzy celebrity endorsement, rendering certain causes noble and legitimate in the eyes of consumer-donors in the West who wish to help. Similarly, the Richard Gere–endorsed organization has been instrumental in keeping Tibet on the map, both literally and figuratively, in an array of competitively worthy global causes. The pop-up window on the home page for International Campaign for Tibet prompts prospective donors to give with slogans such as "Don't Let China Wipe Tibet Off the Map. Save Tibet for Generations to Come" (accessed June 21, 2017). The website also publishes a series of prisoner files, like this one below:

> Name: Tsering Tsomo (F), nun, 27
> Sentence: 2 years
> Details: On June 8, 2008, public security officials in the seat of Drango (Chinese: Luhuo) county, Kardze (Ganzi) TAP, Sichuan province, beat and detained a nun who staged a peaceful solo protest. At approximately 9:00 a.m., nun Tsering Tsomo (or Tsering Tso), aged 27, of Samtenling nunnery (Watag nunnery) began distributing leaflets and shouting slogans calling for Tibetan freedom and the Dalai Lama's return to Tibet. Security officials kicked, punched, and beat her with rods before taking her to the county detention center, according to a report by the Tibetan Center for Human Rights and Democracy (TCHRD). Later the same day, more than 200 Samtenling nuns attempted to march to the county government offices to protest Tsering Tsomo's detention, but security forces allegedly blocked the nuns and then beat and detained "scores" of them. No information is available about their current whereabouts. The Luhuo County People's Court later sentenced Tsering Tsomo to two years in prison on unknown charges.

Publishing and circulating prison files with names, times, dates, and places provides proof and justification for the resistance movement. The act of writing as a form of resistance happens on a smaller scale as well. As Palden from the Yak Café says, "I tell ex–political prisoners who just arrive that they need to write an account of what happened in Tibet." He implored me to do the same: "Sara-la, if you hear of someone who died because of the Tibet issue, you need to write it down and share the stories with other Americans. This is very important to achieve our aims."

As Tibetan youth seek to join the resistance movement, new forms of protest using social media, music, and video have come under Chinese scrutiny. A handful of Tibetan pop stars have been arrested since 2008, such as Tashi Dondrup, whose album "Torture without Trace" was banned in the PRC, landing him a year and seven months in prison. Another singer, Lo Lo, was arrested in 2012 for writing songs that called for the return of the Dalai Lama to Tibet. Many pop singers are careful not to criticize the PRC, but instead skate on the thin edge of "separatism," lamenting the loss of traditional Tibetan customs and culture (Diehl 2002). The immense popularity of VCD (video compact discs) give singers an emotionally heightened platform to circulate political discourse; even some monasteries have begun producing them in attempts to propagate Buddhist values among youth (Gayley 2016). Some pop stars adopt a stereotyped Western rock look with leather jackets and spikey hair. Others, particularly women singers, wear formal Tibetan dress, but in their videos all seem to feature a monolithic background with scenes of yaks out on the Tibetan plateau, footage of traditional prayer festivals and horse races, images of devoted older people prostrating, and the Dalai Lama's abandoned Potala Palace that is now draped with red Chinese banners.

The soulful youth sing for the return of a culture they fear losing. Indeed, when I lived in Dharamsala I spent most evenings with Tibetan friends watching the VCDs that people swapped with one another around town. The guys who worked at the Yak Café shared an old hand-me-down iPad left by an American girlfriend and used the cafe's Wi-Fi to watch YouTube videos of stars like Sherten sing "Protecting Mother Grassland," or "I Dreamt Panchen Lama" by Yardong. The Panchen Lama is the incarnate lama who was kidnapped by the Chinese government as a young child and has not been seen since. Whereas Yardong's music is ostensibly about devotion to a religious lama, it is coded to signal resistance and to galvanize allegiance to Tibetans' endangered culture. Likewise, songs like "Mother's Tsampa" by Lobsang Tashi and "Missing Lhasa" by Pemsi and Tenzin Seungyi coach their peers to resist the draw to materialistic and worldly things in exile culture and implore one another to listen to their parents and grandparents back in Tibet who are seen as morally superior. The Buddhist revitalization that is sweeping across the Tibetan plateau is at once a call for spiritual, cultural, and political agency in the face of an oppressive regime.

Watching music videos allow residents in Dharamsala to both consume and perform their Tibetanness, a category that begs defending not just inside Tibet, but to one another in exile. Pop music is shared and adored by both the laity and their monastic neighbors. As religion scholar Holly Gayley asserts, "In monastery-produced VCDs, a new technology is being harnessed not only to revitalize the traditional centrality of devotion in Tibetan Buddhism but also—through advice to the laity and asserting Tibetan identity in Buddhist terms—to address distinctively modern issues as Tibetan society undergoes rapid change under Chinese rule" (2016, 44). Within Tibetan Buddhism, monasticism is more highly integrated into everyday communal life than outsiders may imagine. Monasteries and nunneries are often at the center of village life, and when people choose a monastic career, they continue to interact with their friends and relatives, even if they live inside the monastery walls. Very few choose a more renunciant path that involves meditating in remote caves or retreat huts. And within the political life of Tibet, monastics have long played a prominent role in politics. The Tibetan government-in-exile's parliament of forty-five members created two seats each for representatives of the four schools of Tibetan Buddhism as well as the pre-Buddhist Bön religion. As of 2017, the speaker is a *khenpo*, a monk with a high degree from a monastic college. In addition, monks and nuns are often among the most radical in their political activities, including those who choose to self-immolate for a Free Tibet.

Self-Immolations

During my fieldwork between 2011 and 2012, nearly forty Tibetans set themselves on fire to protest the Chinese occupation of Tibet. It is estimated that between 2009 and 2018, there have been over 150 self-immolations in total. Self-immolation as a form of protest is new to Tibet (McGranahan and Litzenger 2012; Shakya 2012), and one that escalated rapidly following the 2008 crackdown and subsequent mass protests across the Tibetan Plateau. As Charlene Makley argues, "State efforts to erase the deaths of protesters in 2008 in fact helped unleash the specter of the Maoist dead, raising again moral questions about painful complicities that haunted all Tibetan elders and their kin" (2015, 457). That is, once protesters' bodies were disappeared, the complicit and resentful silence among Tibetans not to discuss violent histories bubbled to the surface, breaking literally into flames. Self-immolation protests are not an expression of individual anguish, but of cultural grief.

Most of the immolators have been monks and nuns (including a *tulku*, incarnate lama); students and laymen and laywomen with families immolate as well. Many believe these acts will alert the international community to the severity of suffering within Tibet; once people know, they say, of course they will help. And yet, *Time Magazine* called the immolations in Tibet the number-one underreported story of 2011 (cited in McGranahan and Litzinger 2012).

On March 26, 2012, a young Tibetan student named Jamphel Yeshi set himself on fire during a protest in New Delhi just hours before the Indian government welcomed Chinese president Hu Jintao for a visit. And unlike in the restricted area of Amdo where most of the previous immolations occurred, hundreds of bystanders, including reporters for Reuters Press, captured the horrific images that went viral. Images such as the one below were almost immediately printed on large banners and hung throughout town in Dharamsala. Tibetan shopkeepers closed their stands and joined the hundreds of monks, nuns, and students who began to gather outside the Dalai Lama's temple. Although there had already been thirty or forty immolations that year, this one, which occurred on the streets of New Delhi, struck a wounded chord in the heart of Dharamsala residents because it happened in India.

Word traveled quickly that Jamphel Yeshi's body was on its way to Dharamsala. When the corpse arrived early in the morning on March 30, a group of middle-aged Tibetan men drove motorcycles through town. One held a megaphone and announced loudly that the *mi rigs kyi dba-wo* (national hero) was inside the Dalai Lama's temple. I lived along a steep path that wove past Jamyang Choling Nunnery and Kirti Monastery; the shortcut to the main temple tucked away from tourist hotels was a quiet respite from the honking cars of Indian taxis below. Not walking with anyone in particular, I joined my Tibetan neighbors making their way up and over the path down to the Dalai Lama's temple where townspeople and monastics were already filing in. A group of *ama-la* (honorific term for mother or woman) handed out *bag leb* (homemade bread), and some monks poured Tibetan tea from huge metal teapots, as is customary during religious teachings.

The slow-moving line into the temple was somber. Many grasped a *mala* (prayer beads) in their hands, quietly mouthing *om mani padme hum*, the mantra of compassion. As we moved from the courtyard and upstairs to the main *tsuglakhang* (temple), rows of school children stood quietly in their blue and green uniforms as if waiting for morning assembly. I learned later that this was the first time a corpse had been brought to the Dalai Lama's temple. While political activity is generally discouraged inside the complex, today seemed an exception. Hundreds of Tibetans came, one by one, to offer a *khatag* (ceremonial silk scarf), which are typically offered to high lamas or other dignitaries. There were two monks standing by who periodically had to clear the towering stack of *khatags* off the coffin that was draped with the Tibetan flag, military style.

Eight or nine parliament members arrived and there were a number of speeches commending the boy for his heroism. The sentiments were echoed in news articles such as "Tibet Self-Immolation Is the Highest Form of Non-Violent Struggle" (*Tibet Post* 2013), which proliferate Tibetan popular views. The article and others like it emphasize that "the self-immolators have not harmed a single Chinese person but have simply voiced their protest" (*Tibet Post* 2013); those who self-immolate are seen rather uncritically as selfless heroes. But within the PRC, the silence was deafening. As Kevin Carrico (2012) points out, "Even the *Global Times* (Huanqiu shibao), known for its characteristically outspoken state-nationalist viewpoint, seems to have stumbled in search of words to characterize [self-immolations], claiming in an odd editorial that there is 'no need to sweat over minor unrest.'" The reports that came out of China tended to dismiss the Tibetans as hooligans propagating treasonous rhetoric as part of the "Dalai Clique"; some reports claim that immolations are orchestrated by the Dalai Lama himself.

Despite the relative silence from the international community, many Tibetans across the globe seem to believe, unequivocally, that the horrific acts will capture the attention of the rest of the world, justifying a life lost. It is also assumed that the motivation for taking one's own life for the benefit of the Tibetan cause is always noble. Although suicide within the *vinaya*, Buddhism's moral code of ethics, is clearly forbidden and thought to propel a person into a hell realm, the residents of Dharamsala see self-immolation as distinct from suicide. In fact, it is seen as an act that leads to a good rebirth because of the tremendous merit (good karma) accrued. Indeed, my friend Yangzom was emphatic that self-immolations are wholly distinct from suicides.

"This is different. It is not a suicide." She explained that when people are so anguished they want to die, their negative state of mind at death brings them to a hell realm.

"Your state of mind at death will tell you what your next life will be like," she says. Someone who is so generous, brave, and selfless to give their own life serves as evidence that they are not ordinary people. Great beings, like bodhisattvas (*jangchub sems-pa*) who work tirelessly for the benefit of other sentient beings will accumulate tremendous merit and will not be reborn in a lower realm. Those who self-immolate are greatly admired and are seen to possess great virtue.

During this time, many Tibetans with whom I spoke about the immolations told me a story about the Buddha's previous life from the Jataka Tales, where he allegedly gave his body to a tigress to feed her cubs. This parallel is evoked both by scholars of Tibet who make such connections (Craig 2012b; Gyatso 2012) and among ordinary Tibetans who point out that offering one's body is a deep form of generosity and evidence of the great merit and realization that a person must possess to accomplish such a feat. In this way, they are lauded as cultural heroes and spiritual warriors.

Just three months before Jamphel Yeshe self-immolated in New Delhi, I was in Bodhgaya for the Kalachakra Initiation given by the Dalai Lama, a ten-day Vajrayana group practice that empowers practitioners to perform a tantric practice. With more than three hundred thousand people crammed together in the tiny streets of Bodhgaya, the place where the historical Buddha sat underneath the Bodhi tree, it was impossible to walk down the street without slowly trudging forward pressed up against a wall of people. Working my way through the crowd, I felt my mobile phone vibrating. It was a text message from my Tibetan research assistant: "Sara-la, I met one monk, same county as me in Tibet, he try to self-immolate before in Nepal. You want to interview?"

I made my way through the crowded street to the stupa where we agreed to meet. Thousands of people were doing *khora*, circumambulating around the huge *chörten*[2] (stupa). Despite the mass of people, it felt calm and serene, unlike the street. I found my assistant and we continued walking the *khora* while we waited for the monk to arrive. My assistant said: "He is, um, a little bit, maybe *nyönpa* [crazy]. He is a little bit funny," using a mix of English and Tibetan to convey his discomfort. I asked him to say more. My assistant was silent and seemed uncomfortable. "Well, he is a monk. But we don't know. Maybe he wants to change." This is a euphemism for saying he suspects that the monk wants to sleep with women (meaning he would no longer be a monk); it can also mean that he is already sleeping with women but continues to wear robes. Although giving up monastic vows is shameful as an adult,[3] it certainly does not make one *nyönpa*. I pressed my assistant. "Well, he . . . we don't know his intention. Those who self-immolate for Tibet, they have very pure hearts." It seemed incommensurate to him that someone who attempts self-immolation might not have the purest of values.

We managed to find the monk in the crowd and walked out to a grassy area, moving slowly because he walked with a cane, and we found a log on which to sit. After chatting for a bit, he lifted his robes to show me the burns scarred on his extremities.

"I did it. I was on fire," he said. "The Tibetan people nearby tried to shield me so I could continue to burn when the Nepali police stormed in to extinguish the flames." There are a number of established Tibetan communities near Kathmandu. The monk, who lived in a nearby monastery went to the heart of a Tibetan neighborhood near a sacred stupa to perform his immolation. The townspeople shielded him to support his heroic act, but he was quickly extinguished by police who often linger near the stupa, and then transported to the state hospital in Kathmandu.

I asked, "What happened next?" He described how after a few weeks, recovery in the state hospital he was sponsored by the Tibetan government-in-exile in Dharamsala to be moved from Nepal to India. He spent two months in the Delek Hospital in Dharamsala recovering from the burns, where he was given a special room. Many visitors, including important lamas, came to see him. When I asked why he chose to self-immolate, he looked at me as if it were obvious: "We need to show the world our suffering. Tibetans can no longer withstand this oppression." In this way, there is a certain irony that individual citizens willingly take on an unthinkable pain for the greater social good.

Although there is no specific historical tradition of self-immolation in Tibet, religion scholar Janet Gyatso (2012) points out that a parallel may be drawn to other instances of spiritual virtuosos withstanding pain—evidence of their superior qualities and the power of Buddhism. Specifically, Gyatso calls to mind the Tibetan tradition of *gtum'mo* where highly practiced yogis withstand freezing conditions wearing only thin, cotton robes by generating intense inner heat through meditation. These practitioners survive sometimes for years—even decades—in icy, Himalayan cave retreats. Such practices, accomplished through sustained purity and discipline (Gyatso 2012), serve as inspiration for lay Tibetans. Generating this remarkable inner fire was not an end in itself, but rather an indication of a highly realized person. My impression of the monk I met who attempted self-immolation was somewhat neutral. He did not strike me as remarkable (unlike some other practitioners with whom I conducted interviews); he also did not strike me as *nyönpa* (crazy), as my Tibetan assistant asserted. It seems to be his ordinariness, juxtaposed with the extraordinary acts that only a highly selfless person could accomplish, that created the uncanny feeling of doubt among his Tibetan peers. The speculation that he might have broken his vow of chastity only further exposes his ordinary human character.

Although it seems at first glance that all Tibetans are uncritical of the immolations and believe that it will help their political cause, there are those who condemn these acts. A notable voice is that of the seventeenth Karmapa (head of the Karma Kagyu school), who published an open letter denouncing the immolations; other high lamas have also come forward emphasizing that such acts do not uphold the sanctity of life (Makley 2012). Some criticize the Dalai Lama for not doing the same. When asked directly in a series of interviews, he stated he was in a difficult position. Although he does not encourage the immolations, he remarked that the friends and families of those who immolated might be upset if he speaks out against them.

Numerous scholars of Tibet have tried to make sense of this new form of protest. Many argue that the self-immolations are different from other political suicides, such as suicide bombing, in important ways. Rather than an act of terror meant to scare, they are seen instead as "horror intended to induce empathy" (Shakya 2012). The body is not a weapon, but a medium for communication (Makley 2012). As my friend Yangzom explained to me, "suicide means that you want to die; or at least you don't want to live." Here, it is precisely *because* the activist is able to put the Tibetan cause before his or her desire to live that they are heroic. From this vantage point, those who let go of "self-cherishing" are spiritually superior and worthy of admiration. "As understood by Tibetans, self-immolation constitutes a moral act, a refusal of the Chinese presence, and a sacrifice of the individual for the collective" (McGranahan 2016b). To exemplify this, McGranahan cites the words of Lama Soba, a *tulku* who self-immolated in 2012: "I'm giving my body as an offering of light to chase away the darkness, to free all beings from suffering" (International Campaign for Tibet, cited in McGranahan 2016b, 339). Here, Tibetans not only refuse to accept their occupation, but the framing of self-immolation in religious terms constitutes a refusal that is even more brash:

they cannot control my will to offer, to help other sentient beings, and to fight for what is just.

It may be precisely because of the inaction of the international community that Tibetans have resorted to this radical form of protest. For without international attention, their resistance campaign cannot flourish. As an older man named Dhondrup explained:

> When I was in prison, I was tortured very badly. As my body is composed of flesh and blood, it is sure that I would have had pain. But I felt very proud that I experienced this suffering for Tibetan people. Generally, when I was in prison, I felt worried and suffered a lot. But as I felt great encouragement and a sense of nationalism I didn't feel too upset. Sometimes when relatives come to visit prisoners and deliver food, they would say that the American government supports the Tibetan issue, so maybe you will be released soon. Or, maybe soon the problem will be solved. And then I would feel very happy and experience great hope that I might be released. But I came to India almost eighteen years ago; inside Tibet, people still experience great suffering. When I think about prisoners experiencing this hardship, I feel very sad. Also, I recall everything that happened in prison [he cries and stops speaking for some time]. Most difficult in my life is when I remember the Tibetan people who are in prison right now. This is my greatest source of suffering. My hope or wish is that people around the world will see the truth of the Tibet issue and help us to liberate those in prison. I don't have anything else to say.

Refusal in Dharamsala

In this chapter, I articulate a cultural paradox and dilemma where on the one hand Tibetans in Dharamsala argue a person exposed to traumatic events should see what happened as illusory and use their suffering as a way to generate compassion for others. Cultural wisdom suggests they should resist chronicity and cultivate a big mind to recover and move on. Yet they understand that such sentiments will not fuel a successful resistance movement worthy of global attention. What I found, however, is that this dilemma remains largely unresolved—not because a solution has yet to be found, but because of flexible thinking. I argue that the cultural reticence to construct fixed narratives of the past, which sits alongside cultural savvy to use trauma narratives to galvanize global sympathy, reveals epistemologies that are at once multiple, flexible, and fluid, as well as highly pragmatic in the world.

Theories that elucidate an anthropology of refusal is a way to make sense of such seeming contradictions. When Audra Simpson's Mohawk interlocutors expressed repeatedly, "no one seems to know," when asked pointed questions about the limits of citizenship and belonging, she came to read such utterances ("it is enough; what I have said is enough") as a refusal to comply with a set of codes and parameters embedded in a settler-colonial framework they resist. In her writing, Simpson as an ethnographer, and as a member of the community in which she works, refuses "to tell the story of their struggle. But [she consents] to telling the story of their constraint" (2016, 328). As an outsider in Dharamsala, my decisions about what to write and how to portray resilience and struggle were not straightforward. Many Tibetans seemed proud of the ways their culture cultivated resilience, noting that their practices of compassion were special and unique. They hoped what I wrote would inspire other refugee populations. And at the same time, my interlocutors would implore and encourage me: "Tell them it is bad. Tell them how much Tibetans suffer."

Whereas part of the story I hope to tell in this book is how a community may demonstrate resilience alongside suffering—and that resilience and suffering are not either-or experiences, it seems that Tibetan activists came to worry that their stories of resilience may diminish their deservingness of help and even their status as a refugee population. Here, they quietly sought to see distress as illusory, whereas on the public stage they emphasized its severity and chronicity.

I observed many Tibetans speak in different ways at different times, not only to different audiences but even within the same interview. For instance, a monk named Sherab at the beginning of our interview explained how the best thing a person can do is to minimize how bad they think their problems are, which would only make things worse. And in that same interview when I asked him to describe his first few days in India, he said:

> Due to the restrictions and destruction in the monastery, which caused me a lot of problems and suffering, I left Serta Monastery and came to India. Myself, and my friend arrived in India's capital, Delhi, from Tibet and a human rights center organized a press conference. At that time, journalists from about thirty different countries came, including CNN and BBC journalists. During

this press conference, myself and my friend got to express our experiences of the restrictions and destruction in the monastery and the real situation in Tibet. Additionally, the photos and video we had were put on display, which meant that the whole world could see the torture and merciless destruction taking place. I took many risks coming from Tibet, but I felt it was worthwhile to show the world what is happening there and how profound our suffering is.

I read this seeming contradiction through the theoretical lens of "refusal," where cultural actors play with paradox as an agentive move. Sherab understands the utility and pragmatism of reporting his traumatic past to news cameras even if on the personal level he insists that people should minimize its severity as a resilience practice.

Anthropological writings on refusal tend to focus on the "generative and strategic" (McGranahan 2016a, 319) stances marginalized communities make against oppressive sociopolitical institutions. Here, I draw on these theories to suggest that refusal may also serve an interpersonal and *intrapersonal* function. What I observed in Dharamsala was a kind of double refusal: the refusal to solidify distress, which could cause illness, and the refusal to be bound by seeming contradiction. Indeed, Tibetan activists saw no problem at all with encouraging their countrymates to generate trauma narratives while simultaneously insisting that talking about problems is not helpful for recovery. As I describe in the next chapter, this kind of flexible thinking is emblematic of Tibetan forms of resilience. After all, samsara itself is but an illusion, and at the same time, people must live and work and function. Buddhist practitioners all come to face a certain epistemological conundrum, that is, how at once things both matter and fundamentally do not matter. As great Tibetan Buddhist masters coach their students: the only place of safety, the only thing a person should count on and direct their lives toward, is compassion for others.

Chapter 5

OPEN SKY OF MIND

Now in her early twenties, Tashi Lhamo came to Dharamsala from eastern Tibet with her mother when she was sixteen years old. We walk up the steep, poorly paved road after buying vegetables at the Indian bazaar. Today we stop at a tea stall on the side of the road to rest and drink a small glass of peppery Indian chai. Tashi Lhamo zips up her purple hooded sweatshirt, the autumn weather sunny but chilly, and squints back at me. "These problems you always want to discuss," she teased, holding my hand, "it's better to ignore the problems in your life. Don't pay them any mind. Instead, we should try to have *sems pa chen po* [big or vast mind] and not focus on problems." Like many of my Tibetan friends, Tashi Lhamo, although very open, was reticent to discuss specific details of hardship and difficulties in her life, claiming that others had it much worse than she.

Despite spending eight months in a Chinese prison after being caught by border police, Tashi Lhamo does not consider herself an ex–political prisoner or even a political activist. "Ex–political prisoners, these are people who suffered very badly," she explains. "When difficult things happen in life, we should just to do our best and move on. Or we can become very upset and make things even worse. Negative emotions can be very dangerous." In a sense, for Tashi Lhamo, the anger, fear, and anxiety occasioned by political violence are considered more dangerous and toxic than the actual events. The events are over, and thus one should not continue to think about them endlessly, which would only bring about more suffering. Not only do many Tibetans maintain a typical style of humility according to which it would be arrogant to talk openly about withstanding violence, but I argue that they skillfully and purposefully sidestep taking on an identity as a "survivor." As Didier Fassin notes, "trauma produces the traumatized person just as humanitarianism produces the victim" (2012, 203). There is no shortage of Tibetan political activists in Dharamsala, and yet many people who seemingly fall into the category of political refugee resist this label unless they are speaking for a public audience for whom they are compelled to justify their suffering.

In this chapter, I challenge existing theory on structural violence and social suffering, which tends to overemphasize victimhood, bypassing the ordinary (and extraordinary) ways that people find agency in extreme situations. The case of Tibetan refugees complicates these theories because this is a culture that argues that freedom can only be found or constrained within one's own mind. And simultaneously, Tibetan exiles are fighting a global battle for human rights, only complicating how they conceive of agency and the power (or lack thereof) of structural oppression. This chapter grapples with the meaning of agency, asking how the quest to find liberation and freedom within individual minds clashes with—or resolves—questions of structural inequity and power.

A Look Away from the Self

Typical paradigms in structural violence theory speak to ways that those in marginalized and oppressed positions lack agency, choice, and unfettered access to self-determination. From the viewpoint of Euro-American theorists, placing limits on individual self-hood is itself evidence of violence (Bourdieu 1999; Farmer 2001). And yet, when Tibetans find themselves in difficult circumstances, they argue that one should actually take the focus *off of the self* to skillfully cope with the problem. They should contemplate emptiness and impermanence to recognize that fundamentally the self is an illusion. And those who are seen as most resilient seem to focus on wishing happiness for others—the supreme method among Tibetan Buddhists for mitigating suffering. As I argued earlier in this book, this way of thinking could be considered a kind of north star that guides a way: it would be a gross mischaracterization to assume that all Tibetan Buddhists think in this way. But these methods reveal important cultural distinctions in trauma appraisal, recovery, and resilience.

Tashi Lhamo's claim that people should strive for *sems pa chen po* and not focus too much on problems seemed to stem from ordinary cultural wisdom about what resilient people ought to do in difficult moments. In addition, she is a young person who is deeply religious, so her narrative reveals the ways lay Tibetan Buddhists make use of religious teachings to cope with suffering in everyday life. As I discussed earlier, whereas Tibetan cultural life is steeped in devotional practices such as mantra recitation, circumambulation, and making offerings, most people are not particularly interested in Buddhist philosophy or teachings on emptiness and karma. Tashi Lhamo was atypical in this regard. In fact, we first became acquainted in a daily philosophy class held at the Tibetan library given by the late Geshe Sonam Rinchen. The daily teachings were based on high philosophical texts of great Indian pandits such as Nagarjuna and Shantideva who were influential in *madhyamika prisanghaka* (middle way) schools of Mahayana Buddhism. Geshe Sonam Rinchen, a highly respected lama, devoted much of his life to working with his longtime translator, Ruth Sonam, on translating important philosophical works into English. In their daily classes, Geshe-la would sit on a traditional Tibetan teaching throne and slowly present commentary on seminal texts while Ruth translated in English for a mostly foreign audience. A handful of Tibetans joined the classes, however, including Tashi Lhamo, for there were fewer opportunities for lay Tibetans outside of monasteries to access philosophical teachings than one might expect.

We often walked back up the hill together after class, talking about the material. When studying Shantideva, a Buddhist master who is known for *lojong* teaching, Tashi Lhamo, expressed how interesting it was to learn its formal logic.

This is what my *mo-lag* (granny) lectures us about! We will just be more and more miserable if we focus on the self. Thinking about others is the only thing that makes sense. It is what Gyalwa Rinpoche [the Dalai Lama] says, but learning now how emptiness and compassion fit together is very good for more training. Many Tibetans just think about using this logic to approach life's problems very naturally. I think these Buddhist ideas are just a part of how we think. But I see more and more that, actually, this way of thinking is very special.

I agreed that *lojong* is a very unique and special way of thinking, and told her that I imagined people back in the United States might think that putting others before yourself is just ignoring the problem and not fighting injustice. "But does it help?" Tashi Lhamo asks. "Going on and on about things that happen. Does it really change things?" I sheepishly thought of Hillman and Ventura's wry psychology text, "We've Had a Hundred Years of Psychotherapy—And the World's Getting Worse" (1993), in which they ask something similar. Her question is a logical one.

In this regard, the story of how Tibetans in Dharamsala understand resilience raises fundamental questions about the extent to which one should focus all of one's attention on "the self" to recover. This question seems to be a major distinction between psychotherapy-based interventions and the religious variety in Dharamsala where people are coached to do the exact opposite: that is, to take focus *off the self*. The field of psychological anthropology has long investigated cross-cultural differences in notions of self and personhood, where it is understood that Euro-American cultures have a rather extreme view of autonomy, individualism, privacy, and boundedness. That is, for many cultures across the globe, a hyperfocus on the primacy of self would be "alien, a bizarre idea cutting the self off from the interdependent whole" (Shweder and Bourne 1984, 194). Actively cultivating attention away from the self is the explicit imperative of *lojong* approaches, which coach people to consider all of life's problems (even atrocities like torture and imprisonment) as inherently workable on the basis of a well-known Tibetan idiom: "If you want to be miserable, think about yourself. If you want to be happy, think about others."

A nun, Ani Seldron, explained how she used such logic when she first came to Dharamsala ten years ago.

I was so miserable when I came here. I couldn't tolerate the food and weather; I was sick all the time and struggled with the intense schedule inside the nunnery. The more I thought about my misery, the more miserable I became.

But then I started to think that there were many people around the world who, just like me, were coping with a new environment. Actually, many people in the world are suffering even more than me. I began to notice the many Indian beggars around town who did not have food and shelter provided for them. Gradually, this helped me not to get caught within my own narrow view.

Although Ani Seldron does not report practicing *lojong* by name, this is an example of how Tibetans lessen personal suffering by thinking about others.

An abbot of a local nunnery told me that the first thing the Tibetan community did when they came to Dharamsala in the early 1960s was to build a *lhakhang* (Buddhist temple), a place for devotion. "They had nothing," she said. "But they just got on with it." Devotion provides something outside oneself on which to focus, which for Tibetans, is at the heart of successful coping. This idea of simply "getting on with it" is difficult for Westerners to swallow. Somehow there is a felt sense that people cannot cope without talking about past trauma at great length.

Although many Tibetans struggle with long-lasting effects of violence (both physically and psychologically), they mitigate distress through cultivating *sems pa chen po*, allowing them to take a wider view rather than processing discursive narratives that focuses on the ways the self was harmed. This cultural sensibility, which helps people to avoid taking their pain and misfortune too seriously—to instead hold lightly—helps to explain why the genre of testimony is not seen as particularly therapeutic. As I discussed in chapter 3, Tibetan temporalities that emphasize impermanence, a central ontological framing of reality, helps to explain why it is nonsensical to think that recovery can be achieved by retrospectively processing past events. For Tibetan Buddhists, resisting the fact of impermanence actually keeps them trapped in a samsaric mind-set where one desires to keep one's possessions and loved ones permanently fixed in time. Therefore, narratives of the past— what happened, why they were wronged, what someone's motivations were for harming them—should be seen as fluid and flexible. This is a resilient take on past suffering. Based on Buddhist sensibilities, many Tibetans explain that the more one can let go of a conventional hold on things and see the self as "empty," the more content one will be.

Phuntsok, a twenty-four-year-old born to a nomad family in Amdo says: "Did you ever notice how something can happen and one family member is okay, while another person within that same family holds on to a lot of suffering and does not recover? The difference is probably that the one who is okay is reflecting on emptiness and impermanence, which helps us remember that everything is constantly changing. Once something has happened, we should think—'okay, it is over now!' We shouldn't go over it again and again in our minds."

This passage reflects how seemingly high Buddhist philosophical concepts such as "emptiness" permeate the lived social world of Tibetans who may or may not practice formal Buddhism. This pragmatic orientation to life's problems (seeing the illusory nature of reality), does not lead Tibetans to become despondent. Actually, the fact that reality is empty of inherent existence and not fixed offers an intriguing sense of freedom: we do not know what will happen.

Agency in an Unjust World

In this chapter, I am concerned with articulating how the Buddhist notions of compassion and emptiness generate agency in an unjust world for Tibetans in exile. How is it that Tibetans can be deeply political in the struggle for justice and equity when their religious values point them to compassion, empathy, nonviolence, and letting go? Whereas typical studies of structural violence ask how people manage to resist despair, anger, depression, and hatred (evidence of their grit), this book reveals how a refugee population may, in fact, be resiliently sad and resiliently angry. The "grit" approach asks those who are wronged to bravely plow through unscathed—that is, "teach how to fish in spite of the polluted waters" (Evans and Reid 2014, 33). There is much to be wary of in the ways that resilience is promoted. Critical resilience scholars do not automatically see resilience as something desirable because it may inevitably ask the most vulnerable members of society to remain docile rather than dismantle oppression, as Julian Reid (2012) asserts in his article, "The Disastrous and Politically Debased Subject of Resilience." And yet the project of resilience for Tibetan Buddhists seems to point to something that is quite distinct from this paradigm altogether. It asks for connecting deeply with humanity not in spite of suffering, but because of it, and through it.

The practice of contemplating emptiness as a way to move through suffering is a particularly difficult concept for a Western audience, in part because the translation of *shunyata* (a Sanskrit term) is a rather ill fit. The term "emptiness" in the English language seems more akin to what Angela Garcia (2010) describes in her ethnographic work on heroin addiction in New Mexico than a recipe for resilience. In Garcia's work, she explores how diffuse and enduring unequal social conditions are re(produced) in the hearts and minds of those who live in the Rio Grande, perpetuating empty despair. She suggests that her interlocutors aim to *lose themselves* through their drug use, to disappear from the world. They want to become numb and not feel anything. She asks, "What does this form of self-exile communicate in terms of the (broken) interdependencies of self and other?" (2010, 11). This parallel between the self and the environment is to be expected. Thus, when Tibetans explained that their views on emptiness helped them to cultivate contentment and equanimity, it was not immediately apparent to me why such a view would bring about resilience, let alone spiritual attainment.

But the kind of broken or empty self that Garcia (2010) describes is categorically different from what Tibetans mean when they refer to emptiness and the ways that ego clinging yields misery. Here, emptiness is fundamentally a view that relates to interdependence because it suggests that nothing is inherently or independently existent. Everything (including the self) is dependent on other arising phenomena. This is known as *tendrel*, or "dependent origination," the way that certain karmic causes and conditions hang together. In the space of emptiness, particular karmic form arises: accidents, illness, loss, misfortune. Buddhist teachings and practices such as *lojong* help practitioners to take such events in stride. See them, feel them, and then let go. The display of mind and its reactions to the forms of life will naturally ebb and flow. It is human; it is natural.

Clouds of Emotion

For many Tibetans coping with the aftermath of violence and the difficulties inherent in exile, *btang snyom*, or "equanimity," is their most important value. They do not think oppression and discrimination are acceptable, evidenced by the long-standing political struggle and international resistance campaign for Tibet. And yet, an important (but theoretically controversial) aspect of mitigating what might be called structural violence is to choose equanimity—a view that refugees in Dharamsala found empowering. As

Tseyang, a sixteen-year-old student said: "I remember my *Ama-la* [mother] saying to me when I was little: 'you always have a choice.' No matter what, it is up to you. In a bad situation, you should try to find a solution, but the most important thing is not to let it affect your peace of mind too much." This is similar to my elderly neighbor whose advice to me no matter the situation always seemed to be: "self is the protector of self."

Tibetans do not view such flexible attitudes as submissive or indicative of internalized oppression. Rather, they see this approach as savvy, agile, and skillful. Such perspectives, which purport that "self is the protector of self" might sound somewhat lonely, and as noted earlier, could even be misinterpreted as a neoliberal call for self-reliance. But here I see these forms of resilience as reflective of culturally sanctioned understandings of health and more broadly what it means to find contentment in an unstable world. That is, there is always a choice at any moment to let go of suffering. And to do so is to be in accordance with the lived reality of impermanence. Within the Tibetan diaspora, those who are not bound by traumatic memory or cling to past events are considered the healthiest within society. They are people who make good use of compassion to work with life's greatest challenges (Ozawa-de Silva and Ozawa-de Silva 2011). To put it within a local idiom, resilient people are those who identify with the vast blue sky that is eternal rather than the ever-changing clouds.

An abbot of a monastery relied on this metaphor to explain how to cope with adversity. He told me that if someone is very attached to every passing thought and every passing emotion, there will be great instability within the mind. Those who can learn to identify with the vast blue sky behind the clouds will not be swayed too much by the passing of weather (difficult emotions). "You don't have to ignore them, and pretend they are not there," he said. "But you don't have to identify with them either. We might *have* difficult emotions, but we wouldn't say that we *are* them. It is not good to say, I am angry. It is better to think, okay, right now, at the moment, there is a feeling of anger passing by." This orientation to the self helps Tibetans to view mental distress as something that comes and goes: it is part of being human.

From the Tibetan perspective, emotions, time, memories, and even the coherence of the self are impermanent and changing moment by moment. Therefore, solidifying traumatic narrative by going back to "work through" past events is counterproductive because it traps a person in illusion. The Tibetan cultural concept of time in relation to the person is highly complex in that past, current, and future lives are at once illusory and intimately connected through karma (Gerke 2011). The history of experience is not merely a personal story but entails a long project of being in the world that predates one's birth and extends beyond death. Studies of cultural temporalities such as these may be a fruitful site for pushing the boundaries of how we understand trauma, the body, and the workings of mind. Understanding that one should not place too much weight on current suffering seems to coincide with their expectation of suffering in life—that is, all sentient beings suffer, and as a political refugee one should necessarily expect that things will be tough.

Collective Suffering, Collective Will

Typically, within the scientific literature, status as a refugee denotes risk, but some researchers have questioned whether collective struggles of various kinds may in fact bolster resilience, perhaps alongside suffering. For example, Wexler, DiFluvio, and Burke (2009) investigate the ways that discrimination might serve to orient people in overcoming those very disparities; in other words, the effects of marginalization status are not always negative. When activated, there seems to be something about collective struggle that provides strength. Elsewhere, Brian Barber (2008) conducted a study among Palestinian and Bosnian youth, comparing their experiences. Here, experiences of war were far from uniform. Whereas Palestinian youth relied on strength passed down across generations and felt they contributed to something larger than themselves, the narratives of Bosnian youth in Sarajevo centered around individual trauma with little connection to broader historical and cultural context (2008, 289). Wexler, DiFluvio, and Burke (2009) argue that oppressed populations that share a collective purpose may actually *use their oppression* to inspire and motivate their fight. In this light, resilience is not the final accomplishment but a dynamic process heavily dependent on interpretation of difficult life events.

My study did not aim to investigate whether Tibetans in Dharamsala experience trauma symptoms to a lesser extent than other refugee groups, but it does show how they think about trauma differently. A person's appraisal of trauma is an important ingredient in how they move beyond it. For example, I asked Ani Peldron, a nun in her early thirties who was imprisoned for two years, if she has ever heard of anyone having nightmares or reliving traumatic events. She said:

> I think some people might have these problems, but I haven't witnessed it. When Tibetans have these problems, they think that it is the result of a past life; it is only the result of my past actions. As for political prisoners, they made the decision to sacrifice themselves for Tibetan issues, so whatever happens, it is no problem. Even torture and imprisonment don't get them down because they already made this decision. They think that even if they experience great suffering and difficulties, then they did something very great for the nation and their people. Generally, when Tibetans protest against the Chinese army and police, they say they want freedom of religion. Old Tibetans know that after they do this, they will probably be imprisoned and tortured. They already know to expect this, so when it happens they don't mind too much. As for me, I decided this already. So in prison after experiencing great hardship and torture, I still didn't regret my protest. I think that other political prisoners feel the same way; we kept each other going by sharing this kind of advice.

Stories such as these throw the question of agency into dispute in that the normal binary of victimhood and oppressors seems not to apply. Without question, Tibetans are marginalized in their homeland. Their languages, religions, cultures, and chances of decent livelihood are threatened by Han Chinese suppression. But do structural violence and social suffering theories adequately explain how Tibetans themselves understand their plight?

Beyond Social Suffering

Since the 1990s, there has been a major paradigm shift in medical anthropology to investigate "social suffering" (Bourdieu 1999; Kleinman, Das, and Lock 1997) and the structural causes of illness, war, and misery (Farmer 2001; Link and Phelan 1995). Over time, a number of scholars have complicated the debate, asking how to conceptualize the role of subjectivity, agency, caring, and individual experience (Biehl, Good, and Kleinman 2007; Garcia 2010). Many authors of foundational writings on social suffering have also been instrumental in developing new theories on subjectivity (Das 2000; Good, Subandi, and DelVecchio Good 2007; Kleinman 2011) that consider personal agency in the face of structural violence. Although these perspectives provided a launching point from which I theorize this book, they provide only a limited framework for thinking through suffering in the Tibetan exile community, in part because there are fewer obvious lines of stratification in Tibetan communities and because they view suffering in ways that are incommensurate with a highly bounded notion of personhood. Whereas many studies of structural violence articulate zones of abandonment (Biehl 2005) where the agency of particular groups is constrained by the state, this model of inequity and oppression plays out differently for Tibet and its diaspora population.

To highlight these differences, it was instrumental to consider the ways that Tibetans approached poverty in contrast to their Indian counterparts. Economically speaking, most Tibetan residents have very little but rely on Buddhist-based notions of charity and generosity to get by. Many of my friends and neighbors spoke ill of Indians, citing examples of child-beggars as evidence of their poor moral character. On a particularly wet day in August, I walked slowly up the hill with Palden, a Tibetan friend in his mid-twenties who worked at the Yak Café. It was monsoon, and although everyone carries large umbrellas, the streets become so flooded that no one bothers to avoid sloshing through puddles. The pace on the streets of Dharamsala is always slow, in part because one is always walking up or down a steep hill. We passed by a young Indian woman dressed in a dirty, torn sari, holding an infant. "Milk! No money. Milk!" she said to me in a pleading tone, holding out her hand and gesturing to her infant and a nearby shop. There is a well-known group (some pejoratively call it a "beggar mafia") that comes from Rajasthan to engage in organized begging among foreign tourists. Living in a shanty town of tents and cardboard shelters nearby, small groups of young women walk into town every day, each carrying an infant. They approach unsuspecting tourists, sometimes very persistently, even aggressively, and convince them to purchase a large bag of powdered milk, which is then resold for a profit. Palden clucked in disapproval, as if to say, *what a shame.* "You never see Tibetans begging, do you?" he asked.

Sometimes the ex-pats who lived in Dharamsala instructed new tourists not to give them money or purchase milk. "You know, some Tibetan monks started a foundation for them," one German woman said. "But they won't even let the kids go to school; they're more of an asset to be used in begging." It is not the case that Tibetans are never reduced to begging (although it is true that one generally only sees Indians and not Tibetans begging in Dharamsala), but many of my friends and neighbors around town seemed to think they were morally superior to Indians in this regard. "Many Tibetans are very poor, we have nothing," Palden continued. "But we would never live this way or let a neighbor or family member live this way."

One day, my research assistant remarked that there were four people staying in his room. He explained that a small group from his county in Kham arrived six months ago and have not yet found jobs. There was a strong sense of belonging and clansmanship connected to one's county of origin in Tibet. Despite never meeting these individuals before, my assistant pointed out that they were "from my same county," as if it would be obvious why he would host a group of men for six months or more in his one-room flat. When Tibetans talked about Indian beggars, it was often with a sense of incredulousness and superiority. They did not necessarily look down on individual beggars, as much as the society or culture that does not look after its own (Ward 2013). As I became more integrated into the community and began receiving invitations to come to neighbors' homes for dinner, I observed that Tibetans rarely dined alone. Groups of friends, classmates, neighbors, and families often pooled food and cooked large meals together. This stretched food supplies as well as gas—a scarce resource in Dharamsala. "Why would everyone in the neighborhood be using gas at dinner time, all cooking alone?" a neighbor asked. In all my time spent in the homes of Tibetans, however, there was never an Indian person invited to dinner.

Although no one much liked to give to the Rajashtani "milk ladies," there were other sorts of beggars around Dharamsala, like those with serious disabilities from polio. It was not uncommon for Tibetans, including monks and nuns, to offer money. This was especially true on Saga Dawa and other Buddhist holy days where merit from good deeds is thought to be multiplied millions of times. The Tibetan cultural and religious sense of generosity and making offerings shapes many everyday practices. Making offerings to monks and nuns is a rather simple way to generate merit and something that is commonly found across Buddhist and Hindu cultures of South Asia. Whenever I would come along with friends and neighbors to pay someone a visit—particularly if the host was a monk or nun—it was requisite to stop along the way and purchase some juice, biscuits, or fruit to offer on arrival.

Likewise, as a guest one is offered tea or food, without exception. This became somewhat of an amusing problem if I was conducting a number of interviews inside private homes. By the end of a day, I was so full of tea and biscuits I could not stomach anymore. There is a built-in sense that generosity and good fortune are inextricably linked. Being stingy or miserly is dangerous, not only in the karmic sense, but as one woman remarked, "we never know when we might need the help, and if we don't have the habit of helping others, they may not be there when we are in need." Given these cultural norms, it is difficult to imagine what a Tibetan zone of abandonment would look like. The Tibetan government-in-exile offers a six-month stipend and job training to new arrivals, but much of the assistance people receive is informal among friends, neighbors, and especially from countymates who hail from their local regions of Tibet. Because misfortune and struggle are considered to be just a part of life, it is obvious to people that they should construct a society that offers collective support.

Among the North American middle class, there is an unacknowledged sense of entitlement to near constant health, happiness, and well-being. Becoming sick, feeling unhappy, or losing a job or loved one feels not just painful, but somehow wrong. *Why do bad things happen to good people?* some ask. But this book grapples with a culture that insists that difficulty, illness, and disruption are just a part of life. In Dharamsala, no matter how bad things get, personal and collective karma provides an ordering principle to explain difficult life events such that nothing is senseless. Far from implying that anyone who is imprisoned or violated somehow deserves it, the system of karma reminds this community that in the endless sea of past lifetimes, we have all been murderers, rapists, and oppressors at one time. When my Tibetan interlocutors argue that constructing polemic categories such as "the oppressed" and "the oppressors" misses something more fundamental—that suffering is a core *human experience*—the usual models of structural violence seem to lose traction.

Theories of structural violence and social suffering are ways of understanding how the agency of individual citizens (in general, those who are marginalized) are constrained by unequal social conditions. In seeing inequity as a "fundamental cause" of illness and disenfranchisement (Link and Phalen 1995), critical studies of race, gender, and sexuality reveal how structural conditions shape individual experience. And yet, these theories are an awkward mismatch for how Tibetans themselves understand their plight, because for them, accepting suffering as a natural part of life actually promotes agency and internal freedom.

By seeing moments of suffering as purifying a karmic debt, or even trying to view one's enemies as one's greatest teacher, Tibetans are born into a
culture that has a lot to say about how to manage in unthinkable situations.
The notion that there may be positive outcomes or opportunities for growth—
what is called "bringing adversity onto the path" in traditional Buddhist
texts—is a culturally unique way of meeting suffering. The correct attitude
for bringing adversity onto the path is one of flexibility. The suffering that a
person faces acts as fuel for his or her spiritual advancement, providing a felt
sense of compassion for others facing exactly the same thing—grief, loss, anger, disillusionment. And yet, at the same time, those who are suffering are
coached to recognize the illusory nature of emotions and ultimately not to
take themselves or their problems too seriously.

The Trap of Hope and Fear

The flexibility that is required to see the illusory nature of life in samsara
and to be an actor in the world with desires calls into question the matter of
hope. With desire comes hope and fear: the hope it will work out and the
fear it won't. There are numerous Buddhist texts that caution practitioners
against the trap of hope, and its counterpart, fear, seen as two sides of the
same coin. That is, wishing for things to go a certain way in the future, and
conversely, fearing things will turn out differently from what one wishes. Although hope outside of Buddhist contexts seems to be a universally positive
quality, hope, for Tibetans, is a complicated matter. A classic Buddhist teaching known as the Eight Worldly Concerns (*jig rten chos brgyad*) suggests
that hope and fear are essentially what drives human beings to suffer in samsara. This suffering is explained in four categories: hope for happiness and
fear of suffering, hope for fame and fear of insignificance, hope for praise
and fear of blame, and hope for gain and fear of loss (explicated further in
Arya Nāgārjuna's [c. 150–c. 250 CE] classic text, *Letter to a Friend*). The point
made by Nāgārjuna and other Buddhist masters is not that people should
feel nothing and be devoid of emotion but that they should remember that
life contains many ups and downs, and thus, they should try not to get swept
away.

Such sentiments were readily repeated and echoed in Dharamsala as
everyday cultural knowledge. For example, Dekyi says: "As we are Buddhist,

we believe very strongly in karma and its results. Therefore, if we obtain great happiness, we don't particularly gain great excitement. Likewise, if something bad happens, we don't get extremely upset. I think this is a special ability for Tibetans." By hoping and wishing for happiness, fame, praise, and gain (as outlined in the Eight Worldly Concerns), Tibetans believe this will only lead to suffering. A related *lojong* slogan is "Abandon any hope of fruition—Don't get caught up in how you will be in the future, stay in the present moment." Slogans like this help to continually train the mind to lessen attachment to outcomes.

But how do Tibetans in Dharamsala take heed and avoid the trap of hope without falling into nihilism or apathy, particularly in dire contexts of torture, violence, and imprisonment? It is not the case that those who are imprisoned feel nothing and lose hope. Rather, people encourage one another to focus their attention on compassion, a kind of protective salve. Dorje, who was imprisoned for two years, told me: "You have to use your intelligence and meditate deeply on the Dharma in prison. Otherwise, you will become *nyönpa* [crazy]. You shouldn't hope for things to become better; that will just make you miserable when it doesn't work out. Instead, we tried to focus on the happiness and well-being of others, which is the only thing that guarantees happiness in the mind."

Such moments of discovery—that compassion and care for others may be the only true refuge in prison—have been articulated elsewhere, particularly in Holocaust memoirs. In Viktor Frankl's *Man's Search for Meaning*, an autobiographic account of Auschwitz, Frankl offers his own psychological analysis of hope and apathy in dire circumstances. He argues that apathy can become a psychological defense from vacillating back and forth between paralyzing hope and fear. Apathy becomes a psychological safe place where there is no risk. Frankl writes a moving account of a sudden realization where he realizes that love, specifically his love for his wife, cannot be taken from him. His writing speaks to what he calls "the last of human freedoms—to choose one's attitude in any given set of circumstances, to choose one's own way. Every day, every hour, offered the opportunity to make a decision, a decision which determined whether you would or would not submit to those powers which threatened to rob you of your very self, your inner freedom; which determined whether or not you would become the plaything of circumstance, renouncing freedom and dignity to become molded into the form of the typical inmate" ([1946] 1992, 104). The kind of freedom and dignity that Frankl writes of is primordial and cannot be denigrated by external forces.

It is this kind of freedom that Tibetan political prisoners also pointed to and why some later said that their greatest fear was that they would lose compassion for their torturers. Because Tibetans are trained through their religion to look outward and generate compassion in times of distress, they are primed to use such strategies in dire contexts. But whereas hope is precarious, it is also ubiquitous—especially within the political domain.

Political activism is based on investing in hope for things to change, which on the surface seems at odds with Buddhist perspectives that warn against the traps of hope and fear. This is a question often put to the Dalai Lama: If Buddhists are to remain in equanimity, detached from outcomes, then why bother engaging in activism? His response is that if activism is motivated by fighting racism, sectarianism, and oppression, it can be enlightened action. The political fight for Tibetan freedom is imbued with hope, particularly in the ways that members of the diaspora insist that their people will one day return to Tibet. "To refuse [citizenship elsewhere] is to hope for a different Tibet, one to which you may go home, regardless of your politics—of either independence/*rang btsan* or autonomy/*dbu ma'lam*" (McGranahan 2016b, 338). What McGranahan points to is the ways a stance of refusal automatically, and by definition, reveals a kind of hope. Therefore, the tension I elucidate in this chapter speaks to the ways that resilience practices in Tibetan Buddhism are predicated on letting go of outcomes while simultaneously fighting for what one believes is right and just.

And to be sure, all resistance stories within political conflict are imbued with hope of some kind—the hope to find work, to find religious freedom, or in cases of forced migration and trafficking, the hope to make it through alive. In this way, migration is always a future-oriented process (Pine 2014), where hope becomes one's currency or fuel to press on. And yet hope is always closely aligned with fear and dread, the other side of the coin. This danger was investigated by Eaves, Nichter, and Ritenbaugh (2016) among individuals with chronic pain. The team found hope to be a highly complex and multifaceted concept, which was often experienced as paradoxical in that those with intractable pain needed to "[hope] enough to carry on while keeping hopes in check to avoid the ever-present possibility of despair" (2016, 35). Those with terminal illness likewise must transform the meaning of hope and what is possible—hoping for things to change, hoping for the strength to cope. These contexts complicate an overly simplistic definition of hope that is more akin to positive thinking. Likewise, the kinds of coping methods used by Tibetan political prisoners that people found most emblematic of resilience had little to do with changing outcomes. Instead, they were much deeper and interconnected, like wishing to take on the pain for the benefit of all sentient beings.

Many Tibetans in Dharamsala talked about their "special way of thinking" when referring to teachings that suggested putting other before self or seeing the illusory nature of reality. Even when comparing themselves to Buddhists in other traditions, they discussed how the Vajrayana methods of Tibetan Buddhism has a unique approach that has been called "crazy wisdom" (Trungpa 1991). There is acknowledgment that what is being asked, to fight for the benefits of others while abandoning hope and fear, is a rather tall order.

Crazy Wisdom

Yeshe chölwa, or "crazy wisdom," entails approaches that use unorthodox or outrageous methods to shake students from fixed and habitual views. In particular, these sorts of teachings challenge overly puritanical or rigid worldviews that prevent practitioners from experiencing the world without projection (Khyentse 2008; Trungpa 1973, 1991). Crazy wisdom teachings often appear in historical allegory and folktales, but even today there are lamas known as crazy wisdom masters; often they are *ngakpas* (yogis) or "householder" lamas who may reside in or outside of monasteries. Their teachings defy convention as a way to wake up their students and reveal their fixed mind-set.

For example, a thirty-year-old *tulku* (high incarnate lama) named Phakchok Rinpoche writes provocative yet inspiring quotes on his Facebook page, such as: "Genuine practitioners don't run from their emotions, they chew them, they eat them, and they transform them"; "Hope is going to kill you!"; and "Next time you are angry, turn all that energy into something beautiful." These pith quotes are examples of everyday *lojong*, or mind training, where people tenaciously take suffering onto the path and transform it. And they are also somewhat unorthodox in their presentation. Another lama, Dzongsar Khyentse Rinpoche, is not only the head of major monasteries and highly respected *shedras* (monastic colleges) in Bhutan and India but he is also an award-winning filmmaker and has been known to show up to important religious events wearing wigs or silly sunglasses. A book Khyentse Rinpoche wrote to help his students learn how to relate to one's Buddhist teacher is called *The Guru Drinks Bourbon* (2016), which explains that the job of a true master is to help destroy the ego of his or her students, sometimes through outrageous measures. For example, he has been known to periodically ignore and even insult his close students out of kindness, to break them out of habitually seeking praise and external validation.

There is a story about a beloved lama named Patrul Rinpoche (1808–87), author of *Words of My Perfect Teacher* (2010), and a renowned yogi who used crazy wisdom methods. As told by Pema Chodron (2001, 125), one day, Patrul Rinpoche went to visit a hermit known for his austerity who had been practicing in a cave for twenty years. Patrul Rinpoche showed up and the hermit humbly and sweetly welcomed him in. He asked, "Tell me, what have you been doing in here?" The hermit replied, "I've been practicing the perfection of patience." Putting his face very close to the hermit's face, Patrul Rinpoche taunted him relentlessly: "But a pair of old scoundrels like us, we don't care anything about patience, really. We only do this to get everyone's admiration, right? We just do this to get people to think we are big shots, don't we? I'll bet they bring you a lot of gifts, don't they? Well?? Do they?"

At this point, the hermit stood up and screamed, "Why did you come here? Why are you tormenting me? Go away and leave me in peace!" And then Rinpoche said, "So now, where is your perfection of patience?"

Many crazy wisdom stories take on a humorous tone, such as this one. The sense of being "crazy" also connotes something like the outrageous courage or confidence that is needed to act fully for the benefit of others. But whereas great *mahasiddhas* (masters with great accomplishments) have the spiritual attainment and selfless devotion to utilize such methods to train their students, the neologism "crazy wisdom" has also been dangerously used to justify harm, including sexual abuse of women who are led to believe that becoming a consort to their guru is for their own spiritual development (Gayley 2018). Indeed, Vajrayana Buddhism is itself steeped with warnings instructing students to investigate a potential guru before entering into a formal teacher–disciple relationship. As Dzongsar Khyentse argues in the opening of *The Guru Drinks Bourbon*: "Guru devotion is the head, heart, blood, spine, and breath of the incredible Vajrayana, the path of Buddhist tantra. The Vajrayana is not a safe stroll in the countryside. In fact, safety is probably the least of our concerns. The Vajrayana's way of dealing with ego and the emotions is hazardous. The methods are sometimes even reckless" (2016, front matter). Ultimately, the role of the guru is to help students understand that their egos and harmful emotions are illusory, and what is fundamental and eternal is their buddhanature: the brilliant blue sky behind the stormy clouds of samsaric grasping.

When my Tibetan interlocutors shared stories about those with deeply spacious minds, they did so with the understanding that all human beings are innately capable of enlightenment. Awakening is admired, but not romanticized. This recognition stems from an understanding of buddhanature, or *tatagathagarba* (Sanskrit). Whereas Christians believe in "original sin," Buddhists believe the exact opposite; that the true nature of the mind is all-knowing, compassionate, and stainless. No matter how much negative karma obscures the mind, the true nature of every being is a mind of enlightenment. Therefore, people do not need to acquire something they do not yet possess to become enlightened—they need to recognize the true nature of the mind, which is primordial.

Freedom and Agency

The concept of agency has become increasingly important in cultural anthropology. In general, agency is discussed in terms of a social actor's capacity to act freely, often in opposition to the state. In my view as an American researcher, I noticed how important it seemed to me that corrective action should be taken to correct corruption and inequity, and thus, I sometimes found it unsettling when I witnessed injustice and unfair treatment in Dharamsala. When Tibetans praised The Middle Way Policy that embraces nonviolence and dialectical logic, I wondered if stronger action was not called for. But for many of my interlocutors, the project of finding equanimity— the path to freedom within the mind—was at the heart of their goals (even if achieving it imperfectly). While I sat on the wooden bench fuming with indignation while the Indian visa officers drank tea and purposely ignored us, my Tibetan friends teased me for my illogical anger. "Who is the person who is suffering the most right now? It is you!" Their quest for equanimity was found through a flexible mind. And though theories of structural violence and social suffering help to make sense of how the forces of inequity create real suffering, the Tibetan case reveals some limitations of these approaches.

An ideal life from the vantage point of structural violence theories would be someone who is unconstrained by external forces, such that they have the freedom to act as highly autonomous and independent actors. But for Tibetans, a highly autonomous and independent agent, free to act in the world however he or she wishes does not describe their highest ideals. If Tibetans do not place a high premium on personal independence, liberty, and autonomy, then what are the qualities they admire most? Tibetan cultural heroes seem to have a number of qualities in common. Perhaps most central is that heroes willingly take on the suffering of others. They also act with humility and kindness. Those imbued with ideal qualities might consider sickness and even severe adversity, such as imprisonment, as an opportunity to purify negative karma and generate compassion.

Tibetologist Geoffery Samuel (2005), who writes on one of Tibet's heroes, Gesar of Ling, the beloved enlightened warrior king of Tibet, points out that the Tibetan concept of warriorship is not about dominance and aggression, but about a willingness to face enemies with gentleness. That is the meaning of bravery here. Being brave does not suggest that there are no negative feelings or experiences. Rather, my interlocutors describe highly resilient and heroic people as those who take a humanistic attitude toward suffering, understanding that their own suffering can bring them closer to other sentient beings. They use painful experiences to generate compassion for everyone who suffers.

A modern-day hero is Palden Gyatso, a Tibetan monk who spent thirty-three years in a Chinese prison and who is often referred to as an exemplar of resilience. Gyatso stated soon after his release that his greatest fear during captivity was that he might lose compassion for his torturers. As he describes in his autobiography (Gyatso 1997), wishing compassion for those who harm you does not make you weak and complicit; it makes you free of the toxic effects of hatred. Gyatso has given talks across the world in human rights forums, often supplying graphic accounts of his torture. Sometimes he offers a demonstration of how various implements of torture were used, such as how electric rods were put into his mouth. For Tibetans and foreign activists alike, this discourse juxtaposed with a compelling rhetoric of compassion and forgiveness challenges conventional notions about freedom and agency. As Schröder argues, in such narratives, "the categories of 'culprit and victim' do not necessarily fit" (2011, 153). From this perspective, true freedom is not measured against social constraint, but rather, *inner constraint*. Gyatso offers a stark example of what is possible in these circumstances.

My interlocutors describe very resilient people as those with great confidence and dignity, citing examples of *nyam chung*, or "humble," individuals, who could bear anything because of their compassion.

In her book on ordinary ethics, Veena Das (2007) claims that healing is a process that occurs not through rising up to the transcendent, but rather, sinking down into the ordinary. I am reminded of how often my Tibetan interlocutors say, "These are *human problems*, we are *all* suffering." Having the flexibility and space to see things from different angles helps Tibetans to work with suffering in their minds. From one point of view, Tibetans in a prison might be seen as the victims. But as a man named Tashi points out: "The Chinese guards who maltreat prisoners are the ones accruing all this negative karma. So we should feel compassion for them. Taking the broad view, we can see that they are the real victims in this situation." In coming to see the human infallibility of their oppressors, they feel a sense of interdependence through the system of karma. Karma is a social construct, showing how cause and effect brings people together in particular situations. Classic Buddhist advice suggests that those who are harmed should think, *may I willingly take this on, to purify the karmic debt between us*. This approach to life is emphasized in Mahayana traditions including Tibetan Buddhism, which are oriented toward achieving enlightenment for the sole purpose of helping others.

The question of agency in relation to karma is an interesting one. One might expect that those who believe in karma would feel powerless. But actually, I found the opposite to be true. Among Tibetans in exile, it gives a sense of increased agency insofar as one can be certain that one's actions will have demonstrable effects in the future. Through this spiritual effort and work, Tibetans experience increased agency and sense of self-efficacy because it is their own action that determines what comes next. In addition, there is always the possibility of purifying negative karma that has already accumulated. This is what makes karma different from a position of fatalism—karma may be purified because like everything else, it is ultimately empty and thus its causal power is both definitive and flexible. The flexible nature of reality itself is central to how Tibetans find agency within unjust conditions.

Flexible Minds

Researchers have explored the concept of "flexibility" in a variety of ways, in terms of bodies (Martin 1994), citizenship (Ong 1999), and personhood Shir-Vertesh (2012). In a section titled "Learning to Be Manic" in her book *Bipolar Expeditions: Mania and Depression in American Culture*, Emily Martin writes on the dark side of flexibility: when it is cultivated to reinforce the oppressive constraints of markets (2007). For instance, she observed a retreat for members of a Fortune 500 corporation where twenty-two thousand employees engaged in team-building exercises such as an obstacles ropes course. The objective of these activities was to cultivate flexibility, agility, and fearlessness—the challenge of the ropes course was meant to mimic stressful and challenging situations in the workplace, which hard-working and tenacious employees were enticed to overcome. Although these traits sound adaptive and healthy, Martin argues that these skills were purposefully cultivated to enable workers to rapidly adjust to continuously changing work conditions such as downsizing (2007). She argues that in the United States, exuberant energy even to the point of mania is celebrated and admired among traders and others in high-pressure jobs struggling to get ahead. For David Harvey (1991), this kind of flexible bending in service to the demands of capitalism is a defining feature of our postmodern era and a harbinger of neoliberalism where individuals contort themselves to meet harmful structural conditions.

In the Tibetan context of trauma and resilience, the concept of flexibility is markedly different. Here, it refers to the capacity to avoid clinging or holding too tightly to anything—including suffering. And although it might seem counterintuitive why anyone would hold onto suffering, as one lama explains: "Even though we may be miserable, having big and very important problems gives us the feeling that we, ourselves, are big and important. Most people prefer that to seeing clearly that their emotions and fixations are not such a big deal." This sense of spaciousness and flexibility, many Tibetans argue, is the best state of mind for approaching life's ups and downs.

An important part of flexible thinking involves looking at troubling situations from different vantage points and considering how one's own suffering might not be such a big deal. In Karen Seeley's ethnographic research in lower Manhattan during and after 9/11, she found that something occurred that surprised the mental health professionals who had come to help. Finding themselves in what she calls "simultaneous trauma" (2008), psychotherapists found it increasingly difficult to maintain professional boundaries that tend to discourage much in the way of personal disclosure or display of too much emotion. And yet, amidst the community-wide horror, many found themselves grappling with the same psychological responses as their clients. This became a source of struggle for many therapists whose identities were built on their capacities for professional distance and efficacy.

Whereas seeing one's own infallibility was a source of discomfort for New York City therapists, Tibetans readily contemplate the likeness of others in one's same situation as a healthy method of coping. This not only helps to cultivate compassion but is an effective way to work very directly with difficult emotions. Rather than moving away and desperately avoiding pain, classic Buddhist advice on managing negative emotions actually suggests that one should move in closer to one's own experience. It is often the resistance to experiences that make us suffer most. Tibetans argue that the most resilient people use pain as an opportunity to connect with their own vulnerability and tenderness, which automatically connects them to the humanity of others. As the anthropologist Michael Jackson argues, "human beings strive to go beyond themselves, consummating their singularity in relation to universality, variously construed as the social, the cosmic, the historical, or the ideological" (2009, 101). For Tibetans in unthinkable situations, it is only through seeing the humanity, even the ordinariness, of their torturers that allows them to maintain a sense of compassion for the whole situation, that is, the very humanness of our nature.

Being Humble, Being Confident

Another important aspect of flexible thinking is the capacity to simultaneously manifest the cultural ideals of *nyam chung*, or "humbleness," and *sang tham*, or "confidence," which are important values within Tibetan culture. An American Buddhist nun named Pema Chodron describes an experience she had during a religious teaching in Nepal. She was a guest of one of the high lamas who organized the weeklong series of empowerments. One day, she was ushered up next to the teacher's throne and asked to come in a special door. The next day, she was told, "oh, no, no, you go and sit with the other nuns on the floor." This continued for days and she did not understand her status. Finally, she said to her host: "I just don't know who I'm supposed to be." He said: "Well, you have to learn to be big and small at the same time" (Chodron 2001). These themes of humility, confidence, and self-reliance provide Tibetans with particular tools for resilience in that a person should both take their emotions seriously and at the same time recognize that one's own suffering is just like everyone else's. It is neither denying nor aggrandizing an emotional response.

The Vajrayana practices within Tibetan Buddhism are distinct in many respects from Zen and the Theravadan traditions of Southeast Asia. Rather than slowly and methodically working to reveal an enlightened mind—the way one might polish a tarnished piece of silver—Vajrayana practitioners attempt to relate to the world as if they were already enlightened (also known as the resultant path). Although the shining silver is still covered with a lot of muck, there is great faith that the true nature of mind is nonetheless, there, shining underneath. A traditional analogy is to imagine the brilliant blue sky; even when it is covered by clouds or it is nighttime—the blue sky still exists behind the clouds. No matter the weather, the nature of the sky does not change.

Tibetan religious beliefs and the cultural practices based on them instill a sense of confidence and faith, not in an external God, but in one's own mind. In late summer, I interviewed two nuns who had just days prior come out of a four-year solitary retreat in a cave shelter near Lahoul. They practice in the Drikung Kagyu tradition and while in retreat did not cut their hair. It was quite unusual to sit with two nuns with long hair since their heads are normally shaved. As is traditional, they remained largely confined to a wooden "meditation box," so they were able to sleep sitting up. Many advanced meditation practices such as *milam,* or "dream yoga," involves working with *rlung* (winds), which can more easily be brought into the central channel if one's spine is straight. Incidentally, practitioners at the time of death attempt to remain in the sitting meditation posture to practice *phowa,* a practice that gives one more control in the rebirth process. I recalled the times that my Tibetan interlocutors explained how you can sometimes detect a person's inner state by their radiance. Indeed, the nuns had an uncanny glow, their eyes were shining and their skin seemed almost luminescent. At the same time, there was an ordinariness in the way they carried themselves. And while I found it very impressive that they had just completed a four-year solitary retreat, there seemed to be no trace of pride or accomplishment.

I asked them, "What advice do you have for other women?" The answer one gave was a bit unexpected, as I anticipated a comment on compassion or the benefits of devotion. She said: "We need to relax. The more we can relax, the more confidence we have. This would be good."

Although concepts such as space and relaxation have not been of much concern to anthropologists, these ideas may reveal something important about human flourishing. For example, the psychoanalyst Donald Winnicott (1971) articulates a concept known as "holding space" or "potential space," a process he considered crucial for healthy development. The kind of healthy aloneness that children need to thrive comes from an environment that is "safe but unobtrusive" (Epstein 1998, 39). For meditation practitioners, generating space in the mind helps to accommodate any and all experience— including difficult emotion. With spaciousness, one does not get caught up in emotion but rather allows it to rise and fall away naturally. Long retreat is also said to bring about confidence in that practitioners can experience *rigpa*, the vast blue sky behind the stormy clouds of thoughts and emotion. Those experiences of the fundamental nature of mind help to put the problems of life into perspective. This is what is deemed "big mind."

When Tibetans describe those who are resilient as "very humble," and also "very confident," they mean that they do not have to build themselves up because they have trust in their own minds. Arrogance is seen as a sign that there is a lack of inner confidence because self-worth is dependent on external confirmation and praise. This trust and inner confidence in their own minds are so strong that when faced with difficulty, their negative emotions do not destabilize their confidence. Resilient people in this context may experience anger, fear, sadness, grief, or even rage, but they understand it to be temporary, fundamentally illusory, and empty of inherent existence.

During a teaching in Dharamsala, I heard the Dalai Lama recount a well-known anecdote. He was at a conference in North American when a psychologist asked what to do about chronic problems with "low self-esteem." His Holiness leaned over to his translator and asked for help; the translator tried to explain, but still he did not fully understand what this concept of "low self-esteem" was all about. In fact, he was astounded when his American colleagues described what was meant by low self-esteem. He responded by saying that Tibetans have many problems and can act in harmful ways, but they do not, he explained, question their inherent worth. The psychologists at this conference came away wondering if the very notion of self-esteem, something that seems rather basic and universal, is in fact a culturally constituted concept.

Buddhanature

Because of buddhanature, the notion that underneath one's confusion is a mind of enlightenment, Tibetans seem to have a built-in sense that things will be fundamentally okay even when there is chaos in the present. A traditional analogy is a poor man despondent about living in poverty all the while there is abundant gold beneath his dirt floor, unbeknownst to him. The framework of buddhanature also suggests that on the ultimate level, all sentient beings share something fundamental in common. In this way, compassion is not just about garnering good-natured feelings toward others, but actually recognizing that inherent sameness. As Jason Throop describes in the context of arguing for a person-centered anthropology of moral experience: "Arising from the nexus of the suffering of compassion and the suffering of the other that can never be my own, there is, ironically, the basis for the most primordial forms of human connectedness. Non-useless suffering, what I have termed suffering-for, is compassion for that which I can never assimilate to my self-experience or fully understand, for that which outstrips the limits of my own particularity" (2010, 220). Because of the Buddhist path, Tibetans are trained early on to look at most forms of suffering as the type of "non-useless suffering" that Throop describes.

Life events can be torturous and a person may simultaneously feel they will be okay in the end. Consider this story from a monk at Kirti Monastery about his life back in Tibet:

> Every single day, the Chinese government would come to the monastery and call a meeting where they would talk to us about Chinese nationalism, "Love your country!" They would come directly to our dormitories and check our belongings. They would intimidate us. Then me and my two friends wrote some papers about freedom for Tibet and spread them around the monastery and the town. So I was arrested by the Chinese police and sentenced to five years in prison from 1996 to 2001. I was released on May 1. At that time,

I had two friends with me. One is now at Sera Monastery in South India. The other friend died in Chamdo as a result of severe torture in prison.

In prison, I was tortured as well and experienced great hardship. There were three of us who were interrogated in different rooms, so we didn't know what the others were saying. Finally, the police learned that I was the one who wrote the fliers because of the handwriting. I was sentenced to five years and my friends, only two years.

On June 2, 1996, my friends were taken to a large playground near a middle school where the guards hung a sign on our necks saying that we were trying to destroy the country. They paraded us around for everyone to see. On October 1, 1996, we were taken to Lhasa from Chamdo; this took only one week. From Chamdo to Riwoche, and then from Riwoche to Tsawa Parcchu, we stayed in prisons all along the way. From Dhamo to Richi, one day and one night in prison. From Mendogangka, we stayed one night in another prison, and from there, we went to Lhasa. On October 16, 1996, finally I ended up in Dargi Prison in Lhasa.

If I talk endlessly about prisons, this will be a waste of time, but I'm just giving you an idea. When I first went to prison, I had to go to the hospital so they could take my blood because I was young and healthy. I didn't consent, but they forced me and took a lot of my blood. This wasn't to check my health; it was just to take my blood for the Chinese army to stock their blood bank. Due to taking a lot of blood, I became very weak and exhausted.

In Dagri Prison, there are seven different sections. In the third and fifth sections are all the political prisoners. The rest of the sections are for people who stole, raped women, and committed other crimes. The fifth section is for male political prisoners and the third is for female political prisoners. On May 1, 1998, in Dagri Prison, many political prisoners gathered together on the grounds near one Chinese national flag. We protested all together. This protest was known all throughout China and Tibet. At that time, my friends from Ganden Monastery, Lobsang Wangchuk and Kedep, and one from Kharmar Monastery, Lobsang Chumdu—three monks—were killed at that time. They were beaten to death. Three nuns were also tortured and beaten to death. Two nuns committed suicide. At that time, a few hundred Chinese soldiers came into the prison and used many weapons, such as electric rods to beat us. After they cleaned the ground, it was still filled with blood. At that time, the Chinese government increased the sentences of twenty-seven political prisoners.

After 1998, for three years, the prisoners who protested were put in small rooms without toilets or windows. We had to use one bucket for a toilet and keep it in our small cell. We all became sick and experienced great hardship.

But since we know a bit about Buddhism, it was beneficial for our minds. Before I was a monk, I was a herdsman, and at that time, I beat the yak and sheep very harshly. When I was tortured by the police, I thought about how I beat animals, so now I am getting the results. So I just tried to remain patient. The police and army beat the prisoners and sometimes we felt very scared and startled. Sometimes they would bang on the metal doors when the prisoners were inside, so we became temporarily deaf. They would rip the doors open and people became very scared; they would almost faint. But I just tried my best to stay patient; things always fall apart in samsara and we have to do our best and practice the Dharma.

This account shows the ways that Tibetans use Buddhist concepts and principles, such as karma, in the moment in ways that seem both ordinary and extraordinary. The monk does not disavow his suffering, but it is contextual in how he understands that it is natural for things to fall apart in samsara. This may, again, be an example of what Jason Throop (2010) refers to as "non-useless suffering" where pain simultaneously brings a dawn of compassion.

Similar sentiments are described by another man, Tsering Norbu, a sixty-four-year-old man who sells sweaters out of a cart along the road. He says:

We all have buddhanature. His Holiness the Dalai Lama always reminds us of this. The problem is that we don't know it, so we do all kinds of harmful actions. But underneath, just like the sun shining behind a sky full of clouds, is a vast, spacious, and radiant mind. That is buddhanature. You asked me some questions earlier about what I do to cope with difficulties in my life. I am not a good practitioner. But if I were a better practitioner, I would always try to meditate on my own buddhanature and the buddhanature of others. Many great lamas were thrown into prison by the Chinese. Some have been there for over thirty years. When I was in prison, there was a very humble monk who always tried to help me. He advised me that when I was being beaten and tortured, I should meditate on compassion for all beings. I told him I cannot because I am not a great lama. He challenged me and said that because of my buddhanature, I can. This immense compassion exists whether I can see it or not. This gave me great confidence.

Others also mentioned that just knowing—if only intellectually—that they already have buddhanature, a mind that is stainless and pure, was a source of great strength. Studies that investigate local experiences of resilience may be a fruitful site for pushing the boundaries of how we understand human freedom and agency.

Inner Agency

In this chapter, I have discussed the ways that the Tibetan Buddhist notions of emptiness and compassion bolster agency in times of distress. But whereas anthropologists are highly attuned to local differences across cultures when it comes to suffering and oppression, there is a tendency to conceive of agency in ways that are limited to Euro-American contexts. It is assumed that enhanced agency will promote individuality, personal choice, and personal freedom—values that are highly praised in North America. Instead, I look to Kim Hopper's description of agency, which is not culturally bound or limited to individualistic perspectives. Hopper suggests that agency is a moral category in that it measures the extent to which a person is able to achieve what he or she understands to be a good and decent life (Hopper 2007; see also Lewis, Hopper, and Healion 2012 and Myers 2016). This perspective helps to theorize agency in a context where the moral good appears foreign against the backdrop of global human rights discourse and social justice perspectives.

The Tibetan moral imperative to put others before self, even making aspirations to willingly take on the negative karma of those who wrong you, runs counter to ways that most anthropologists conceptualize social harm and retribution. Socially engaged anthropologists strive to reveal insidious power structures that marginalize and oppress based on race, gender, sexuality, or ethnicity. Therefore, when Tibetans in Dharamsala explain how they work to see prison guards as human beings and loving parents and friends— just like them, seeking happiness—it is a stretch to understand these approaches as a moral good, imbued with agency. Whereas Tibetan political activists increasingly seek to join a global network of human rights practices, everyday Tibetan people, including those same activists, place much more emphasis on what might be called "inner agency"—the capacity to be free and unconstrained by harmful negative emotion.

Conclusion

Dekyi and I walked the *khora* one afternoon in autumn, the sun finally peeking out behind the clouds after months of monsoon rain. Dekyi, the sixty-year-old mother of a *tulku*, had become a good friend and she seemed to like having a young person to look after. As we walked, she would often tell me stories of life back in Tibet or sometimes about topics she thought might be related to my research project. Often these stories were different versions of a similar story—a humble, noble person was wronged in some way and yet through deep Buddhist practice, they ultimately prevail. For example, she said:

> Usually ex–political prisoners seem very happy and do not exhibit much sorrow; they smile a lot and look radiant. Also, they often sing and recite prayers for most of the day. Some ex–political prisoners will try to do [mantra] recitation and prostrations when they have difficulties to alleviate their mental suffering. From my county, for example, one *tulku* called Gawochi was arrested and imprisoned for seven or eight years. After his release, we went to

meet him at the prison bearing *khatag* [silk scarves for offering]. His face was radiant and his body seemed very light. Later we learned that when he was in prison, he used it as an opportunity to do many prostrations and prayers. For this reason, he was mentally and physically sound during his stay in prison. Some prisoners don't know anything about Buddhism and when they are tortured, they cannot tolerate the suffering and even commit suicide. I think whether people can cope with problems or not depends on their understanding of Buddhism, particularly how *sems-gya* [spacious] their mind is.

As I listened, I thought back to when I first met Dekyi at the Tibetan reception center, where she cried throughout our first interview. Sometimes it seemed that the stories she told me were more for her benefit than mine.

"So, these stories seem to help you," I said simply.

"Yes, we can do our best to look up to these humble people, and follow their example," she said. We continued walking silently, Dekyi holding a *mala* and reciting mantras easily under her breath.

"But what if people cannot live up to this spacious mind," I asked. "What if they struggle a lot and don't feel any compassion at all, like the ones you talked about, the ones who might even commit suicide?"

"What about them?" she asked.

"Well," I tried to explain. "It is not their fault they are imprisoned."

"But it is their karma," she interjected. "It is so important to train our minds toward the Dharma so that we can find it easily in our next lifetime. When our minds are well trained in any difficult situation, we will naturally recall our practice. People who commit suicide in prison probably did not practice very much in their previous lifetime and now when they need it most, their minds are untrained. But we should practice *nying-je* [compassion] on behalf of others and wish that they will train their minds."

"But," I prodded further. "In your own life, when you struggled with losing family members and witnessing violence, how did you feel when it was not easy to find *sems pa chen po*?"

She explained, "I am not a good practitioner, so it is only natural that I have some difficulties. Like when we first met, my mind was very disturbed. My relatives in Dharamsala who helped me when I arrived told me many times, 'don't make yourself sick!' They reminded me and warned me that I should not hold on to anger and agitation. Past is past. It is good to think like this, and compassion protects the mind. You can take something like anger and wrap it in compassion—compassion for yourself, for others in that same situation, and for all sentient beings. Have you ever tried it, Sara-la? It works."

My aim in writing this book was to elucidate the ways that members of the Tibetan diaspora understand resilience in a context of violence, oppression, and rapid social change. This study does not suggest that Tibetans are more resilient than other cultural groups (despite many of them believing this to be true), but rather it reveals an alternative system of trauma appraisal and a highly developed approach for meeting distress, which they see as inevitable as a human being. Specifically, Tibetans in Dharamsala understand difficulties in life as the ripening of karma and are reticent to generate more negative karma and risk illness by reacting too strongly. Instead, they understand they have purified a karmic debt and try to let go of negative emotions. To do so, there is recognition that one needs to transform one's relationship to difficulty. Transforming difficult experiences involves cultivating *sems pa chen po*, a vast and spacious mind, which comes from generating compassion, seeing things flexibly, and reflecting on emptiness. This process is moderated by Buddhist concepts of impermanence. But as I argue throughout the book, *sems pa chen po* is better understood as a guiding principle and a horizon than an absolute outcome that is easily achieved. It is a way of orienting oneself toward recovery in moments of darkness, and a perspective the binds Tibetans together through their Buddhist faith.

Many previous studies in medical anthropology have considered the difficulties inherent in attempting to equate mental distress that is spiritual, or even existential in nature, with psychiatric diagnostic categories (Csordas, Storck, and Strauss 2008; Good 1994; Storck, Csordas, and Strauss 2000). In the Tibetan context, mental distress, including that which is occasioned by political violence, tends to be more of a spiritual problem than a medical problem. In fact, the way that members of the Tibetan exile community view human suffering transcend the overly simplified binaries of that which is "medical" and that which is "religious." Their view is instead much more humanistic: it entails understanding that all people are suffering, and that political violence and the suffering that ensues is emblematic of samsara. This reminds Tibetans in Dharamsala that there is nothing special or notable about their misfortune because all beings have suffered endlessly in samsara. Perhaps paradoxically, the sense that this is nothing special actually seems to give people the strength to let go and move on by feeling connected to other human beings through suffering.

Reframing Resilience

In 2010, the National Institutes of Mental Health began the Grand Challenges in Global Mental Health, an initiative to direct new research priorities. The major goals identified by a large and fairly diverse team of experts center around early intervention and expanding access to mental health care across the globe. Much of global mental health care is aimed at enhancing "mental health literacy," that is, raising awareness about mental health and combatting stigma to promote help seeking. However, mental health literacy is assumed to mean familiarity with and acceptance of biomedical perspectives (Watters 2010), even in contexts where local concepts of mental distress are quite distinct from psychiatric illness.

The Tibetan exile community offers a case study for understanding how pushing a biomedical agenda that is meant to help may inadvertently ignore and bypass the ways that foreign counseling methods using talk therapy may be seen as antithetical to healthy coping. For Tibetans, talking about distress and examining it over and over again runs counter to what they understand to be a resilient approach to meeting adversity. But whereas studies in medical anthropology have produced a broad range of perspectives that elucidate differences in suffering and illness across cultures, there have been fewer studies that investigate how concepts of resilience differ from culture to culture.

The Tibetan approach to trauma appraisal and resilience reveals a unique perspective on how to think about stress. The practices and approaches I described in this book employ Buddhist notions of compassion and emptiness to meet stress head on in ways that may at first appear contradictory. Seeing the world as flexible and illusory, Tibetans try to think that their difficulties are fleeting and not particularly special. Likewise, compassion, the wish for others to be well and happy, provides something outside the self on which to focus, which people in Dharamsala see as integral for healthy coping.

The Stress of Stress

Stress may be understood as a reaction to painful or difficult events; these events might be external, such as a work deadline, or internal, such as a feeling of anxiety in the dark night. Buddhist psychological approaches explain that whereas stress feels automatic in the face of difficulty, there are actually two steps or phases. First, is the basic perception or feeling. Second, comes the interpretation or how we react to our reactions, sometimes called the "second arrow." Whereas it seems natural that people should merely avoid stress (understood to be harmful and undesirable), researchers today are developing more subtle understandings of stress and its impact on the body.

A Stanford University health psychologist, Kelly McGonigal, has been a leading voice in changing the ways the biomedical research community thinks about stress. McGonigal's studies have led her to believe that the near universal message that "stress is the enemy" is actually doing more harm than good. She began to rethink her stance on stress after noticing a series of public health research reports indicating that high levels of stress increased a person's risk of death by 43 percent—but, and here is the interesting part—this was only true of those who believed that stress was harmful. The people who saw their stress as a minor setback, something fleeting that they could handle, had the lowest risk of death in the study. In other words, mortality rates were not affected by the severity of stress but the *appraisal* of the stress itself (McGonigal 2016). Her research suggests that people who see a stress response as their body's way of meeting a challenge are far more likely to avoid long-lasting effects of stress on the body. In this way, it is important to avoid thinking of stress as necessarily chronic, intractable, and severe.

McGonigal's research findings have subsequently led her to partner with colleagues investigating how Tibetan Buddhist compassion practices might combat stress in laboratory settings. In a randomized control trial, American adults were offered a course on Buddhist practices of mindfulness and compassion. The findings demonstrate that after only nine weeks, those in this condition reported an increase in happiness and a decrease in worry and emotional suppression (Jazaieri et al. 2014). The study investigators surmise that the power of this intervention is linked with increased psychological flexibility, where purposively thinking about others' well-being in moments where one is flooded by one's own distressing emotions provided something akin to what I have described in this book. Despite the fact that clinical adaptations of mindfulness have goals that may be quite different from the Buddhist cultures in Asia from where they derive (see Cassaniti 2018), such practices and perspectives are revolutionizing the way we think about the mind in clinical settings (Condon et al. 2013; Kaklauskas et al. 2008; Wegela 2010). Thinking about others was a powerful method for cutting through worry, rumination, and negative affect—harmful mental states that increase depression and anxiety (McLaughlin, Borkovec, and Sibrava 2007).

Whereas most scholars understand that how a person interprets suffering will impact his or her experience, it is still the case that many researchers understand both physical and emotional pain as a universal feature of being human. And yet anthropological evidence presents a more complex picture. In Jason Throop's long-term ethnographic investigations of pain in Yap, he has found that pain itself is culturally configured. Specially, there seems to be a difference when pain is in the "form of 'mere-suffering,' unwanted and without meaning, or it can be experienced as 'suffering-for,' transformed into a key cultural virtue that provides individuals with a moral connection to others" (2010, 144). For Tibetan Buddhists, any form of suffering presents an opportunity—that is, the opportunity to use it to see reality more closely and to generate compassion. In this way, cultural training provides a wider and more spacious understanding of how, and why, humans suffer.

Studies like these emphasize that suffering does not evaporate—and that resisting and looking for ways for suffering to disappear may actually make things worse. Instead, these perspectives suggest that reframing and looking at pain differently may help to train in building resilience, which is more of a process than a trait. This is where flexibility becomes important because it helps to diminish fixation. Flexibility and the capacity to experience paradox helps people to see that they can experience their own suffering but put it into a larger context of interconnectedness through thinking about others. In this way, resilience is not a mere absence of suffering. Rather, a person may be resiliently sad and resiliently in pain.

Resilient Trauma?

I opened this book by proposing that resilience is not the inverse of suffering, which would mean that a person could experience the deep effects of a traumatic past in a way that is resilient. In other words, I would like to propose that there may be such a thing as a resilient trauma response. But I have also argued that "trauma" is a concept that is a rather new idea, and one that is a largely Western concept insofar as it is understood as a psychiatric illness or psychological problem. Readers may struggle with what may seem like a contradiction, particularly if they feel that I am suggesting that trauma is not real if it is socially constructed. There are neurobiological realities (namely, a flight, fight, freeze or fold response) found across all animals, including human animals, when faced with serious threat or atrocity (Levine 2010). And bodies may continue to act as if there is still threat long after returning to safety. Might it be better to understand intractable reactions to traumatic events like hypervigilance and nightmares as a normal and even healthy response than a mental disorder? There is now evidence to suggest that viewing trauma in this way—as something that was actually protective, normal, and *not* disordered could be an important way forward for those recovering from life changing events (Van der Kolk 2014).

The conflating of resilience with positivity reveals the ingrained belief that resilience means a person has overcome, withstood, or resisted adversity. And thus, there are few examples within the literature about how people may be both resilient and suffering. Because Tibetans tend to treat suffering as an ordinary part of life and something that is expected, the notion that difficulty can be *related to* resiliently was more natural for them. A neighbor, Tenzin, who has a small stall on the side of the road where he sells religious *puja* items told me:

> When I first arrived here, I had an audience with the Dalai Lama. I was so happy I cried. But after leaving the reception center, we had to stand up on our own feet. So there were some problems. I went to Norbulingka [an area about twenty minutes away from Dharamsala] because there was someone there from my county and he helped a few of us find work as laborers. There is one little company that collects people to clean, work on buildings, or do painting. Sometimes I would sell carpets on the street or do building work. But we got only one hundred rupees each day. My two children are in Massouri TCV boarding school, so they need clothes and other things. But we didn't have enough money. Then I started selling Tibetan bread. I would stay up all night making bread so I could sell it in the morning at the temple. This was very difficult to stay up all night. Then I started making vegetable *momos* instead. We managed to save around twenty thousand rupees, so I bought

some *malas*, blessing cords, and *khatas*, and set up my stall. Now we are doing okay. But sometimes the Indian police will come and say that we can't sell our things here. They will ask for bribes and otherwise will shut us down. The police will say, "you can't do this" and "you can't do that," but we can't do anything. We also cannot go back to Tibet. Here we don't go hungry because of the kindness of the Dalai Lama. We will never have an empty stomach. When I see the Dalai Lama, I feel very happy. But otherwise, we aren't so happy here. At the same time, we just stay patient and try not to let it affect our peace of mind too much. A person doesn't need happiness all the time.

The sense of equanimity, or *btang snyom*, that Tenzin and others discuss is an important aspect of the Tibetan style of resilience. One does not need to act like everything is fine when it is not, but the imperative is to stay patient and not solidify one's thoughts and emotions.

And yet somehow this attitude runs counter to notions of recovery, resilience, and social justice in the Global North where it is assumed that people should talk, share, and debrief. In addition, it drums up a dangerous (yet mistaken) notion that individuals are at fault if, for whatever reason, they are not able to find sources of resilience. Instead, what I have shown in this book is how Tibetan Buddhists see an opening for awakening through the doorway of suffering. It may be another kind of grit, where instead of forsaking and valiantly resisting pain—bouncing back unscathed—a resilient person is one who is deeply changed and transformed. As resilience research in psychology, which has largely focused on individuals, enters into conversation with community resilience perspectives (Berkes and Ross 2013), it will be critical to understand how the vulnerability of trauma may provide essential cues for social connectedness and justice.

As I have discussed in this book, trauma is a particular kind of temporal suffering where the past speaks through forms of haunting the present (Good 2015). This pervasive and persistent haunting only serves to legitimize its veracity, creating looping effects between society and individual trauma survivors, for as scholars like Hacking (1998) and Foucault (1965) attest, the social production and fueling of disorders in the public imagination reify the ontological status of categories themselves. As is evident in conversations around trigger warnings in college classrooms and a controversial discourse on what it means to be "trauma informed," the general public has become increasingly aware of how women, sexual minorities, and people of color disproportionately experience harm. Despite the relatively new awareness of structural oppression in the popular imaginary, scholars have long been investigating concepts such as intergenerational and historical trauma (Argenti and Schramm 2010) among Holocaust survivors and their descendants (Feldman 2010; Kidron 2010), and among Native American and First Nations communities (Gone 2013; Gone and Trimble 2012; Kirmayer, Gone, and Moses 2014). In addition, African American activists and scholars point out that disproportionate rates of incarceration, mental illness, and poverty must be understood within the context of slavery in the United States; the intergenerational trauma paradigm explains how present-day individual suffering is exponentially and contextually linked with community-wide and historical trauma of past generations alongside the present experience of systemic racism (Fullilove 2004; Hejtmanek 2015).

Clinical researchers such as Bessel van der Kolk (2014) and Mark Wolynn (2017) have written award-winning books that are emblematic of how new scientific research on trauma has permeated the cultural zeitgeist. These works detail the neurobiological effects of trauma, including the ways that maladaptive stress responses may be passed down from generation to generation. In *It Didn't Start with You* (2017), Wolynn offers stories such as a woman who inexplicably becomes plagued with anxiety that she will harm her baby when she becomes pregnant. The fear was unfounded and confusing until she learned that her grandmother accidentally set fire to her house and lost her own infant daughter. In Wolynn's view, the notion of history repeating itself is deeply encoded within the body. Such stories echo those collected and analyzed by Carol Kidron (2010, 2015), whose ethnographic work among Holocaust survivors and their descendants details the ways that silent traces of traumatic memory are passed through generations. She offers the following account of Emma (2015, 147):

E: The one aspect of daily life that I can link to the Holocaust was that every night, at a very young age, maybe six or seven, I would prepare my shoes, placing them next to my bed, so that if the Nazis came, I would have shoes ready. I would also fold my clothes in a way that would be easy to put on.

C: Do you know where you got this habit?

E: I remember placing the shoes in the center of the floor in front of my bed so that if I had to get up and I had to wear the shoes in a hurry, I would be able to. Why were shoes so important? My mother apparently told me how she walked in the snow. I remember her saying how cold it was, how she almost froze. Now I know it was the Death March. Then it didn't matter what it was, just that it was something terrible. Then I just desperately wanted to have shoes handy . . . so that I wouldn't have to walk barefoot in the snow, so I would prepare it in such a way, so that if the Nazis came. . . . I specifically took the Nazis as the enemy, because it was so terrible. Now it wasn't that my mother sat me down and told me what had happened to her. I think I just picked up on all sorts of things that floated in the home.

Kidron draws on the work of Bakhtin (1981) and his writings on "micro-moments and micro-acts" to make sense of how the descendants of Holocaust survivors take up traumatic memory, not through explicit storytelling, but in "silent mundane practices" (2015, 147) of the everyday.

The uncanny transference of memory is deeply and synergistically a social and biological phenomenon. The field of epigenetics, which reveals the ways the environment changes the expression of our genes has not only shed compelling light on the deleterious effects of trauma but has changed the paradigm of so-called nature versus nature debates. Previously, we thought that the influence of genes moved only in one direction: that is, the genetics we inherited would influence our behavior. Epigenetics presents a much more complex and highly plastic picture, where our genes, our behavior, and the environment reciprocally respond to and modify the expression of our genetic blueprint.

The groundbreaking work of Rachel Yehuda, a professor of psychiatry and neuroscience at Mt. Sinai School of Medicine, demonstrates how through genetic inheritance, epigenetic changes to particular genes that likely play a role in stress responses may be passed on to offspring. Yehuda and colleagues have investigated this phenomenon among Holocaust survivors and their children (2016), and among pregnant women who lived in Lower Manhattan during 9/11, whose children now display similar epigenetic changes to those observed in their mothers at the time of the attacks (2005). Genes themselves do not change, but these findings suggest that the expression of some genes may be more flexible than others, which Yehuda (2015) believes can explain why the children of Holocaust survivors are three times more likely to develop PTSD than their peers who did not have parents who survived the Holocaust. These results have been simultaneously praised and dismissed (skeptics point to low sample size and other conflating variables); yet these new paradigms undeniably reveal the complex ways we might inherit a troubled past.

To be sure, we do not come into this world as blank slates and the ways we inherit norms, assumptions, power, and privilege may both protect and harm. Alexis Shotwell (2016) argues that the notion of "personal purity," a belief that we may disavow a custodial relationship to the past and to our social, biological, and familial environments is a politically dangerous myth. Shotwell argues that we are all implicated through hereditary transference of various sorts. If we apply this assertion to the case of trauma, we might consider the ways that we are all recipients of various harm encoded in the body through culture, epigenetics, karma, socialization, and language. Because the slate has never been clean, so to speak, we can acknowledge this interconnected web of suffering, and of liberation (Shotwell 2016). As I conclude this book, I wish to propose that all that we inherit, including trauma, may not be wholly negative.

When Rachel Yehuda speaks of her research on the epigenetics of trauma, she argues that trauma is simply something that changes you—and not necessarily for the worse. She says: "When something cataclysmic happens, people say, I am changed. I am not the same person I once was" (Yehuda 2015). There is a certain wisdom or intelligence to be found in trauma, including the wisdom to learn how to let it soften you, to deepen you, yet to know when to let go. I am reminded of something a Tibetan *amchi*, Dr. Dorjee, once said to me, "People may have the karma to get sick, but they can also have the karma to recover."

Social Action as Recovery

The question of how to best recover from trauma—and whether certain cultural groups recover in different ways—remains an open question. A group of clinicians at the Bellevue Clinic for Torture Survivors in New York City working with Tibetan torture survivors learned rather quickly how this cultural group differed in their approach to healing. As part of a political asylum case, the group was offered counseling services. But an interesting series of events occurred instead. Rather than accepting the psychotherapy that was offered, the group requested assistance in forming a coalition within their local neighborhood in Queens, New York. As one of the clinicians, Jack Saul, recounts: "For many [Tibetans], their priority was not just to receive support from the group; they also wanted to help other recently arrived refugees and asylum seekers . . . [they] valued helping others as an adaptive way of dealing with the trauma and loss they had experienced as a result of torture and migration, and separation from their families" (2014a, 34). This style of cultivating resilience through helping others is emblematic of healthy coping from the Tibetan point of view. Focusing on one's problems alone is not wrong, but it is not seen as particularly effective either. Incidentally, the notion that helping and being of benefit to others might actually be more therapeutic than simply *consuming* and being the beneficiary of services was something I had previously investigated in the context of peer-run recovery-oriented mental health treatment (see Lewis, Hopper, and Healion 2012). Seeing altruism, service, and compassion as a pathway to care was something that also intrigued the clinicians at Bellevue, prompting the group to travel to Dharamsala to learn more about Tibetan approaches to health.

When Saul and colleagues came to Dharamsala, they asked a Tibetan nurse who was an established and prominent member of the community to assemble a group of Tibetan torture survivors. She gathered a group of nuns from a few of the local nunneries; most did not know one another and were not aware of their common history of having been tortured. The aim of their meeting was not to process trauma, but rather to form a support group and to share strategies that have helped them to adapt to life outside of Tibet. The nuns were keen to share their ideas when they learned of Saul's work with Tibetans back in New York City. They were also curious about how other groups around the world have managed oppression, loss of homeland, and environmental destruction; they took particular interest in the historical and present-day experiences of Jews (Saul 2014b). The clinicians from New York also became aware that many of these nuns who had been imprisoned did not consider themselves to be trauma survivors or political refugees.

Likewise, at the beginning of my study it seemed like a fruitful idea to compare the experiences of those who were political refugees and those who came to Dharamsala for economic or educational reasons. However, I quickly found that many Tibetans who told me they were not ex–political prisoners would later mention rather neutrally, without much fanfare, that they had been imprisoned. To identify oneself as someone who had been exposed to severe events might be to aggrandize oneself as a hero. As Saul recounts (2014a), many torture survivors from around the world—Mauritania, Sierra Leone, Iran, Iraq, Jordan, Palestine, Afghanistan, Tibet, China, the Philippines—are not accustomed to talking about their experiences as is done in psychotherapy. When immigrant and asylum seekers across the globe come into contact with foreign mental health services, there is often a schism between what service users feel they need and what service providers think is most beneficial. Those who find their way to social services often do not seek mental health services, but rather legal assistance, housing, and medical care. Many global mental health programs also "[assume] that the client is willing to disclose and rationally discuss his or her deepest emotions to a professional stranger" in clinical contexts (Calabrese 2008, 342). And yet the social service organizations in Dharamsala started by Tibetans for Tibetans are not structured around emotion work. Rather than processing the details of violence and formulating trauma narratives, social service organizations started by Tibetans help people focus on the material aspects of resettlement. Friends and relatives encourage one another to swiftly "get over" or "move on" from negative emotions. This might be called repression in the West, but in Dharamsala this sensibility is connected to what Tibetans call "broad thinking." Tibetan approaches to meeting life's challenges are deeply inscribed with such cultural wisdom. As Norbu explains:

> The people who come to India through Nepal experience a lot of hardships and difficulties. They have to cross many high mountains in their journey to India and are in constant fear of arrest by the border police. We also don't have enough food and drink. Second, Tibetans inside Tibet don't have any human rights or freedom of religion and culture. For example, you don't have the right to keep photos of the Dalai Lama and Karmapa. In general, we keep these photos very secretly. When Chinese government authorities come to inspect our houses, we take down the photos and hide them in a box. Tibetans have a very unique culture. The kindness and advice of Buddhism helps us to avoid hurting any others. It teaches us to be patient even in the face of adversity; this is our habit—being patient with problems. Also, I think since Tibetans are innocent, we are proud to struggle for our freedom since it is

truth. Third, those who experience many difficulties, such as Tibetans, become accustomed to bearing hardship. Fourth, the Dalai Lama gives good advice through his teachings, helping us to keep strong hope.

But whereas there are strong cultural cues on how to work with suffering at this individual level, the Tibetan exile community has come to understand that their practices of un-remarking will not fuel a human rights campaign.

The path forward is not at all agreed upon among Tibetans. In his lecture to the American study abroad students gathered on meditation cushions around him, Sonam Tashi, after recounting his own torture experiences, explained:

> Sometimes entire families will be arrested altogether for being suspected of engaging in political activities. Or if one family member was killed, the entire family will go to the Chinese office and protest, and they will all be arrested. Some Tibetans have sacrificed everything, including their bodies and lives; some have even self-immolated. [He calls them, *Cho-me*; the same term as butter lamps offered in religious temples.] Some Tibetans think all that we do doesn't matter; they are hopeless and do not think it will have much effect. Many people both in Tibet and in exile just continue to live their lives and don't get involved. But this only means that we have no hope at all of things improving in Tibet. But most Tibetans hope that one day Tibet will gain its freedom. There are four or five different perspectives on the Tibet issue: (1) [the] Middle Way (*Uma-lam*); (2) self-decision (*rang-ta rang-gyi*); (3) persistence of truth (*den-be u-tsu*); (4) regional autonomy (*den-ta se*); (5) TYC (Free Tibet). Nuns and monks from the monastery are held in prisons with remarkable patience. They don't have anger and hatred. Anyway, most Tibetans entrust their faith in the Dalai Lama and hope the international community will help. You also need to abandon hope and fear.

A young woman raised her hand. "Why would you abandon hope if the Dalai Lama helps to restore hope? I think I am confused!"

The others nodded in agreement. "Yeah, isn't all political activism about fighting for what is right? Why would you abandon hope?"

As a monk trained in philosophical debate, Sonam Tashi seemed to relish these kinds of conversations. He smiled and said, "His Holiness the Dalai Lama always tell us that we have to fight hard for justice in this world, what we could think of as enlightened action. But then we cannot be attached to the result. Once we have attachment to a certain result—this is the trap of hope and fear—we will suffer when we do not achieve it."

"How do you know what to fight for? There are always many different sides," one student asked.

Sonam Tashi paused. "Before you take any action, or speak anything, if you stop and question whether your motivation is to help others, to help all sentient beings, you will not go astray. The wish for others' happiness will always protect you." The students sat in silence. Their questions were not fully resolved, but something had shifted.

NOTES

Introduction

1. See Audra Simpson 2014 and Carole McGranahan 2016b on the anthropology of refusal. These concepts are explored in more depth in chapter 4.

2. See chapter 1 for extended discussion on how *rlung* (wind) disorders, particularly among torture survivors, are glossed as PTSD.

1. Life in Exile

1. "Oracles" are monastic or lay tantric practitioners who go into trance and become possessed by particular deities. The deity Pehar is thought to have long possessed the Nechung Oracle, which historically consults closely with the lineage of the Dalai Lamas. To this day, the Dalai Lama and the government-in-exile Parliament members in Dharamsala consult the Nechung Oracle before making important political decisions (see Bell 2016).

2. The Kalachakra (meaning Wheel of Time in Sanskrit), is a tantric Buddhist empowerment ceremony that accompanies an intricate sand mandala that is ceremoniously destroyed to symbolize emptiness upon completion of the ten-day initiation. Those who

receive the empowerment are said to become enlightened in no less than sixteen lifetimes. In general, it is considered an enormous blessing that purifies negative karma. When it is given in Bodhgaya, the place where the Buddha is said to have attained enlightenment, hundreds of thousands from all over the world come to attend.

3. *Maha* (Sanskrit) meaning greater or bigger. In some cases, adherents of the Mahayana traditions have understood this school to be superior to the Hinayana, called with derision, "the lesser vehicle." Buddhist scholars, however, argue that Mahayana is more aptly translated as "wider" not *better*, to infer that practitioners may continue to take rebirth even when they achieve enlightenment to work for the enlightenment of all sentient beings.

4. CNN interview aired on April 25, 2012.

5. *Baksheesh* is a "tip" that is more analogous to a bribe. The practice is common throughout India. Particular institutions, such as utility companies, the postal service, and a range of government agencies may deny services until *baksheesh* is paid. In some cases, parents can make "donations" that allow their children to be admitted to medical schools or prestigious colleges.

6. Tibetans often place *lags* (pronounced "la") at the end of a person's name to communicate respect.

2. Mind Training

1. A pseudonym.

2. Breaking *samaya* (tantric vow with one's guru) is to go against one's root lama or teacher or abandon sacred view, which brings negative karma.

3. The *jig rten chos brgyad*, or "eight worldly concerns," in Buddhism are related to avoiding pain, criticism, and blame, and seeking out fortune, praise, and pleasure.

4. Tibetan Buddhist practitioners take this vow as a matter of course; it is not reserved for those with special qualities or qualifications.

5. *Nagas* are harmful spirits that are associated with bodies of water. They are easily disturbed by not respecting the land and cause ailments such as skin diseases and mental illness if angered. Daily protector chants that appease *nagas* and other spirits are performed daily by monasteries and nunneries on behalf of the community.

6. Burning dried herbs on or just above the body to promote healthy circulation and the flow of energy.

7. *Pujas* are religious rituals that often span several hours and involve elaborate prayers, mantra recitation, and visualization of particular deities. Monasteries and nunneries undertake a variety of *pujas* throughout the day on behalf of the community. Generally, protector *pujas* are performed daily and seek to appease wrathful deities who fiercely protect practitioners from harm. Other deities, such as the Medicine Buddha and Green Tara, have particular days within the lunar calendar on which it is traditional to recite mantras and make offerings that are particular to these deities.

8. Within the culture and personality period of anthropology in the early twentieth century, scholars equated psychiatric categories with local categories of distress across cultures, referring to some cultures as "depressive" or "anxious" societies. It has also been

fashionable to falsely deduce that possession and trance states are cultural manifestations of multiple personality disorder or schizophrenia.

3. Resisting Chronicity

1. Structural violence is a theoretical concept, which explains how unequal social structures, poverty, racism, and other forms of oppression harm individuals and communities (Farmer 2001). A related construct, symbolic violence explicates how agency is constrained through hegemonic knowledge and practices (Bourdieu 1999).

2. In the next chapter, I complicate this assertion in that Tibetan political activists have learned the importance of bolstering human rights campaigns with trauma narratives.

3. All foreigners, including Tibetans, are required to check in to the Foreign Registration Office at the police station every six months to renew their documents.

4. The Paradox of Testimony

1. There are very high rates of tuberculosis in Dharamsala, likely made worse by people living in close quarters in boarding schools, monasteries, and nunneries.

2. A structure that commemorates a holy person or event that occurred, usually in connection to the historical Buddha. Stupas sometimes contain ashes or relics. The stupa in Bodhgaya sits adjacent to the bodhi tree where the Buddha is said to have attained enlightenment.

3. It is not uncommon for young monks to give up their monastic vows after receiving their education, which is usually acceptable. Likewise, there are times when laypeople will take monastic vows later in life after having been householders. However, engaging in sexual activity and continuing to wear robes is extremely shameful. Most people will not directly criticize monastics, which is considered disrespectful to the institution of monasticism. But there are many euphemisms and subtle gestures to indicate that a monk or nun is breaking vows.

REFERENCES

Adams, Vincanne. 1998. "Suffering the Winds of Lhasa: Politicized Bodies, Human Rights, Cultural Difference, and Humanism in Tibet." *Medical Anthropology Quarterly* 12 (1): 74–102.

———. 2001. "The Sacred in the Scientific: Ambiguous Practices of Science in Tibetan Medicine." *Cultural Anthropology* 16 (4): 542–75.

———. 2013. *Markets of Sorrow, Labors of Faith: New Orleans in the Wake of Katrina.* Durham, NC: Duke University Press.

Adams, Vincanne, Suellen Miller, Sienna Craig, and Michael Varner. 2005. "The Challenge of Cross-Cultural Clinical Trials Research: Case Report from the Tibetan Autonomous Region, People's Republic of China." *Medical Anthropology Quarterly* 19 (3): 267–89.

Adams, Vincanne, Michelle Murphy, and Adele E. Clarke. 2009. "Anticipation: Technoscience, Life, Affect, Temporality." *Subjectivity* 28 (1): 246–65.

Adams, Vincanne, Mona Schrempf, and Sienna R. Craig. 2013. *Medicine between Science and Religion: Explorations on Tibetan Grounds.* New York: Berghahn Books.

Ager, Alastair. 1997. "Tensions in the Psychosocial Discourse: Implications for the Planning of Interventions with War-Affected Populations." *Development in Practice* 7 (4): 402–7.

Allen, James, Kim Hopper, Lisa Wexler, Michael Kral, Stacy Rasmus, and Kristine Nystad. 2013. "Mapping Resilience Pathways of Indigenous Youth in Five Circumpolar Communities." *Transcultural Psychiatry* 51 (5): 601–31.

American Psychiatric Association. 2013. *Diagnostic and Statistical Manual of Mental Disorders DSM-5.* 5th ed. Washington, DC: American Psychiatric Association.

Andreasen, Nancy C. 1980. "Post-Traumatic Stress Disorder." In *Comprehensive Textbook of Psychiatry,* edited by Harold Kaplan, Alfred Freedman, and Benjamin Sadock, 1517–25, 3rd ed. Baltimore, MD: Williams and Wilkins.

Antze, Paul, and Michael Lambek. 1996. *Tense Past: Cultural Essays in Trauma and Memory.* New York: Routledge.

Appadurai, Arjun. 1990. "Disjuncture and Difference in the Global Cultural Economy." *Public Culture* 2 (2): 1–24.

Argenti, Nicolas, and Katharina Schramm. 2010. *Remembering Violence: Anthropological Perspectives on Intergenerational Transmission.* New York: Berghahn Books.

Back, Anthony L., Susan M. Bauer-Wu, Cynda H. Rushton, and Joan Halifax. 2009. "Compassionate Silence in the Patient-Clinician Encounter: A Contemplative Approach." *Journal of Palliative Medicine* 12 (12): 1113–17.

Bakhtin, Mikhail M. 1981. *The Dialogic Imagination.* Austin: University of Texas Press.

Barber, Brian K. 2008. "Contrasting Portraits of War: Youths' Varied Experiences with Political Violence in Bosnia and Palestine." *International Journal of Behavioral Development* 32 (4): 298–309.

Barrett, Lisa Feldman. 2017. *How Emotions Are Made: The Secret Life of the Brain.* Boston: Mariner Books.

Bateson, Gregory. 1972. *Steps to an Ecology of Mind.* New York: Ballantine Books.

Beasley, Margaret, Ted Thompson, and John Davidson. 2003. "Resilience in Response to Life Stress: The Effects of Coping Style and Cognitive Hardiness." *Personality and Individual Differences* 34 (1): 77–95.

Bell, Christopher. 2016. "Divination, Prophecy and Oracles in Tibetan Buddhism." In *Prophecy in the New Millennium: When Prophecies Persist,* edited by Sarah Harvey and Suzanne Newcombe, 124–35. London, Routledge.

Benedict, Adriana Lee, L. Mancini, and M. A. Grodin. 2009. "Struggling to Meditate: Contextualising Integrated Treatment of Traumatised Tibetan Refugee Monks." *Mental Health, Religion & Culture* 12 (5): 485–99.

Berger, Peter L., and Thomas Luckmann. 1966. *The Social Construction of Reality: A Treatise in the Sociology of Knowledge.* New York: Anchor Books.

Berkes, Fikrit, and Helen Ross. 2013. "Community Resilience: Toward an Integrated Approach." *Society and Natural Resources: An International Journal* 26 (1): 5–20.

Berliner, Peter, Line Natascha Larsen, and Elena de Casas Soberón. 2012. "Case Study: Promoting Community Resilience with Local Values—Greenland's Paamiut Asasara." In *The Social Ecology of Resilience: A Handbook of Theory and Practice,* edited by Michael Ungar, 387–97. New York: Springer.

Bhatia, Shushum, Tsegyal Dranyi, and Derrick Rowley. 2002. "A Social and Demographic Study of Tibetan Refugees in India." *Social Science and Medicine* 54 (3): 411–22.

Biehl, Joao. 2005. *Life in a Zone of Social Abandonment.* Berkeley: University of California Press.

Biehl, João Guilherme, Byron Good, and Arthur Kleinman. 2007. *Subjectivity: Ethnographic Investigations*. Berkeley: University of California Press.

Bobrzynski, Kuba. Letter to author, July 3, 2012.

Bonanno, George A. 2004. "Loss, Trauma, and Human Resilience: Have We Underestimated the Human Capacity to Thrive after Extremely Aversive Events?" *American Psychologist* 59 (1): 20–28.

Boston Globe. 2017. "UMass Amherst Bars Student from Carrying Tibetan Flag in Commencement Ceremony." May 4.

Bourdieu, Pierre. 1977. *Outline of a Theory of Practice*. Cambridge: Cambridge University Press.

——. 1994. "Doxa, Orthodoxy, Heterodoxy." In *Culture/Power/History: A Reader in Contemporary Social Theory*, edited by Nicholas B. Dirks, Geoff Eley, and Sherry B. Ortner, 155–99. Princeton, NJ: Princeton University Press.

——. 1999. *The Weight of the World: Social Suffering in Contemporary Society*. Stanford, CA: Stanford University Press.

Breslau, Joshua. 2000. "Globalizing Disaster Trauma: Psychiatry, Science and Culture after the Kobe Earthquake." *Ethos* 28 (2): 174–97.

Brox, Trine. 2016. *Tibetan Democracy: Governance, Leadership and Conflict in Exile*. London: IB Tauris.

Cabezón, José Ignacio. 2008. "State Control of Tibetan Buddhist Monasticism in the People's Republic of China." In *Chinese Religiosities: Afflictions of Modernity and State Formation*, edited by Mayfair Mei-hui Yang, 261–94. Berkeley: University of California Press.

Calabrese, Joseph D. 2008. "Clinical Paradigm Clashes: Ethnocentric and Political Barriers to Native American Efforts at Self-Healing." *Ethos* 36 (3): 334–53.

Carlisle, Steven G. 2008. "Synchronizing Karma: The Internalization and Externalization of a Shared, Personal Belief." *Ethos* 36 (2): 194–219.

Carpenter, Ann. 2013. "Social Ties, Space, and Resilience: Literature Review of Community Resilience to Disasters and Constituent Social and Built Environment Factors." Federal Reserve Bank of Atlanta: Community and Economic Discussion Paper, 2–13.

Carrico, Kevin. 2012. "Self-Immolation and Slander-Woeser." Self-Immolation as Protest in Tibet. *Cultural Anthropology Online*. https://culanth.org/fieldsights/self-immolation-and-slander-woeser.

Cassaniti, Julia. 2012. "Agency and the Other: The Role of Agency for the Importance of Belief in Buddhist and Christian Traditions." *Ethos* 40 (3): 297–316.

——. 2015. *Living Buddhism: Mind, Self, and Emotion in a Thai Community*. Ithaca, NY: Cornell University Press.

——. 2018. *Remembering the Present: Mindfulness in Buddhist Asia*. Ithaca, NY: Cornell University Press.

China View. 2013. "The Dalai Clique." www.news.xinhuanet.com. Accessed December 20, 2013.

Cho, Francisca. 2014. "Buddhism, Science, and the Truth about Karma." *Religion Compass* 8 (4): 117–27.

Chodron, Pema. 2001. *Start Where You Are: A Guide to Compassionate Living*. Boston: Shambhala.

Clifford, Terry. 1994. *Tibetan Buddhist Medicine and Psychiatry: The Diamond Healing.* Delhi: Motilal Banarsidass.

Condon, Paul, Gaelle Desbordes, Willa B. Miller, and David DeSteno. 2013. "Meditation Increases Compassionate Responses to Suffering." *Psychological Science* 24 (10): 2125–27.

Connerton, Paul. 1989. *How Societies Remember.* Cambridge: Cambridge University Press.

Cooper, Amy. 2015. "Time Seizures and the Self: Institutional Temporalities and Self-Preservation among Homeless Women." *Culture, Medicine & Psychiatry* 39 (1): 162–85.

Coulthard, Glen. 2014. "Red Skin, White Masks: Rejecting the Colonial Politics of Recognition." Minneapolis: University of Minnesota Press.

Craig, Sienna. 2012a. *Healing Elements Efficacy and the Social Ecologies of Tibetan Medicine.* Berkeley: University of California Press.

———. 2012b. "Social Suffering and Embodied Political Crisis." Self-Immolation as Protest in Tibet. *Cultural Anthropology Online.* http://www.culanth.org/fieldsights/97-social-suffering-and-embodied-political-crisis.

———. 2013. "From Empowerments to Power Calculations: Notes on Efficacy, Value and Method." In *Medicine between Science and Religion: Explorations on Tibetan Grounds*, edited by Vincanne Adams, Mona Schrempf, and Sienna Craig, 215–44. New York: Berghahn Books.

Crane, Johanna T. 2013. *Scrambling for Africa: AIDS, Expertise, and the Rise of American Global Health Science.* Ithaca, NY: Cornell University Press.

Crescenzi, A., E. Ketzer, M. Van Ommeren, K. Phuntsok, I. Komproe, and J. T. de Jong. 2002. Effect of Political Imprisonment and Trauma History on Recent Tibetan Refugees in India. *Journal of Traumatic Stress*, 15 (5): 369–75.

Csordas, Thomas J. 1999. "Ritual Healing and the Politics of Identity in Contemporary Navajo Society." *American Ethnologist* 26 (1): 3–23.

Csordas, Thomas J., Michael J. Storck, and Milton Strauss. 2008. "Diagnosis and Distress in Navajo Healing." *Journal of Nervous and Mental Disease* 196 (8): 585–96.

Dalai Lama. 2019. https://www.dalailama.com/messages/tibet/middle-way-approach. Accessed April 25.

Das, Veena. 2000. *Violence and Subjectivity.* Berkeley: University of California Press.

———. 2007. *Life and Words Violence and the Descent into the Ordinary.* Berkeley: University of California Press.

———. 2015. *Affliction: Health, Disease, Poverty.* New York: Fordham University Press.

Davidson, Richard J. 2000. "Affective Style, Psychopathology, and Resilience: Brain Mechanisms and Plasticity." *American Psychologist* 55 (11): 1196–1214.

———. 2017. "If You Toss a Stone into a Lake: Attention and Emotion in the Brain." In *The Monastery and the Microscope: Conversations with the Dalai Lama on Mind, Mindfulness, and the Nature of Reality*, edited by Wendy Hasenkamp, 211–33. New Haven, CT: Yale University Press.

Davidson, Richard J., Daren C. Jackson, and Ned H. Kalin. 2000. "Emotion, Plasticity, Context, and Regulation: Perspectives from Affective Neuroscience." *Psychological Bulletin* 126 (6): 890–909.

Davidson, Richard J., and Bruce S. McEwen. 2012. "Social Influences on Neuroplasticity: Stress and Interventions to Promote Well-Being." *Nature Neuroscience* 15 (5): 689–95.

Del Vecchio Good, Mary-Jo, Tseunetsugu Munakata, Yasuki Kobayashi, Cheryl Mattingly, and Byron J. Good. 1994. "Oncology and Narrative Time." *Social Science & Medicine* 38 (6): 855–62.

Desjarlais, Robert R. 1995. "Violence, Culture, and the Politics of Trauma." In *Writing at the Margin: Discourse between Anthropology and Medicine*, edited by Arthur Kleinman, 173–89. Berkeley: University of California Press.

———. 2003. *Sensory Biographies: Lives and Deaths among Nepal's Yolmo Buddhists.* Berkeley: University of California Press.

Desjarlais, Robert, and C. Jason Throop. 2011. "Phenomenological Approaches in Anthropology." *Annual Review of Anthropology* 40 (1): 87–102.

Diehl, Keila. 2002. *Echoes from Dharamsala: Music in the Life of a Tibetan Refugee Community.* Berkeley: University of California Press.

Dreyfus, Georges B. J. 2003. *The Sound of Two Hands Clapping: The Education of a Tibetan Buddhist Monk.* Berkeley: University of California Press.

Durkheim, Emile. (1912) 1995. *The Elementary Forms of Religious Life.* New York: Free Press.

Eaves, Emery R., Mark Nichter, and Cheryl Ritenbaugh. 2016. "Ways of Hoping: Navigating the Paradox of Hope and Despair in Chronic Pain." *Culture, Medicine and Psychiatry* 40 (1): 35–58.

El-Shaarawi, Nadia. 2015. "Living an Uncertain Future: Temporality, Uncertainty, and Well-Being among Iraqi Refugees in Egypt." *Social Analysis* 59 (1): 38–56.

Epstein, Mark. 1999. *Going to Pieces without Falling Apart: A Buddhist Perspective on Wholeness.* New York: Broadway.

Evans, Brad, and Julian Reid. 2014. *Resilient Life: The Art of Living Dangerously.* Cambridge, U.K.: Polity Press.

Evans, Dabney. 2008. "Shattered Shangri-La: Differences in Depressive and Anxiety Symptoms in Students Born in Tibet Compared to Tibetan Students Born in Exile." *Social Psychiatry and Psychiatric Epidemiology* 43 (6): 429–36.

Evans-Pritchard, E. E. 1937. *Witchcraft, Oracles and Magic among the Azande.* Oxford: Clarendon Press.

Fanon, Frantz. 1963. *The Wretched of the Earth.* New York: Grove Press.

———. 1967. *Black Skin, White Masks.* New York: Grove Press.

Farmer, Paul. 2001. *Infections and Inequalities: The Modern Plagues.* Berkeley: University of California Press.

Fassin, Didier. 2009. *The Empire of Trauma: An Inquiry into the Condition of Victimhood.* Edited by Richard Rechtman. Princeton, NJ: Princeton University Press.

———. 2012. *Humanitarian Reason: A Moral History of the Present Times.* Berkeley: University of California Press.

Feldman, Jackie. 2010. "Nationalising Personal Trauma, Personalising National Redemption: Performing Testimony at Auschwitz-Birkenau." In *Remembering Violence: Anthropological Perspectives on Intergenerational Transmission*, edited by Nicolas Argenti and Katharina Schramm, 103–34. New York: Berghahn Books.

Felman, Shoshanna, and Dori Laub. 1992. *Testimony: Crises of Witnessing*. New York: Routledge.

Finley, Erin P. 2011. *Fields of Combat: Understanding PTSD among Veterans of Iraq and Afghanistan*. Ithaca, NY: Cornell University Press.

Foucault, Michel. 1965. *Madness and Civilization: A History of Insanity in the Age of Reason*. New York: Pantheon Books.

———. 1980. *The History of Sexuality*. 1st Vintage Books ed. New York: Vintage Books.

Foxen, Patricia. 2010. "Local Narratives of Distress and Resilience: Lessons in Psychosocial Well-Being among the K'iche'Maya in Postwar Guatemala." *Journal of Latin American and Caribbean Anthropology* 15 (1): 66–89.

Frankl, Viktor E. (1946) 1992. *Man's Search for Meaning: An Introduction to Logotherapy*. 4th ed. Boston: Beacon Press.

Free Tibet. "Unsung Heroes." https://freetibet.org/about/human-rights/case-studies/musicians. Accessed, May 28, 2017.

Freud, Sigmund. 1919. "The Uncanny." In *Imago*, translated by Alix Strachey, reprinted in *Sammlung, Fünfte Folge*.

Fullilove, Mindy Thompson. 2004. *Root Shock: How Tearing Up City Neighborhoods Hurts America, and What We Can Do About It*. New York: One World Books.

Galatzer-Levy, Isaac R., Charles L. Burton, and George A. Bonanno. 2012. "Coping Flexibility, Potentially Traumatic Life Events, and Resilience: A Prospective Study of College Student Adjustment." *Journal of Social and Clinical Psychology* 31 (6): 542–67.

Garcia, Angela. 2008. "The Elegiac Addict: History, Chronicity, and the Melancholic Subject." *Cultural Anthropology* 23 (4): 718–46.

———. 2010. *The Pastoral Clinic: Addiction and Dispossession along the Rio Grande*. Berkeley: University of California Press.

Gardiner, Michael. 1996. "Alterity and Ethics: A Dialogical Perspective." *Theory, Culture & Society* 13 (2): 121–43.

Garmezy, Norman. 1991. "Resilience in Children's Adaptations to Negative Life Events and Stressed Environments." *Pediatrics* 20 (1): 459–66.

Gayley, Holly. 2007. "Soteriology of the Senses in Tibetan Buddhism." *Numen* 54 (1): 459–99.

———. 2013. "Reimagining Buddhist Ethics on the Tibetan Plateau." *Journal of Buddhist Ethics* 20 (1): 248–86.

———. 2016. "T-Pop and the Lama: Buddhist 'Rites Out of Place' in Tibetan Monastery-Produced VCDs." In *Religion and Modernity in the Himalayas*, edited by Megan Adamson Sijapati and Jessica Vantine Birkenholtz, 43–62. New York: Routledge.

———. 2018. "Revisiting the 'Secret Consort' (*gsang yum*) in Tibetan Buddhism." *Religions* 9 (179). doi:10.3390/rel9060179.

Gerke, Barbara. 2011. *Long Lives and Untimely Deaths: Life-Span Concepts and Longevity Practices among Tibetans in the Darjeeling Hills, India*. Boston: Brill.

Giddens, Anthony. 1991. *Modernity and Self-Identity*. Palo Alto, CA: Stanford University Press.

Goffman, Erving. (1968) 1990. *Asylums: Essays on the Social Situation of Mental Patients and Other Inmates*. New York: Doubleday.

Gone, Joseph P. 2013. "Redressing First Nations Historical Trauma: Theorizing Mechanisms for Indigenous Culture as Mental Health Treatment." *Transcultural Psychiatry* 50 (5): 683–706.

Gone, Joseph P., and Joseph E. Trimble. 2012. "American Indian and Alaska Native Mental Health: Diverse Perspectives on Enduring Disparities." *Annual Review of Clinical Psychology* 8 (1): 131–60.

Good, Byron J. 1977. "The Heart of What's the Matter: The Semantics of Illness in Iran." *Culture, Medicine and Psychiatry* 1 (1): 25–58.

———. 1994. *Medicine, Rationality, and Experience: An Anthropological Perspective.* Cambridge: Cambridge University Press.

———. 2012. "Phenomenology, Psychoanalysis, and Subjectivity in Java." *Ethos* 40 (1): 24–36.

———. 2015. "Haunted by Aceh: Specters of Violence in Post-Suharto Indonesia." In *Genocide and Mass Violence: Memory, Symptom and Recovery*, edited by Devon Emerson Hinton and Alexander Laban Hinton, 58–82. Cambridge, MA: Harvard University Press.

Good, Byron J., Subandi, and Mary-Jo DelVecchio Good. 2007. "The Subject of Mental Illness: Psychosis, Mad Violence, and Subjectivity in Indonesia." In *Subjectivity: Ethnographic Investigations*, edited by João Biehl, Byron J. Good, and Arthur M. Kleinman. Berkeley: University of California Press.

Green, Linda. 1994. "Fear as a Way of Life." *Cultural Anthropology* 9 (2): 227–56.

Gyatso, Janet. 2012. "Discipline and Resistance on the Tibetan Plateau." Self-Immolation as Protest in Tibet. *Cultural Anthropology Online.* http://www.culanth.org/fieldsights/96-discipline-and-resistance-on-the-tibetan-plateau.

Gyatso, Palden, and Tsering Shakya. 1997. *The Autobiography of a Tibetan Monk.* New York: Grove Press.

———. 1998. *Fire under the Snow: True Story of a Tibetan Monk.* London: Harvill Press.

Hacking, Ian. 1998. *Rewriting the Soul: Multiple Personality and the Sciences of Memory.* Princeton, NJ: Princeton University Press.

———. 1999. "Making Up People." In *The Science Studies Reader*, edited by Mario Biagiolo, 161–71. New York: Routledge.

———. 2002. *Mad Travelers: Reflections on the Reality of Transient Mental Illnesses.* Cambridge, MA: Harvard University Press.

Hallisey, Charles, and Anne Hansen. 1996. "Narrative, Sub-Ethics, and the Moral Life: Some Evidence from Theravada Buddhism." *Journal of Religious Ethics* 24 (2): 305–27.

Harvey, David. 1991. *The Condition of Postmodernity: An Enquiry into the Origins of Cultural Change.* Malden, MA: Blackwell.

Hejtmanek, Katie Rose. 2015. *Friendship, Love, and Hip Hop: An Ethnography of African American Men in Psychiatric Custody.* New York: Palgrave MacMillan.

Herman, Judith Lewis. 1992. *Trauma and Recovery.* New York: Basic Books.

Hillman, James, and Michael Ventura. 1993. *We've Had a Hundred Years of Psychotherapy—And the World Is Getting Worse.* New York: Harper.

Hinton, Devon E., Alexander L. Hinton, Kok-Thay Eng, and Sophearith Choung. 2012. "PTSD and Key Somatic Complaints and Cultural Syndromes among Rural

Cambodians: The Results of Needs Assessment Survey." *Medical Anthropology Quarterly* 26 (3): 383–407.

Hinton, Devon, Susan Hinton, Khin Um, Audria Chea, and Sophia Sak. 2002. "The Khmer 'Weak Heart' Syndrome: Fear of Death from Palpitations. *Transcultural Psychiatry* 39 (3): 323–44.

Hinton, Devon E., Stefan G. Hofmann, Edwin Rivera, Michael W. Otto, and Mark H. Pollack. 2011. "Culturally Adapted CBT (CA-CBT) for Latino Women with Treatment-Resistant PTSD: A Pilot Study Comparing CA-CBT to Applied Muscle Relaxation." *Behaviour Research and Therapy* 49 (4): 275–80.

Hinton, Devon E., and Laurence J. Kirmayer. 2017. "The Flexibility Hypothesis of Healing." *Culture, Medicine, and Psychiatry* 41 (1): 3–34.

Hinton, Devon E., and Roberto Lewis-Fernández. 2011. "The Cross-Cultural Validity of Posttraumatic Stress Disorder: Implications for DSM-5." *Depression and Anxiety* 28 (9): 783–801.

Hinton, Devon E., Ria Reis, and Joop de Jong. 2015. "The 'Thinking a Lot' Idiom of Distress and PTSD: An Examination of their Relationship among Traumatized Cambodian Refugees Using the 'Thinking a Lot' Questionnaire." *Medical Anthropology Quarterly* 29 (3): 357–80.

Hinton, Devon, Khin Um, and Phalnarith Ba. 2001. "*Kyol Goeu* (Wind Overload)," part 1, "A Cultural Syndrome of Orthostatic Panic among Khmer Refugees." *Transcultural Psychiatry* 38 (4): 403–32.

Hirsch, Marianne, and Nancy K. Miller. 2011. *Rites of Return Diaspora Poetics and the Politics of Memory*. New York: Columbia University Press.

Holecek, Andrew. 2013. *Preparing to Die: Practical Advice and Spiritual Wisdom from the Tibetan Buddhist Tradition*. Boston: Snow Lion.

Hollan, Doug. 2004. "Self Systems, Cultural Idioms of Distress and the Psycho-Bodily Consequences of Childhood Suffering." *Transcultural Psychiatry* 41 (1): 62–79.

Holling, Crawford. 1973. "Resilience and Stability in Ecological Systems." *Annual Review of Ecology and Systematics* 4 (1): 1–24.

Holmes, Seth, and Heide Castañeda. 2016. "Representing the European Refugee Crisis in Germany and Beyond: Deservingness and Difference, Life and Death." *American Ethnologist* 43 (1): 12–24.

Holtz, T. H. 1998. "Refugee Trauma versus Torture Trauma: A Retrospective Controlled Cohort Study of Tibetan Refugees." *Journal of Nervous and Mental Disease* 186 (1): 24.

Hooberman, Joshua B., Barry Rosenfeld, Dechen Lhewa, Andrew Rasmussen, and Allen Keller. 2007. "Classifying the Torture Experiences of Refugees Living in the United States." *Journal of Interpersonal Violence* 22 (1): 108–23.

Hopper, Kim. 2007. "Rethinking Social Recovery in Schizophrenia: What a Capabilities Approach Might Offer." *Social Science & Medicine* 65 (5): 868–79.

Hussain, Dilwar, and Braj Bhushan. 2011. "Posttraumatic Stress and Growth among Tibetan Refugees: The Mediating Role of Cognitive-Emotional Regulation Strategies." *Journal of Clinical Psychology* 67 (7): 720–35.

Husserl, Edmund. 1970. *The Crisis of European Sciences and Transcendental Phenomenology: An Introduction to Phenomenological Philosophy*. Evanston, IL: Northwestern University Press.

International Campaign for Tibet. https://www.savetibet.org/. Accessed April 25, 2019.

Jackson, Michael. 2009. *The Palm at the End of the Mind: Relatedness, Religiosity, and the Real*. Durham, NC: Duke University Press.

———. 2013. *The Wherewithal of Life: Ethics, Migration, and the Question of Well-Being*. Berkeley: University of California Press.

Jacobson, Eric. 2007. "'Life-Wind Illness' in Tibetan Medicine: Depression, Generalised Anxiety Disorder, and Panic Attack." In *Soundings in Tibetan Medicine: Anthropological and Historical Perspectives*, edited by Mona Schrempf, 225–27. Boston: Brill.

James, Erica. 2008. "Haunting Ghosts: Madness, Gender, and *Ensekirite* in Haiti in the Democratic Era." In *Postcolonial Disorders*, edited by Mary-Jo Delvecchio Good, 132–56. Berkeley: University of California Press.

Janes, Craig R. 1995. "The Transformations of Tibetan Medicine." *Medical Anthropology Quarterly* 9 (1): 6–39.

———. 1999a. "Imagined Lives, Suffering, and the Work of Culture: The Embodied Discourses of Conflict in Modern Tibet." *Medical Anthropology Quarterly* 13 (4): 391–412.

———. 1999b. "The Health Transition, Global Modernity, and the Crisis of Traditional Medicine: The Tibetan Case." *Social Science and Medicine* 48 (12): 1803–20.

Jazaieri, Hooria, Kelly McGonigal, Thupten Jinpa, James R. Doty, James J. Gross, and Philippe R. Goldin. 2014. "A Randomized Controlled Trial of Compassion Cultivation Training: Effects on Mindfulness, Affect, and Emotion Regulation." *Motivation and Emotion* 38 (1): 23–35.

Jenkins, Janis H. 2015. *Extraordinary Conditions: Culture and Experience in Mental Illness*. Oakland: University of California Press.

Kaiser, Bonnie N., Emily E. Haroz, Brandon A. Kohrt, Paul A. Bolton, Judith K. Bass, and Devon E. Hinton. 2015. "'Thinking Too Much': A Systematic Review of a Common Idiom of Distress." *Social Science & Medicine* 147: 170–83.

Kaklauskas, Francis J., Susan Nimanheminda, Louis Hoffman, and MacAndrew S. Jack. 2008. *Brilliant Sanity: Buddhist Approaches to Psychotherapy*. Denver, CO: University of Rockies Press.

Kashdan, Todd B. 2010. "Psychological Flexibility as a Fundamental Aspect of Health." *Clinical Psychology Review* 30 (7): 865–78.

Keller, Allen. 2006. "Traumatic Experiences and Psychological Distress in an Urban Refugee Population Seeking Treatment Services." *Journal of Nervous and Mental Disease* 194 (3): 188–94.

Keller, A., D. Eisenman, J. Saul, G. Kim, J. Connell, and T. Holtz. 1997. *Striking Hard: Torture in Tibet*. Boston: Physicians for Human Rights.

Kenworthy, Nora J. 2014. "A Manufactu(RED) Ethics: Labor, HIV, and the Body in Lesotho's 'Sweat-Free' Garment Industry." *Medical Anthropology Quarterly* 28 (4): 459–79.

Ketzer, Eva, and Antonella Crescenzi. 2002. "Addressing the Psychosocial and Mental Health Needs of Tibetan Refugees in India." In *Trauma, War, and Violence: Public Mental Health in Socio-Cultural Context*, edited by Joop Jong, 283–315. New York: The Springer Series in Social/Clinical Psychology.

Khyentse, Dzongsar Jamyang. 2008. *What Makes You Not a Buddhist*. Berkeley, CA: Shambhala.

——. 2016. *The Guru Drinks Bourbon*. Boulder, CO: Shambhala.

Kidron, Carol A. 2010. "Embracing the Lived Memory of Genocide: Holocaust Survivor and Descendant Renegade Memory Work at the House of Being." *American Ethnologist* 37 (3): 429–51.

——. 2015. "Embodying the Distant Past: Holocaust Descendant Narratives of the Lived Presence of the Genocidal Past." In *Genocide and Mass Violence: Memory, Symptom, and Recovery*, edited by Devon E. Hinton and Alexander Hinton, 137–56. New York: Cambridge University Press.

Kirmayer, Laurence J. 1989. "Cultural Variations in the Response to Psychiatric Disorders and Emotional Distress. *Social Science & Medicine* 29 (3): 327–39.

Kirmayer, Laurence J., Stéphane Dandeneau, Elizabeth Marshall, Morgan Kahentonni Phillips, and Karla Jessen Williamson. 2011. "Rethinking Resilience from Indigenous Perspectives." *Canadian Journal of Psychiatry* 56 (2): 84–91.

Kirmayer, Laurence J., Joseph P. Gone, and Joshua Moses. 2014. "Rethinking Historical Trauma." *Transcultural Psychiatry* 51 (3): 299–319.

Kirmayer, Laurence J., and Norman Sartorius. 2007. "Cultural Models and Somatic Syndromes." *Psychosomatic Medicine* 69 (9): 832–40.

Kirmayer, Laurence J., Megha Sehdev, Rob Whitley, Stéphane F. Dandeneau, and Colette Isaac. 2009. "Community Resilience: Models, Metaphors and Measures." *International Journal of Indigenous Health* 5 (1): 62–117.

Kleinman, Arthur. 2011. *Deep China: The Moral Life of the Person: What Anthropology and Psychiatry Tell Us about China Today*. Berkeley: University of California Press.

——. 2015. "What Does Trauma Do?" In *Genocide and Mass Violence: Memory, Symptom, and Recovery*, edited by Devon E. Hinton and Alexander L. Hinton, xiii–xiv. New York: Cambridge University Press.

Kleinman, Arthur, Veena Das, and Margaret M. Lock. 1997. *Social Suffering*. Berkeley: University of California Press.

Kleinman, Arthur, and Byron Good. 1985. *Culture and Depression: Studies in the Anthropology and Cross-Cultural Psychiatry of Affect and Disorder*. Berkeley: University of California Press.

Kloos, Stephan. 2012. "Processing Exile-Tibetan Identity: The Alchemy of Tibetan Medicine's Pharmaceutical and Political Efficacy." *Curare* 35 (3): 197–207.

——. 2016. "The Recognition of *Sowa Rigpa* in India: How Tibetan Medicine Became an Indian Medical System." *Medical Anthropology Theory* 3 (2): 19–49.

Kobasa, Suzanne C. 1979. "Stressful Life Events, Personality, and Health: An Inquiry into Hardiness." *Journal of Personality and Social Psychology* 37 (1): 1.

Kohrt, Brandon A. 2005. "'Somatization' and 'Comorbidity': A Study of Jhum-Jhum and Depression in Rural Nepal." *Ethos* 33 (1): 125–47.

Kohrt, Brandon A., and Emily Mendenhall. 2015. *Global Mental Health: Anthropological Perspectives*. New York: Routledge Press.

Kongtrul, Dzigar. 2009. "Have Courage and a Sense of Humor." In *In the Face of Fear: Buddhist Wisdom for Challenging Times*, edited by Barry Boyce, 129–36. Boston: Shambhala.

——. 2013. "Shenpa: The Juice of Self-Centered Emotions." *Mangala Shri Bhuti* (blog), December 14.

Kongtrul, Jamgon. 2005. *The Great Path of Awakening: The Classic Guide to Lojong, a Tibetan Buddhist Practice for Cultivating the Heart of Compassion.* Translated by Ken McLeod. Boston: Shambhala.

Krieger, Nancy. 1994. "Epidemiology and the Web of Causation: Has Anyone Seen the Spider?" *Social Science & Medicine* 39 (7): 887–903.

Kulick, Don. 2006. "Theory in Furs—Masochist Anthropology." *Current Anthropology* 47 (6): 933–52.

Laird, Thomas. 2006. *The Story of Tibet: Conversations with the Dalai Lama.* New York: Grove.

Langford, Jean M. 2013. *Consoling Ghosts: Stories of Medicine and Mourning from Southeast Asians in Exile.* Minneapolis: University of Minnesota Press.

Lazarus, Richard S., and Susan Folkman. 1984. *Stress, Appraisal, and Coping.* New York: Springer.

Lempert, Michael. 2012. *Discipline and Debate: The Language of Violence in a Tibetan Buddhist Monastery.* Berkeley: University of California Press.

Lester, Rebecca J. 2005. *Jesus in Our Wombs Embodying Modernity in a Mexican Convent.* Berkeley: University of California Press.

——. 2013. "Back from the Edge of Existence: A Critical Anthropology of Trauma." *Transcultural Psychiatry* 50 (5): 753–62.

Leung, Mei-Kei, Chetwyn C. H. Chan, Jing Yin, Chack-Fan Lee, Kwok-Fai So, and Tatia M. C. Lee. 2012. "Increased Gray Matter Volume in the Right Angular and Posterior Parahippocampal Gyri in Loving-Kindness Meditators." *Social Cognitive and Affective Neuroscience* 8 (1): 34–39.

Levine, Peter A. 2010. *In an Unspoken Voice: How the Body Releases Trauma and Restores Goodness.* Berkeley, CA: North Atlantic Books.

Lewis, Sara E. 2013. "Trauma and the Making of Flexible Minds in the Tibetan Exile Community." *Ethos* 41 (3): 313–36.

——. 2018. "Resilience, Agency, and Everyday Lojong in the Tibetan Diaspora." *Contemporary Buddhism* 19 (2): 342–61. doi: 10.1080/14639947.2018.1480153.

Lewis, Sara E., Kim Hopper, and Ellen Healion. 2012. "Partners in Recovery: Social Support and Accountability in a Consumer-Run Mental Health Center." *Psychiatric Services* 63 (1): 61–65.

Lhewa, D. 2007. "Validation of a Tibetan Translation of the Hopkins Symptom Checklist 25 and the Harvard Trauma Questionnaire." *Assessment* 14 (3): 223–30.

Link, Bruce G., and Jo Phelan. 1995. "Social Conditions as Fundamental Causes of Disease." *Journal of Health and Social Behavior* 35 (1): 80–94.

Livingston, Julie. 2012. *Improvising Medicine: An African Oncology Ward in an Emerging Cancer Epidemic.* Durham, NC: Duke University Press.

Lock, Margaret M. 2001. "The Tempering of Medical Anthropology: Troubling Natural Categories." *Medical Anthropology Quarterly* 15 (4): 478–92.

Lopez, Donald. 1998. *Prisoners of Shangri-La: Tibetan Buddhism and the West.* Chicago: University of Chicago Press.

Luhrmann, Tanya M. 2000. *Of Two Minds: The Growing Disorder in American Psychiatry*. New York: Alfred A. Knopf.

——. 2010. "Review of the Empire of Trauma: An Inquiry into the Condition of Victimhood." *American Journal of Psychiatry* 167 (6): 722.

——. 2012. *When God Talks Back: Understanding the American Evangelical Relationship with God*. New York: Alfred A. Knopf.

Luhrmann, Tanya M., Ramachandran Padmavati, Hema Tharoor, and Akwasi Osei. 2015. "Differences in Voice-Hearing Experiences of People with Psychosis in the USA, India and Ghana: Interview-Based Study." *British Journal of Psychiatry* 206 (1): 41–44.

Lutz, Antoine, Lawrence L. Greischar, David M. Perlman, and Richard J. Davidson. 2009. "BOLD Signal in Insula is Differentially Related to Cardiac Function during Compassion Meditation in Experts vs. Novices." *NeuroImage* 47 (3): 1038–46.

Lutz, Catherine A. 1988. *Unnatural Emotions: Everyday Sentiments on a Micronesian Atoll and Their Challenge to Western Theory*. Chicago: University of Chicago Press.

Makley, Charlene. 2005. "'Speaking Bitterness': Autobiography, History, and Mnemonic Politics on the Sino-Tibetan Frontier." *Comparative Studies in Society and History* 47 (1): 40–78.

——. 2007. *The Violence of Liberation: Gender and Tibetan Buddhist Revival in Post-Mao China*. Berkeley: University of California Press.

——. 2012. "The Political Lives of Dead Bodies." Self-Immolation as Protest in Tibet. *Cultural Anthropology Online*. http://www.culanth.org/fieldsights/95-the-political-lives -of-dead-bodies.

——. 2015. "The Sociopolitical Lives of Dead Bodies: Tibetan Self-Immolation Protest of Mass Media." *Cultural Anthropology* 30 (3): 448–76.

Martin, Emily. 1994. *Flexible Bodies: Tracking Immunity in American Culture from the Days of Polio to the Age of AIDS*. Boston: Beacon Press.

——. 2007. *Bipolar Expeditions: Mania and Depression in American Culture*. Princeton, NJ: Princeton University Press.

Mattingly, Cheryl. 2010. *The Paradox of Hope: Journeys through a Clinical Borderland*. Berkeley: University of California Press.

——. 2014. *Moral Laboratories: Family Peril and the Struggle for a Good Life*. Berkeley: University of California Press.

Mattingly, Cheryl, and Linda C. Garro. 2000. *Narrative and the Cultural Construction of Illness and Healing*. Berkeley: University of California Press.

McGonigal, Kelly. *The Upside of Stress: Why Stress is Good for You, and How to Get Good at It*. New York: Penguin.

McGranahan, Carole. 2010a. *Arrested Histories: Tibet, the CIA, and Memories of a Forgotten War*. Durham, NC: Duke University Press.

——. 2010b. "Narrative Dispossession: Tibet and the Gendered Logics of Historical Possibility." *Comparative Studies in Society and History* 52 (4): 768–97.

——. 2016a. "Theorizing Refusal: An Introduction." *Cultural Anthropology* 31 (3): 319–25.

——. 2016b. "Refusal and the Gift of Citizenship." *Cultural Anthropology* 31 (3): 334–41.

McGranahan, Carole, and Ralph Litzinger. 2012. "Self-Immolation as Protest in Tibet." Self-Immolation as Protest in Tibet. *Cultural Anthropology Online*. http://www.culanth .org/fieldsights/93-self-immolation-as-protest-in-tibet.

McHugh, Ernestine. 2001. *Love and Honor in the Himalayas: Coming to Know Another Culture*. Philadelphia: University of Pennsylvania Press.

McKinney, Kelly. 2007. "Breaking the Conspiracy of Silence: Testimony, Traumatic Memory and Psychotherapy with Survivors of Political Violence." *Ethos* 35 (3): 265–99.

McLaughlin, Katie A., Thomas D. Borkovec, and Nicholas J. Sibrava. 2007. "The Effects of Worry and Rumination of Affect States and Cognitive Activity." *Behavior Therapy* 38 (1): 23–38.

Mendenhall, Emily. 2012. *Syndemic Suffering: Social Distress, Depression and Diabetes among Mexican Immigrant Women*. Walnut Creek, CA: Left Coast Press.

Mendenhall, Emily, and Shane A. Norris. 2015. "When HIV Is Ordinary and Diabetes New: Remaking Suffering in a South African Township." *Global Public Health* 10 (4): 449–62.

Mercer, Stewart W., Alastair Ager, and Eshani Ruwanpura. 2005. "Psychosocial Distress of Tibetans in Exile: Integrating Western Interventions with Traditional Beliefs and Practice." *Social Science & Medicine* 60 (1): 179–89.

Millard, Colin. 2003. "Tibetan Medicine and the Classification and Treatment of Mental Illness." In *Proceedings of the Tenth Seminar of the IATS, 2003*, vol. 10, *Soundings in Tibetan Medicine*, edited by Mona Schrempf, 247–84. Leiden: Brill.

Myers, Neely A. L. 2015. *Recovery's Edge: An Ethnography of Mental Health Care and Moral Agency*. Nashville, TN: Vanderbilt University Press.

———. 2016. "Recovery Stories: An Anthropological Exploration of Moral Agency in Stories of Mental Health Recovery." *Transcultural Psychiatry* 53 (4): 427–44.

Nagarjuna. 2013. *Nagarjuna's Letter to a Friend: With Commentary by Kangyur Rinpoche*. Ithaca, NY: Snow Lion.

National Institute of Mental Health. 2014. Traumatic Stress Research Program. measurement-and-intervention-program/traumatic-stress-research-program.shtml. Accessed January 11, 2014.

Nichter, Mark. 1981. "Idioms of Distress: Alternatives in the Expression of Psychosocial Distress: A Case Study from South India." *Culture, Medicine and Psychiatry* 5 (4): 379–408.

———. 2010. "Idioms of Distress Revisited." *Culture, Medicine and Psychiatry* 34 (2): 401–16.

Nordstrom, Carolyn. 1997. *A Different Kind of War Story*. Philadelphia: University of Pennsylvania Press.

Obeyesekere, Gananath. 1985. "Depression, Buddhism, and the Work of Culture in Sri Lanka." In *Culture and Depression*, edited by Arthur Kleinman and Byron Good, 134–52. Berkeley: University of California Press.

———. 1990. *The Work of Culture: Symbolic Transformation in Psychoanalysis and Anthropology*. Chicago: University of Chicago Press.

The Office of His Holiness the Dalai Lama. 2013. "His Holiness's Middle Way Approach for Resolving the Issue of Tibet." http://www.dalailama.com/messages/middle-way-approach. Accessed December 30, 2013.

Ong, Aihwa. 1999. *Flexible Citizenship: The Cultural Logics of Transnationality*. Durham, NC: Duke University Press.

Ozawa-de Silva, Chikako, and Brendan R. Ozawa-de Silva. 2011. "Mind/Body Theory and Practice in Tibetan Medicine and Buddhism." *Body & Society* 17 (1): 95–119.

Ozer, Emily J., Suzanne R. Best, Tami L. Lipsey, and Daniel S. Weiss. 2003. "Predictors of Posttraumatic Stress Disorder and Symptoms in Adults: A Meta-Analysis." *Psychological Bulletin* 129 (1): 52–73.

Pace, Thaddeus W. W., Lobsang Tenzin Negi, Daniel D. Adame, Steven P. Cole, Teresa I. Sivilli, Timothy D. Brown, Michael J. Issa, and Charles L. Raison. 2009. "Effect of Compassion Meditation on Neuroendocrine Innate Immune and Behavioral Responses to Psychosocial Stress." *Psychoneuroendoncrinology* 34 (1): 87–98.

Pandolfo, Stefania. 2008a. "Testimony in Counterpoint: Psychiatric Fragments in the Aftermath of Culture. *Qui Parle* 17 (1): 62–123.

——. 2008b. "Knot of the Soul: Postcolonial Conundrums, Madness, and the Imagination." In *Postcolonial Disorders*, edited by Byron J. Good, Mary-Jo DelVecchio Good, Sandra J. Hyde, and Sarah Pinto. Berkeley: University of California Press.

Patrul Rinpoche. 2010. *The Words of My Perfect Teacher*. New Haven, CT: Yale University Press.

Phayul. 2013. "China Shuts Down Drongna Monastery in Driru, Arrests Teacher." Phayul.com. http://www.phayul.com/news/article.aspx?id=34413. Accessed June 4, 2017.

——. 2017. "Over 40 Tibetans Arrested after Clash with Police over Water Rights." Phayul.com. Accessed June 4, 2017.

Pine, Frances. 2014. "Migration as Hope: Space, Time, and Imagining the Future." *Current Anthropology* 55 (S9): S95–S104.

Povinelli, Elizabeth A. 2002. *The Cunning of Recognition: Indigenous Alterities and the Making of Australian Multiculturalism*. Durham, NC: Duke University Press.

Proust, Audrey. 2006. "Causation as Strategy: Interpreting Humours among Tibetan Refugees." *Anthropology & Medicine* 13 (2): 119–30.

——. 2008. *Precious Pills: Medicine and Social Change among Tibetan Refugees in India*. New York: Berghahn Books.

Redfield, Peter. 2013. *Life in Crisis: The Ethical Journey of Doctors without Borders*. Berkeley: University of California Press.

Reid, Julian. 2012. "The Disastrous and Politically Debased Subject of Resilience." *Development Dialogue* 58 (1): 67–79.

Rinchen, Sonam. 2001. *Eight Verses for Training the Mind*. Translated by Ruth Sonam. Ithaca, NY: Snow Lion Books.

Robbins, Joel. 2013. "Beyond the Suffering Subject: Toward an Anthropology of the Good." *Journal of the Royal Anthropological Society* 19 (3): 447–62.

Roche, Gerald. 2017. "Linguistic Vitality, Endangerment, and Resilience." *Language Documentation & Conservation* 11: 190–223.

Roche, Gerald, and Hiroyuki Suzuki. 2018. "Tibet's Minority Languages: Diversity and Endangerment." *Modern Asian Studies* 52 (4): 1227–78.

Rosaldo, Renato. 1989. *Culture & Truth: The Remaking of Social Analysis*. Boston: Beacon Press.

Sachs, Emily, Barry Rosenfeld, Dechen Lhewa, Andrew Rasmussen, and Andrew Keller. 2008. "Entering Exile: Trauma, Mental Health, and Coping among Tibetan Refugees Arriving in Dharamsala, India." *Journal of Traumatic Stress* 21 (2): 199–208.

Said, Edward. 1978. *Orientalism: Western Representations of the Orient*. New York: Pantheon.

Samuel, Geoffrey. 1993. *Civilized Shamans: Buddhism in Tibetan Societies.* Washington, DC: Smithsonian Institution Press.

———. 2005. *Tantric Revisionings: New Understandings of Tibetan Buddhism and Indian Religion.* New York: Ashgate.

Saul, Jack. 2014a. *Collective Trauma, Collective Healing: Promoting Community Resilience in the Aftermath of Disaster.* New York: Routledge.

———. 2014b. Letter to author, February 15.

Scheper-Hughes, Nancy. 1998. "Undoing: Social Suffering and the Politics of Remorse in the New South Africa." *Social Justice* 24 (4): 114–42.

Scheper-Hughes, Nancy, and Margaret M. Lock. 1987. "The Mindful Body: A Prolegomenon to Future Work in Medical Anthropology." *Medical Anthropology Quarterly* 1 (1): 6–41.

Scherz, China. 2013. "Let Us Make God Our Banker: Ethics, Temporality, and Agency in a Ugandan Charity Home." *American Ethnologist* 40 (4): 624–36.

Schröder, Nike-Ann. 2011. *Discussing Psychotrauma with Tibetan Healing Experts: A Cultural Translation.* Berlin: Weissensee Verlag.

Seeley, Karen M. 2008. *Therapy after Terror 9/11, Psychotherapists, and Mental Health.* Cambridge: Cambridge University Press.

Seligman, Rebecca, and Laurence J. Kirmayer. "Dissociative Experience and Cultural Neuroscience: Narrative, Metaphor and Mechanism." *Culture, Medicine and Psychiatry* 32 (1): 31–64.

Servan-Schreiber, David, Brigitte Le Lin, and Boris Birmaher. 1998. "Prevalence of Posttraumatic Stress Disorder and Major Depressive Disorder in Tibetan Refugee Children." *Journal of the American Academy of Child and Adolescent Psychiatry* 37 (8): 874–79.

Shakya, Tsering. 2012. "Transforming the Language of Protest." Self-Immolation as Protest in Tibet. *Cultural Anthropology Online.* http://www.culanth.org/fieldsights/94-transforming-the language-of-protest. Accessed on June 1, 2018.

Sharp, Lesley Alexandra. 1993. *The Possessed and the Dispossessed: Spirits, Identity, and Power in a Madagascar Migrant Town.* Berkeley: University of California Press.

Shir-Vertesh, Dafna. 2012. "'Flexible Personhood': Loving Animals as Family Members in Israel." *American Anthropologist* 114 (3): 420–32.

Shore, Bradd. 1996. *Culture in Mind: Cognition, Culture, and the Problem of Meaning.* New York: Oxford University Press.

Shotwell, Alexis. 2016. *Against Purity: Living Ethically in Compromised Times.* Minneapolis: University of Minnesota Press.

Shweder, Richard A., and Edmund J. Bourne. 1984. "Does the Concept of the Person Vary Cross-Culturally?" In *Culture Theory: Essays on Mind, Self, and Emotion*, edited by Richard A. Schweder and Robert A. LeVine, 158–99. Cambridge: Cambridge University Press.

Simpson, Audra. 2007. "On Ethnographic Refusal: Indigeneity, 'Voice' and Colonial Citizenship." *Junctures* 9 (1): 67–80.

———. 2014. *Mohawk Interuptus: Political Life across the Borders of Settler States.* Durham, NC: Duke University Press.

———. 2016. "Consent's Revenge." *Cultural Anthropology* 31 (3): 326–33.

Sontag, Susan. 2003. *Regarding the Pain of Others*. New York: Farrar, Straus and Giroux.

Spiro, Melford E. 1997. *Gender Ideology and Psychological Reality: An Essay on Cultural Reproduction*. New Haven, CT: Yale University Press.

Stephen, Lynn. 2013. *We Are the Face of Oaxaca: Testimony and Social Movements*. Durham, NC: Duke University Press.

Stern, Daniel N. 2004. *The Present Moment in Psychotherapy and Everyday Life*. New York: Norton.

Stevenson, Lisa. 2014. *Life Besides Itself: Imagining Care in the Canadian Arctic*. Oakland: University of California Press.

Stoler, Ann. 2009. *Along the Archival Grain: Epistemic Anxieties and Colonial Common Sense*. Princeton, NJ: Princeton University Press.

Storck, Michael J., Thomas J. Csordas, and Milton Strauss. 2000. "Depressive Illness and Navajo Healing." *Medical Anthropology Quarterly* 14 (4): 571–97.

Sullivan, Brenton. 2013. "The Mother of All Monasteries: Gönlung Jampa Ling and the Rise of Mega Monasteries in Northeastern Tibet." PhD diss., University of Virginia.

Summerfield, Derek. 2012. "Afterword: Against 'Global Mental Health'" *Transcultural Psychiatry* 49 (3/4): 519–30.

Swank, Heidi. 2014. *Rewriting Shangri-La: Tibetan Youth, Migrations and Literacies in McLeod Ganj, India*. Leiden: Brill.

Taussig, Michael T. 1992. *Mimesis and Alterity: A Particular History of the Senses*. London: Routledge.

Taylor, Charles. 1989. *Sources of the Self*. Cambridge, MA: Harvard University Press.

———. 2007. *A Secular Age*. Cambridge, MA: Harvard University Press.

Taylor, Diana. 2007. "Double-Blind: The Torture Case." *Critical Inquiry* 33 (4): 710–33.

Tedeschi, Richard G., and Lawrence G. Calhoun. 1996. "The Posttraumatic Growth Inventory: Measuring the Positive Legacy of Trauma." *Journal of Traumatic Stress* 9 (3): 455–71.

Theidon, Kimberly. 2015. "Pasts Imperfect: Talking about Justice with Former Combatants in Columbia." In *Genocide and Mass Violence: Memory, Symptom and Recovery*, edited by Devon E. Hinton and Alexander L. Hinton, 321–41. Cambridge, MA: Harvard University Press.

Throop, Jason C. 2003. "On Crafting a Cultural Mind: A Comparative Assessment of Some Recent Theories of 'Internalization' in Psychological Anthropology." *Transcultural Psychology* 40 (1): 109–39.

———. 2010. *Suffering and Sentiment: Exploring the Vicissitudes of Experience and Pain in Yap*. Berkeley: University of California Press.

Tibetan Children's Village (TCV). http://www.tcv.org.in/. Accessed February 14, 2017.

Tibetan Review. 2014. "China Shuts Down 3 Tibetan Monasteries in Besieged Driru County." January 9. http://www.tibetanreview.net/news.php?&id=13079.

Tibetan Torture Survivors Program. http://tibet.net/health/#code0slide1. Accessed April 7, 2017.

Ticktin, Miriam. 2011a. *Casualities of Care: Immigration and the Politics of Humanitarianism in France*. Berkeley: University of California Press.

————. 2011b. "How Biology Travels: A Humanitarian Trip." *Body & Society* 17 (2/3): 139–58.

————. 2014. "Transnational Humanitarianism." *Annual Review of Anthropology* 43 (1): 273–89.

Tournadre, Nicolas. 2014. "The Tibetic Languages and Their Classification." *Trans-Himalayan Linguistics: Historical and Descriptive Linguistics of the Himalayan Area* 266 (1): 105–29.

Trungpa, Chögyam. 1973. *Cutting Through Spiritual Materialism*. Berkeley, CA: Shambhala.

————. 1991. *Crazy Wisdom*. Boston: Shambhala.

Tuttle, Gray. 2005. *Tibetan Buddhists in the Making of Modern China*. New York: Columbia University Press.

Tutu, Desmond. 2000. *No Future without Forgiveness*. New York: Random House.

Ungar, Michael. 2011. "Community Resilience for Youth and Families: Facilitative Physical and Social Capital in Contexts of Adversity." *Children and Youth Services Review* 33 (1): 1742–48.

United Nations Human Rights. 2013. Office of the High Commissioner for Human Rights. Committee against Torture. http://www2.ohchr.org/english/. Accessed November 5, 2013.

Upton, Janet. 1996. "Home on the Grasslands? Tradition, Modernity, and the Negotiation of Identity by Tibetan Intellectuals in the PRC." In *Negotiating Ethnicities in China and Taiwan*, edited by Melissa J. Brown, 98–124. Berkeley: University of California Press.

Vahali, Honey Oberoi. 2009. *Lives in Exile: Exploring the Inner World of Tibetan Refugees*. London: Routledge.

Van der Kolk, Bessel. 2014. *The Body Keeps the Score: Brain, Mind, and Body in the Healing of Trauma*. New York: Penguin Books.

Von Peter, Sebastian. 2010. "The Temporality of 'Chronic' Mental Illness." *Culture, Medicine & Psychiatry* 34 (1): 13–28.

Walker, Ana Paula Pimentel. 2013. "Embodied Identity and Political Participation: Squatters' Engagement in the Participatory Budget in Brazil." *Ethos* 41 (2): 199–222.

Walsh, Froma. 2006. *Strengthening Family Resilience*. New York: Guilford Press.

Ward, Shannon. 2013. "Conceiving Modernity." *Medical Anthropology Quarterly* 27 (2): 175–92.

Watters, Ethan. 2010. "The Americanization of Mental Illness." *New York Times*, magazine section, January 8.

Weaver, Lesley Jo, and Emily Mendenhall. 2014. "Applying Syndemics and Chronicity: Interpretations from Studies of Poverty, Depression, and Diabetes." *Medical Anthropology* 33 (2): 92–108.

Weber, Max. (1930) 2004. *The Protestant Ethic and the Spirit of Capitalism*. London: Routledge.

Wegela, Karen Kissel. 2010. *The Courage to be Present: Buddhism, Psychotherapy, and the Awakening of Natural Wisdom*. Boulder, CO: Shambhala.

Weine, Steven M. 2006. *Testimony after Catastrophe: Narrating the Traumas of Political Violence*. Evanston, IL: Northwestern University Press.

Wexler, Lisa. 2009. "The Importance of Identity, History, and Culture in the Wellbeing of Indigenous Youth." *Journal of the History of Childhood and Youth* 2 (2): 267–76.

Wexler, Lisa M., G. DiFluvio, and T. K. Burke. 2009. "Resilience and Marginalized Youth: Making a Case for Personal and Collective Meaning-Making as Part of Resilience Research in Public Health." *Social Science and Medicine* 69 (4): 565–70.

Wexler, Lisa M., and Joseph P. Gone. 2012. "Culturally Responsive Suicide Prevention in Indigenous Communities: Unexamined Assumptions and New Possibilities." *American Journal of Public Health* 102 (5): 800–806.

Whitley, Rob, and Elizabeth Siantz. 2012. "Recovery Centers for People with a Mental Illness: An Emerging Best Practice?" *Psychiatric Services* 63 (1): 10–12.

Wikan, Unni. 1990. *Managing Turbulent Hearts: A Balinese Formula for Living*. Chicago: University of Chicago Press.

Winnicott, Donald W. 1971. *Playing and Reality*. London: Routledge.

Wolff, Jonathan. 2009. "Disadvantage, Risk and the Social Determinants of Health." *Public Health Ethics* 2 (3): 214–23.

Wolynn, Mark. 2017. *It Didn't Start with You: How Inherited Family Trauma Shapes Who We Are and How to End the Cycle*. New York: Penguin Books.

Wool, Zoë H. 2015. *After War: The Weight of Life at Walter Reed*. Durham, NC: Duke University Press.

Wool, Zoë H., and Seth D. Messinger. "Labors of Love: The Transformation of Care in the Non-Medical Attendant Program at Walter Reed Army Medical Center." *Medical Anthropology Quarterly* 26 (1): 26–48.

Yang, Lawrence, and Daisy Singla. 2011. "Use of Indigenous Cultural Idioms by Chinese Immigrant Relatives for Psychosis: Impacts on Stigma and Psychoeducational Approaches." *Journal of Nervous and Mental Disease* 199 (11): 872–78.

Yankey, Tsering, and Urmi Nanda Biswas. 2012. "Life Skills Training as an Effective Intervention Strategy to Reduce Stress among Tibetan Refugee Adolescents." *Journal of Refugee Studies* 25 (4): 514–36.

Yanos, Philip T., and Kim Hopper. 2008. "On 'False, Collusive Objectification': Becoming Attuned to Self-Censorship, Performance and Interviewer Biases in Qualitative Interviewing." *International Journal of Social Research Methodology* 11 (3): 229–37.

Yarris, Kristin. 2014. "'Pensando Mucho' ('Thinking Too Much'): Embodied Distress among Grandmothers in Nicaraguan Transnational Families." *Culture, Medicine, and Psychiatry* 38 (3): 473–98.

Yeh, Emily T. 2013. *Taming Tibet: Landscape Transformation and the Gift of Chinese Development*. Ithaca, NY: Cornell University Press.

Yehuda, Rachel. 2015. "How Trauma and Resilience Cross Generations." *On Being*, radio program with Krista Tippett, July 30. https://www.wnyc.org/story/rachel-yehuda—how-trauma-and-resilience-cross-generations/. Accessed June 17, 2018.

Yehuda, Rachel, Nikolaos P. Daskalakis, Linda M. Bierer, Heather N. Bader, Torsten Klengel, Florian Holsboer, and Elisabeth B. Binder. 2016. "Holocaust Exposure Induced Intergenerational Effects on FKBP5 Methylation." *Biological Psychiatry* 80 (5): 372–80.

Yehuda, Rachel, Stephanie Mulherin Engel, Sarah R. Brand, Jonathan Seckl, Sue M. Marcus, and Gertrud S. Berkowitz. 2005. "Transgenerational Effects of Posttraumatic

Stress Disorder in Babies of Mothers Exposed to the World Trade Center Attacks during Pregnancy." *Journal of Clinical Endocrinology & Metabolism* 90 (7): 4115–18.

Young, Allan. 1995. *The Harmony of Illusions: Inventing Post-Traumatic Stress Disorder.* Princeton, NJ: Princeton University Press.

Zraly, Maggie, Sarah E. Rubin, and Donatilla Mukamana. 2013. "Motherhood and Resilience among Rwandan Genocide-Rape Survivors." *Ethos* 41 (4): 411–39.

Index